Africae Munus

Other Books of Interest from St. Augustine's Press

Maurice Ashley Agbaw-Ebai, *Light of Reason, Light of Faith: Joseph Ratzinger and the German Enlightenment*

Maurice Ashley Agbaw-Ebai, *The Essential Supernatural: A Dialogical Study in Kierkegaard and Blondel*

Peter Kreeft, *Ha!: A Christian Philosophy of Humor*

Peter Kreeft, *If Einstein Had Been a Surfer*

Peter Kreeft, *A Socratic Introduction to Plato's Republic*

Kenneth Weisbrode, *Real Influencers: Fourteen Disappearing Acts that Left Fingerprints on History*

Peter Kreeft, *The Philosophy of Jesus*

Peter Kreeft, *Socratic Logic (3rd Edition)*

Marvin R. O'Connell, *Telling Stories that Matter: Memoirs and Essays*

Jean-Luc Marion, *Descartes's Grey Ontology: Cartesian Science and Aristotelian Thought in the Regulae*

Josef Pieper, *Exercises in the Elements: Essays–Speeches–Notes*

Josef Pieper, *A Journey to Point Omega: Autobiography from 1964*
Winston Churchill on Politics as Friendship

Joseph Bottum, *Spending the Winter*

Richard Ferrier, *The Declaration of America: Our Principles in Thought and Action*

Roger Scruton, *An Intelligent Person's Guide to Modern Culture*

Roger Scruton, *The Meaning of Conservatism: Revised 3rd Edition*

Roger Scruton, *The Politics of Culture and Other Essays*

Roger Scruton, *On Hunting*

Anne Drury Hall, *Where the Muses Still Haunt: The Second Reading*

Chilton Williamson, *The End of Liberalism*

Marion Montgomery, *With Walker Percy at the Tupperware Party*

Africae Munus
Ten Years Later

EDITED BY

MAURICE ASHLEY AGBAW-EBAI

AND MATTHEW LEVERING

ST. AUGUSTINE'S PRESS
South Bend, Indiana

Manufactured in the United States of America.

1 2 3 4 5 6 27 26 25 24 23 22

Library of Congress Control Number: 2022947777

Paperback ISBN: 9781587310119

∞ The paper used in this publication meets the minimum requirements of the American National Standard for Information Sciences – Permanence of Paper for Printed Materials, ANSI Z39.48-1984.

St. Augustine's Press
www.staugustine.net

Table of Contents

Preface

Seán Patrick Cardinal O'Malley, O.F.M. Cap.

Archbishop of Boston

With great foresight and vision for the Church, Pope Emeritus Benedict XVI carefully integrated theological, catechetical and pastoral themes in the Post-Synodal Apostolic Exhortation, *Africae Munus*. Maurice A. Agbaw-Ebai and Matthew Levering, in the introduction to this collection of reflections and studies focused on the Pope Emeritus' themes, affirm the African continent's status as a global center for the growth of the Catholic Church in the twenty-first century and the future of the international Catholic community.

In his Exhortation, the Pope Emeritus also acknowledged that "Africa's memory is painfully scarred as a result of fratricidal conflicts between ethnic groups, the slave trade and colonization... and with new forms of enslavement and colonization." By way of very painful revelations in recent years, Western societies have been called to face the realities Pope Benedict held forth, however difficult that process, and to embark on a path of transparency, responsibility, and reparation. It is notable and even prophetic that the Second Special Synod of Bishops for Africa, the prompting for the Pope Emeritus' Exhortation, focused on reconciliation, justice, and peace.

In the Archdiocese of Boston, we are blessed with vibrant and growing communities of African and African-American Catholics, including substantial populations from Uganda, Kenya, Cameroon and Nigeria. The richness they bring to our practice of the faith, and the high value they place on family, with gratitude to the Lord, is both a gift and, in best sense, a challenge to our parishes and our people. The annual Mass of the Ugandan Martyrs, celebrated at the Cathedral of the Holy Cross, is a powerful highlight of our liturgical year. The Archdiocese is also blessed with priests and religious from throughout Africa, who come to Boston for advanced theological studies. During their years of academic work, they generously assist at our parishes, bringing a vitality, diversity and new perspective of living in witness to the goodness of God.

Building on the vitality and enthusiasm of the Church in Africa, it is important to lift their faith through scholarly research and academic reflections. We cannot fully appreciate the dedication, commitment and perseverance of the Catholic community throughout the African continent if we do not know the truth of their sufferings and persecution and understand their resilience in the light of faith. This collection, drawn from the halls of academia, provides an important contribution to the understanding and advancement of Catholic Africa, following the insights and enlightenment of Pope Emeritus Benedict. It is my hope that these essays will enrich your understanding and experience of the Catholic faith.

Introduction

The continent of Africa contains 236 million Catholics, with a large number of them practicing. This number is almost twenty percent of Catholics worldwide. Moreover, twelve percent of the world's Catholic priests serve in Africa, and thirteen percent of the world's bishops. Many priests serving in the United States and Europe are of African origin, as well. African Catholicism is thus of tremendous importance for Catholicism today and for the future of the Catholic Church.

The present book is a sequel to our 2021 edited volume, *Joseph Ratzinger and the Future of African Theology*. In that volume, which arose from a 2019 conference held at Mundelein Seminary, we gathered African Catholic theologians, alongside some non-Africans, to reflect upon what contributions a dialogue between the theology of Joseph Ratzinger / Pope Benedict XVI and African theological perspectives might make both to the future of African theology and to the future of the theology of the Catholic Church as a whole. It became clear that, unsurprisingly, African theologians have been thinking about and engaging with Ratzinger's theology in important ways, and they have also been absorbing and responding to the magisterial writings of the pontificate of Benedict XVI. Likewise, non-African theologians have been benefiting from the work of African theologians.

After the success of this first conference, we had the idea to invite many of the same scholars, together with some new ones, to a second conference held at Mundelein Seminary of the Archdiocese of Chicago in November 2021. We timed the conference to take place almost ten years to the day after Pope Benedict, while on a visit to Benin, signed his Apostolic Exhortation *Africae Munus* on November 19, 2011, while on a papal visit to Benin.

Pope Benedict promulgated *Africae Munus* in order to sum up and carry forward the results of the Second Special Synod of Bishops for Africa, held in Rome from October 4 to October 29, 2009. The topic of that Synod was "The Church in Africa in Service of Reconciliation, Justice, and Peace."

One of our conference speakers, Paulinus Odozor, C.S.Sp., of the University of Notre Dame, was present at the 2009 Synod as a theological advisor. The African speakers at our conference included scholars from Nigeria, Cameroon, and Uganda. The speakers included doctoral students at various institutions as well as professors at leading American universities, colleges, and seminaries. We have collected a number of the essays delivered at the conference, as well two essays written for the conference but not delivered there.

The eleven essays in the present volume interact with Pope Benedict's *Africae Munus* in a wide variety of ways. Almost all the essays explore in some manner the relationship of particular realities of faith—Jesus Christ, the Triune God, the Church, the liturgy, and so forth—to the concrete pursuit of justice, peace, and reconciliation in Africa and the world.

The volume begins with a summative examination of *Africae Munus* by Paulinus Odozor, grounded in his first-hand knowledge of the Synod and the needs of contemporary Nigeria. Paul Ọlátúbọ̀sún Àdajà then addresses the nature of biblical scholarship with *Africae Munus*'s reading of the parable of the Good Samaritan in view. He argues that biblical scholarship must combine historical-critical rigor with a patristic insistence upon theologically and pastorally applying the text to the situation of the world in which we find ourselves. Maurice A. Agbaw-Ebai turns his scholarly proficiency in Ratzinger's thought to use in reflecting upon *Africae Munus*'s employment of communion ecclesiology. Mary-Reginald Ngozi Anibueze charts a constructive path for African liturgical theology and African liturgies in light of the issues raised by *Africae Munus*. Emery de Gaál draws connections to the theology of Ratzinger's doctoral student Barthélemy Adoukonou, a bishop of Benin who has served since 2009 as the

Secretary of the Pontifical Council for Culture at the Vatican. Andrew Hofer, O.P. reflects upon the Synod's themes of reconciliation, justice, and peace in light of the contributions of the great African theologian Augustine of Hippo. Dennis Kasule explores the challenges that have been increasing over the past decade due to the growth of a politically oriented, often prosperity-focused Pentecostalism. Matthew Levering proposes that the image of the Church as the "family of God," found prominently in Scripture and *Africae Munus*, provides a path by which to understand how a theocentric and Christocentric theology can shape social justice as well. Joseph Lugalambi relates *Africae Munus* to the witness of faith offered by Father Benedict Ssetuuma, Jr., in the context of the explosion of priestly vocations in Uganda. Tegha Afuhwi Nji reconceives "liberation theology" in light of Ratzinger's critique (in the 1980s) of its Marxist forms and the specific needs and cultural contexts of Africa as displayed by *Africae Munus*. Last but not least, Denis Tameh employs the resources of his own specialty, canon law, to underscore that the commitment to justice found in *Africae Munus* must be reflected in the African Church's commitment to ensuring justice within its own ecclesiastical order.

We hope that this book will be of service to accomplishing the ends sought by the African bishops at the Synod and supported by Pope Benedict XVI in his commitment to the Church in Africa. All Catholics who care about faith and justice will benefit from the dialogues with African thinkers and cultures found here.

It remains for us to thank the Benedict XVI Institute for Africa for the work it is doing in service of an ongoing engagement between the thought of Ratzinger/Benedict and African theology. We also wish to thank Mundelein Seminary, especially its Conference Center and its Center for Scriptural Exegesis, Philosophy, and Doctrine. Many thanks also to Cardinal Seán Patrick O'Malley, O.F.M. Cap., for so graciously writing a Preface to this volume, and for St. Augustine's Press, for accepting to publish this text. May the book redound to the glory of Jesus Christ and to the furtherance of the Gospel as a lived reality in the world.

Chapter 1
Africae Munus *as Christian Policy Statement for an African Renaissance*

Paulinus I. Odozor, C.S.Sp.

Introduction

The dawn of the new millennium coincided with a desire for rebirth in Africa, for something the then president of South Africa, Thabo Mbeki, often referred to as an "African Renaissance." This African renaissance was to be "a new contemporary African self-assertion to build an African civilization which would be responsive to the dictates of our times, namely, economic prosperity, political freedom and social solidarity."[1]

Despite concerted development efforts throughout the continent since independence, much of Africa was still mired in crushing underdevelopment and stagnation characterized by dictatorships, the politicization of religion and ethnicity, lack of transparency in public finances, deterioration in press freedom, and the continued undermining of national budgets by means of loans which led to ballooning national debts. There were as well, rising environmental challenges, rising pressures on family and marriage, increased use of drugs, and increase in human trafficking. And, even though the number of wars on the continent had reduced to a trickle (Sudan, Somalia, Niger, and parts of the DRC) as of 2009, there was still plenty of intra-ethnic violence in many countries of the continent.

The dawn of the new century brought new hopes and new desires to set Africa on a more promising course. A new crop of leaders came to office who spoke not only of an African renaissance but also of an African "democracy dividend" implying that it was now time to help African peoples to cash in on the new possibilities which the recent (1989) fall of the Berlin wall and the subsequent clamor for democracy all over the world seemed to suggest were now possible. These leaders put several mechanisms in place on the continent to help Africa face the challenge of alienation and achieve continental integration. To accelerate political integration on the continent, the Organization of African Unity (OAU) metamorphosed into the African Union (AU); while on the economic front a new mechanism, the New Economic Partnership for African Development (NEPAD) was established as a strategic framework for development, while an African Peer Review Mechanism (APRM) was set up to monitor and measure the compliance of the AU members to the development goals which the continent's leaders had set for themselves and their nations. The continent still had its troubles, but there was the feeling that, given a little push, Africa would join the rest of the world to avail of the opportunities which the dawning new millennium seemed to hold for the entire world.

The African Church and the New Millennium

The hopes for a better Africa were not limited to the secular world. It was a shared aspiration in the Catholic Church as well. Therefore, it was in the hope that the Church could help Africa position itself for better things in the new millennium that Pope John Paul II announced a second synod of Africa in 2004, barely 10 years after the first synod of 1994. One remarkable characteristic of the papacy of St. Pope John Paul II was the amount of attention he paid to and interest he took in Africa. He visited the continent thirteen times, covering forty of the fifty-four nations of Africa during these visits. He visited some of the countries more than once. As John Paul II's biographer, George Weigel, has noted, "No world leader in the last two decades of the twentieth century paid sustained attention to Africa as John Paul II."[2] Perhaps there are no other decisions which could indicate this interest in Africa than his convocation of a second synod for Africa despite his failing health and at what was obviously a substantial cost, so soon after the first synod.

Looking back now on the two synods one could say that the tone of the first synod which was held in 1994 was hopeful of Africa's prospects for redemption, despite the egregious situations on the continent at that time. The second synod of Africa had a remarkably different tone than the first. This variance in tone is discernible even from the somber tone of the *Message* of the second synod: "We live in a world full of contradictions and deep crisis.... In all this, Africa is the most hit. Rich in human and natural resources many of our people are still left to wallow in poverty and misery, wars and conflicts, crisis, and chaos. These are very rarely caused by natural disasters. They are due to human decisions and activities by people who have no regard for the common good and this often through a tragic complicity and criminal conspiracy of local leaders and foreign interests."[3] This somber note is also very evident in the homily which Pope Benedict XVI gave at the opening mass of the synod in which he warned that the "deep sense of God" which makes Africa "the repository of an inestimable treasure for the whole world" was itself under attack from at least two dangerous pathologies: practical materialism, combined with relativist and nihilist thinking, and "religious fundamentalism, mixed with political and economic interests by which groups who follow various religious creeds are spreading throughout the continent of Africa: they do so in God's name, but follow a logic that is opposed to divine logic, that is, teaching and practicing not love and respect for freedom, but intolerance and violence." This homily was a clarion call to all and sundry that Africa was in danger on various fronts. What was at stake was the very survival of the continent as a distinct cultural, religious, and political entity. The post synodal exhortation whose 10th anniversary we celebrated in 2020 reflects this sense of urgency and tries to indicate some ways out of this situation in Africa.

The first Synod of Bishops for Africa had identified a set of pastoral priorities for the Church in Africa—evangelization as proclamation, evangelization as inculturation, evangelization as dialogue, evangelization as justice and peace, and evangelization as communication. This first African synod was thus focused around one priority: mission. Borrowing from *Gaudium et Spes,* the synod saw the Church in Africa as the Family of God in Africa; a family made so by one faith, one baptism, one Lord and which shared a bond based on the blood of Christ into whom we are all baptized into this family. In these discussions, *Ecclesia in Africa* was focused on the internal life of the church as evangelizing community. In the second synod, the Church lifted one of those priorities,justice and peace, and developed it in a way that could be used to address the realities Africa was facing at the time, and which secular leaders were trying to grapple with as well.

In this essay I want to discuss some aspects of the Post Synodal Exhortation, *Africae Munus on the Church in Africa in service to Reconciliation, Justice and Peace* which Pope Benedict XVI released on November 19, 2011, at Ouidah, in the Republic of Benin, the birthplace of his old friend and late colleague at the Vatican, Cardinal Bernardin Gantin, who was the Cardinal Prefect of the Congregation for Bishops and Dean of the College of Cardinals when Ratzinger was prefect of the Congregation for the Doctrine of the Faith. I will make my presentation in three broad parts: *Africae Munus* as Christian policy statement for Africa, the role of the Church in the renewal of Africa, and a third concluding section.

Part I
Africae Munus as (Christian) Policy Statement for African Nations.

At a fundamental but most profound level, *Africae Munus* is a blueprint from the Catholic Church concerning the road African societies must travel to arrive at most of the goals which programs like NEPAD and the millennium goals had set forth for the continent. I want to suggest in this essay that *Africae Munus* must be read in a significant way as the Church's broad policy prescription for an African renewal, which is for the African renaissance which African politicians, policy makers, analysts and other segments of African society have long sought for. Paragraph 42 of *Gaudium et Spes* makes the following interesting assertions: "The particular mission which Christ entrusted to his Church is not in the political, economic, or social order: the goal which he set it is in the religious order. And yet this mission of a religious nature produces a function, enlightenment and resources which can be of service in constructing and strengthening the human community in accordance with the divine law." What this means is that although the Church is not a political organization, and should not engage in partisan politics, it "has the capacity to be the primary means by which morality and moral discourse can enter politics."[4] In speaking of *Africae Munus* as a policy directive we mean that in this text the pope offers to Africa some important guidelines through which African societies as a whole can attend to the welfare of their societies by means that are judged to be promotive of individual and societal common goods. Thus, despite its reluctance to be "political," since politics lies outside the direct competence of the Church, the Church refuses to give in to the temptation for "withdrawal or evasion" from participation in discussions concerning proper actions to take for common human welfare (AM 17). As we shall see later in this presentation, there are two broad aspects to Benedict XVI's policy prescriptions in *Africae Munus*—a general exhortatory aspect and a set of specific guidelines on several key issues of the moment in Africa. Put in another way, all actions, both private and public, which have ascertainable public consequences on the maintenance and stability of African societies are indeed proper concerns of this synod and this pope in *Africae Munus*.

What Is Wrong with Africa?

A significant aspect of papal documents of the magnitude and significance of *Africae Munus* is that they usually include the description of what is often referred to as "the signs of the times"—

a more or less brief sociological statement about "the way things are currently," so to speak. In *Africae Munus* the pope begins by acknowledging that the blessings of God on Africa are many and beyond counting (AM, 4). However, he moves quickly to indicating the many situations of concern to him about Africa. Among these are that "Africa's memory is painfully scarred as a result of fratricidal conflicts between ethnic groups, the slave trade and colonization." People in Africa have to face "new forms of enslavement and colonization" (AM.9). Africa "is facing a culture-shock which strikes at the age-old foundations of social life and makes it hard for her to come to terms with modernity. Wars, conflicts, and racist xenophobic attitudes which plague many human societies are also held by a minority to the detriment of entire peoples" (AM 21)—are a reality of African life as are the ravages of drug and alcohol abuse (AM 12). The "plundering of the goods of the earth destroys the continent's human potential" (AM 72). Africa is also grappling with many pandemics and endemic situations such as malaria, HIV/AIDS, and tuberculosis, which, according to the pope, call for serious medical intervention and behavioral changes such as sexual abstinence and fidelity within marriage. These and many more similar situations have led to what the pope famously describes as "an anthropological crisis on the continent, the degradation of the human person in Africa" (AM 11).

Tales of woe about Africa are nothing new and have in many segments of the wider world given rise to so-called Afro-pessimism, the assumption that Africa cannot save itself and is indeed beyond salvaging by anyone. Pope Benedict XVI does not indulge in that kind of attitude. On the contrary, he believes that Africa has the tools it needs to lift itself up. First of these is the much-vaunted sense of the transcendent, the "deep sense of God," which is evident in all aspects of African life, and which makes the continent "the repository of an inestimable treasure for the entire world." Africa needs to work hard to keep this aspect of its life which is under threat from many outside forces. While Africa is maintaining its vertical connections with reality it must also "rediscover and promote the concept of the person and his or her relationship with reality." These discoveries can only come about through "a profound spiritual renewal" (AM 11). At the center of this renewed spiritual focus is a renewed focus on Jesus and on his Gospel. If Africa is "to stand erect with dignity," says Pope Benedict, it "needs to hear the voice of Christ who today proclaims love of neighbor, love even of one's enemies, to the point of laying down one's life: the voice of Christ who prays today for unity and communion of all people of God" (AM 13).

In the first chapter of the first part of his exhortation, Pope Benedict breaks down some of the components of the spiritual renewal he talks about. A first crucial element in this process of spiritual renewal is reconciliation with God and with one another. The absence of peace is in many ways a result of the traumatization of Africa's individual and collective memories. Thus, there is need for restoration through reconciliation both of human relationships with God and human relationships in Africa. Reconciliation is also "the restoration of relationships between people through the settlement of differences and the renewal of obstacles to their relationships in their experience of God's love" (AM 20). Reconciliation is a sure way to achieve lasting peace and it is everyone's responsibility—government authorities, traditional chiefs, and ordinary citizens. Many Africans have been traumatized by wars and other violent and unjust treatments. Thus, there are too many Africans carrying with them memories of deep hurt. It is only through forgiveness that such individuals can come to terms with their traumatic experience.

While the pope speaks of forgiveness and reconciliation he also insists, like the fathers of the synod insist themselves, that effective reconciliation has two sides to it. First it must include the pursuit of those responsible for various crimes on the continent—those responsible for wars and violent conflicts, those involved in various forms of trafficking, and bringing them to account. Secondly, it must be done in a way to give victims the right to truth and justice. Through these "courageous and honest" moves, Africa's memories would be purified, and the continent would be a place "where such tragedies are no longer repeated" (AM 21).

The renewed Africa of Benedict's Exhortation must also be a just Africa. Justice obliges us, as the pope points out, "to render each other his due." This is often not the case in many African societies. Rather, we often have a situation where there is "a plundering of the goods of the earth by a minority to the detriment of entire peoples." The pope declares this "unacceptable" and "immoral." What is needed is to find ways to render justice to everyone. If this is done, that is, if people stop turning public treasuries to private piggy banks, it will become evident that "Africa is capable of providing every individual and every nation on the continent with the basic conditions which will enable them to share in development" (AM 24).

Justice in Africa also demands the creation of societies sustained by the twin principles of solidarity and subsidiarity, by the understanding that for the guarantee of peace and justice, "the abundance of some (must) compensate for the want of some" and that the state should not substitute itself for the initiative of individuals and smaller entities (AM 24). The just society envisaged by *Africae Munus* is one where in the spirit of the beatitudes "preferential attention is to be given to the poor, the hungry, the sick—for example, those with AIDS, tuberculosis or malaria—to the stranger, the disadvantaged, the prisoner, the immigrant who is looked down upon, the refugee or displaced person (cf. Matthew 25:31–46)" (AM 27).

Finally, the pope insists that no society, no matter how efficiently ordered, can exist without love. "It is love which soothes hearts that are hurt, forlorn or abandoned. It is love which brings or restores peace to human hearts and establishes it in our midst" (AM 29).

Some Specific Policy Directives

At the end of their deliberations, the synod fathers drew up fifty propositions—summary and highlights of the issues with which the synod had been preoccupied during its month-long meeting.[5] These propositions form part of the background to the post synodal exhortation of Pope Benedict. While some of these propositions refer to the life of the Church, many of them refer to specific issues which would be necessary for truly flourishing African societies. Many of these propositions found their way into the exhortation as policy directives for African societies. I would like to group these propositions into moral propositions, political propositions, social propositions, and religious directives.

The Moral Propositions

Although there is a certain sense in which one can say that all the propositions of this Exhortation are about morality and how, as I indicated above, morality can enter the political realm in Africa, there are certain issues which for the sake of discussion here I will class as moral concerns as they affect individual lives and particular segments or groups in African societies. These include the family, the elderly, men, women, the young and children. In discussing these entities there is always the exhortatory aspect in which the pope appeals to or encourages them to be of a certain kind of behavior. But there is also always an aspect of the pope's exhortation which is directed at the state and at public authorities regarding how to enhance the welfare of these entities.

In speaking of the family, the pope notes the importance of the family and insists that "by virtue of its central importance and the various threats looming over it—distortion of the very notion of marriage and family, devaluation of maternity and trivialization of abortion, easy divorce and the relativism of a 'new ethics'—the family needs to be protected and defended, so that it may offer society the service expected of it, that of providing men and women capable of building a social fabric of peace and harmony" (AM 43). The pope speaks of the importance of men in the family, of the elderly and of children. Much of what is said about these do not arise to the level of public policy prescription. Not so for his discourse on women. The pope laments that while some progress has been made towards improving the lot of women on the continent, there is still a significant amount of work to do. "Overall, women's dignity and rights as well as their essential contribution to the family and to the society have not been fully acknowledged or appreciated. Thus, women and girls often have fewer opportunities than men and boys. There are still too many practices that debase and degrade women in the name of ancestral tradition." Thus everything must be done to combat all violence against women (AM 56) and to affirm and uphold "the equal dignity of man and woman" as persons utterly unique among all living beings found in the world (AM 56). Following the example of Christ himself, the Church must contribute and champion "the recognition and liberation of women" and help to create opportunities where women's voices would be heard and through which women can express their talents. Through such initiatives which reinforce women's worth, self-esteem and uniqueness, women would be enabled "to occupy a place in society equal to that of men—without confusing or conflating the specific character of each—since men and women are the 'image' of the Creator" (AM 57).

The question of the protection of life on the continent occupies a prominent position in the moral and political discourse in this exhortation. In this regard, the pope laments that "serious threats loom over human life in Africa." He points to the ravages of drugs and alcohol, and the various diseases and pandemics in Africa; many of these demand a change in lifestyle, but others call for clear and unambiguous public policy which respects human life in all its stages and manifestations. In this regard, he mentions abortion in line with universal Church teaching on the matter: "The child in his or her mother's womb is a human life which must be protected. Abortion, which is the destruction of an innocent unborn child, is contrary to God's will, for the value and dignity of human life must be protected from conception to natural death." To ameliorate the scourge of abortion, the pope insists that the Church in Africa must commit "to offering help and support to women and couples tempted to seek abortion, while remaining close to those who have had this tragic experience and helping them to grow in respect for life" (AM 74).

There are also serious concerns about ecology in this text. The pope points to the fact of environmental degradation in Africa and to the fact that this has roots in the greed whose "opulence ... shocks the human conscience" and the poverty and impoverishment of the many, and to many misguided poverty alleviation programs which end up aggravating the situation (AM 79). He speaks also of programs of resource exploitation which pollute the environment, cause deforestation, do damage to nature, to forests, to flora and fauna and put countless species to risk or even cause their extinction. To counter these trends, the pope urges the Church to encourage politicians to enact policies that will protect "the fundamental goods" of land and water for present and future generations (AM 80).

Other Proposals

There are also directives on good governance. Here the pope mentions the need for respect for African traditional rulers and their role in society, for the need for the rule of law, for political participation and the provision of Africa's privileged opportunity for healthy and serene public political debate, marked by respect for different opinions and different political groupings. He calls for free elections and for entrenched systems and avenues for accountability from African leaders (AM 81–83). Also, "independent judiciary and prison systems are urgently needed" for the restoration of justice and the rehabilitation of offenders. He insists that "prisoners are human," and despite their crimes "deserve to be treated with respect and dignity." The Church must provide pastoral care for prisoners and the state must "put a stop to miscarriages of justice and ill-treatment of prisoners." There are other directives from this synod and this pope on how Africa should treat migrants, refugees, and displaced persons, and on how to ensure protection for Africa's cultures in the face of unbridled globalization. The Church, for its part, is eager for the "globalization of solidarity" which inscribes "in commercial relationships the principle of gratuitousness and the logic of gift as an expression of fraternity" (AM 86).

Part II
The Church as Agent of the African Renaissance

As much as *Africae Munus* is about how African states can be renewed in the 21st century through the political process, it is also about the role the Church can and must play to bring about such a renaissance. This expectation is evident in the very theme of the synod itself: *The Church in Africa in Service of Reconciliation Justice and Peace. "You are the Salt of the earth… You are the light of the World" (Matthew 5: 13, 14).* As Benedict XVI puts it, the theme of the synod "made it possible also to reflect on the Church's public role and place in Africa today" (AM 17). The role of the Church is primarily to proclaim the Gospel of Jesus Christ. That role has a social dimension, as is evident in the Church's social teaching. This point needs to be emphasized, because in reading this text it is noticeably clear the impact Catholic social teaching has on both the synod itself and on the post-synodal exhortation of Pope Benedict. In the first place, all the key pillars of Catholic social teaching are evident in this text—consistent ethic of life, that is the need to take care of life at its various points from conception to natural death; the insistence of the rights and responsibilities of everyone; the imperative of special care for the least privileged of society; discussions on the rights of workers and of families; and the need for the special care of creation. One could say that this exhortation was an attempt to "domesticate" Catholic social teaching to suit Africa's needs. *Africae Munus* is therefore a veritable attempt at inculturation, that is, at trying to bring the Gospel of Jesus Christ and the teachings of the Church's magisterium to try to answer Africa's needs and in that way to find a home on the continent as an animator and an engine of Africa's socio-cultural and political development and growth. The engine of that growth and development is of course the Church in Africa. Therefore, the Church looms large in this document—as an agent of the renewal of Africa.

The Church as Essential Element in the Rebirth of Africa

Pope Benedict recalls and reapplies the metaphor "Church family of God in Africa," which was used by the first synod of Africa to describe the Church in Africa. To see the Church as family and as a fraternity "is to recover one aspect of her heritage" and to make it clear that the Church as bearer of good news considers everyone a child of God (AM 8). The aim of the synod and of the exhortation was to transform theology into pastoral care in which the great perspectives found in scripture and in the Church's living tradition find application in the work of every pastoral agent in the Church (AM 10). Africa's challenges are not insurmountable. However, they are challenges which prompt us all, the whole Church, "to draw upon the best of ourselves, our imagination, our intelligence, our vocation to follow without compromise in the footsteps of Jesus Christ to seek God, 'Eternal love and Absolute Truth" (AM 12).

Christ is at the heart of authentic love. Africa needs to hear the voice of Christ which proclaims the love of God and love of one's neighbor, including one's enemies, to the point of laying down one's life; the voice of Christ which continues today to pray for communion and unity of all people in God (AM 13). It is the task of the Church to lead people to this vision of God. Therefore, it chose the theme of the second synod—reconciliation, justice and peace, which brought the Church face to face with its theological and social responsibility and made it possible for her to reflect on "her public role and her place in Africa today" (AM 17).

Given that Africa's memories have been traumatized very badly, one essential task of renewal on the continent is that of reconciliation. This is the task of both the Church and the government; However, the Church has a significant role to play here. First it must work with governments to purify memories. But a major task of the Church is "in forming upright consciences receptive to the demands of justice, so as to produce men and women willing and able to build this social order by their responsible conduct" (AM 22).

In other words, an essential role for the Church regarding public policy in Africa is an educational one through which the Church awakens people's consciences to their civic responsibility. The other aspects to this educational role are to "open the world to the religious sense by proclaiming Christ to be a sign and safeguard of the human person's transcendence," and to enable people "to seek the supreme truth regarding their deepest identity and their questions, so that just solutions can be found to their problems" (AM 23).

Christ

The mission of the Church even in the socio-political sphere is to offer Christ and his vision of reality to Africa as the answer to Africa's challenges. In Jesus God shows us what true justice is. His is the "justice of love" which gives itself to the utmost, taking upon itself "the curse" laid upon humanity and in exchange making it possible for human beings to receive blessings from God (AM 25). Christ is a revolutionary but not in the political or social sense. His is a revolution of love which he brought about by his death and resurrection. The principles of this revolution of love are elaborated in the beatitudes. The Beatitudes "provide a new horizon of justice, inaugurated by the paschal mystery, through which we can become just and build a better world" (AM 26). The beatitudes invite us and therefore African societies to a preferential option for the hungry, the lonely, the abandoned and the sick. Attention to the person and teaching of Christ opens up "the social horizon based on love. Christian love goes beyond the minimalist understanding of justice to the point of giving up one's possessions and laying down one's life for one's brethren just as Christ did" (AM 28). In the midst of the sufferings of this world, some of which are inescapable, "it is love which soothes hearts that are hurt, forlorn or abandoned. It is love which brings or restores peace to human hearts and establishes it in our midst" (AM 29). The Church must be an agent of love for African societies. She must make the voice of Christ heard all through Africa. She must in this way help forge a new Africa in which peace and justice reign. "True peace comes from Christ (cf. John 14: 27). It cannot be compared with the peace that the world gives. It is not the peace of negotiations and diplomatic agreements based on particular interests. It is the peace of a humanity reconciled with itself in God, a peace of which the Church is the sacrament" (AM 30).

Some Reflections

"Public policy has an inherently moral character due to its rootage in existential human ends or goods." It is about the welfare of each individual person, what promotes it and what destroys it. The Church, as an "expert on humanity," is always aware of the need to protect the human person in whatever way possible; in this text the focus is on the human person in Africa with his or her special needs. As the pope puts it in the text, if Africa must make progress, it must first "rediscover and promote a concept of the human person and his or her relationship with reality that is the fruit of a profound spiritual renewal." Here in this exhortation, as we have tried to show, the key ingredient in this anthropological renewal is on the insistence of the age-old truth which is found in Christianity alone: the essential equality of all human beings based on the Judeo-Christian truth of the creation of human beings in God's image and likeness. This anthropology proclaims loudly and clearly that all human beings are essentially equal, and that each human person has a refractoriness about him or her, and therefore cannot be grasped merely based on race, color, gender, or ethnicity, which is at the heart of what Pope Benedict says in this text about the human person on the continent.

Africae Munus is therefore a veritable exercise of reason informed by faith. That is to say that it is a reflection on reality which is 'colored' by the Christian faith. But that does not make it 'unreasonable' or parochial, first of all because "no one speaks from nowhere" and secondly because all that is said here is verifiable and relatable to people who approach these realities from other perspectives. As Richard McCormick put it long ago, "the Catholic tradition reasons about its faith. In the process it hopes to disclose surprising and delightful insights about the human condition as such. These insights are not, therefore, eccentric reflections limited to a particular historical community. For instance, the sacredness of nascent life is not an insight that applies only to Catholic babies, as if it were wrong to abort Catholic babies but perfectly all right to do so with Muslim, Protestant, or Jewish babies. Quite the contrary. Reasoning about the Christian story makes a bolder claim. It claims to reveal the deeper dimensions of the universally human."[6] When the African bishops gathered in Rome, they did not go to advocate for ways to enrich the Church or to increase her wealth and privilege. They gathered to reflect on how they can lift Africans, *all* Africans, up and how they and the Christian believers on the continent can serve the common good of a continent in need of love and sacrifice and in need of whatever help it can get. The exhortation Pope Benedict issued following that synod is nothing more than a reflection of this desire and need to lift all of Africa and every African up in the 21st century.

Chapter 1 Endnotes

1 Nana Akuffo-Addo, Foreign Minister of the Republic of Ghana (2001–2008) Quoted in, The Church in Africa in Service of Reconciliation, Justice, and Peace. "You are the salt of the earth…You are the light of the world" Matthew 5: 13, 14,' Relatio Ante Disceptationem for the 2nd African Synod by Peter Cardinal Turkson (Vatican, 2009), p. 10.

2 Referenced by Emmanuel Ojeifo in *Let the Truth Prevail: Nocturnal Conversations on the Church, the Nation, and the World Today,* John Cardinal Onaiyekan with Emmanuel Ojeifo (Abuja, Lux Terra Foundation, 2021), p. 48.

3 Synodus Episcoporum, II Coetus Specialis Pro Africa, *Nuntius* (E civitate Vaticana, 2009), no.4, 5), p. 2.

4 Christopher F. Mahoney, *Public Virtue, Law, and the Social Character of Religion* (University of Notre Dame Press, 1986), p. 89.

5 See Synodus Episcoporum II Coetus Specialis Pro Africa, *Elenchus Finalis Propositionum* (E. Civitate Vaticana , 23 October 2009). As the synod fathers themselves point out in this text, the synod submitted to the Holy Father other texts as well for his consideration as he prepared his exhortation. These other texts include the "lineamenta," the "instrumeentum laboris," the reports "ante and "post Disceptationem," the texts of the interventions, both those presented in the synod hall and those "in scriptis" and the deliberations in the small groups." *Elenchus Fianlis Propositionum*, p. 3

6 Richard A. McCormick, *The Critical Calling: Reflections on Moral Dilemmas since Vatican II* (Washington, Georgetown University Press, 1989), p. 205.

Happily, for Africans today (at least most Africans), the Bible is still a normative text, and it remains authoritative in addressing *all* affairs of life (and death), and is not just an ancient document that is largely mined for its historical and moral value with little implications for the present.[12] The ultimate goal of this scholarship should be a willingness to be "related to life."[13]

> Many Africans, whether Christian or not, are quite familiar with the Bible since it is one of the most widely translated and read texts in Africa. References to and use of some of its personalities is common. For example, public transport vehicles, so popular in African cities . . . are dotted with biblical words, messages, and texts. The Bible is also viewed as containing messages that are relevant and applicable to the African context, messages that touch on all aspects of life: the cultural, the social and the spiritual. In other words, the Bible serves as a manual of life.[14]

Therefore, to identify only the victim and the Good Samaritan can end up giving a false sense of charity and justice since, according to Benedict XVI in the post-synodal exhortation *Caritas in Veritate,* "Not only is justice not extraneous to charity, not only is it not an alternative or parallel path to charity: justice is inseparable from charity and intrinsic to it." To put all these questions into a larger perspective, it is good to take a look at the history of the interpretation of this passage.

The History of the Interpretation of Luke 10: 25–37

Church Fathers

In a book like this where we pay attention to the works of Joseph Ratzinger, there is no better place to start the appreciation of this passage than with the Church Fathers, given his love of patristics. It is unfortunate that in recent times, there has been in biblical scholarship an attitude that disrespects and devalues the Fathers. Sometimes it almost seems as if biblical scholarship began in the 19th century with the historical-critical method. Luke Timothy Johnson calls such a scholarly dismissal a form of contempt of the past.[15] Writing in 2002, he notes that "among New Testament dissertations produced in the United States today, it is rare to find a dissertation that reviews interpretations in question before the 19th century."[16] One of the dangers of this amnesia is the divorce of biblical scholarship from faith and human life in all its ramifications as earlier noted. Scholarship becomes scholarly but then inert and ineffective. So how did the Fathers interpret this passage?

That Marcion commented on this passage is historically doubtful, but then we have a Syriac manuscript preserved in the British Museum (do not ask me why a Syriac manuscript is in Britain if you do not want me to start talking of robbers). This text is from the 7th century (cod. Add. 17215 fol. 30) and has a saying attributed to Marcion.

> Our Lord was not born from a woman but stole the domain of the Creator and came down and appeared for the first time between Jerusalem and Jericho, like a human being in form and image and likeness, but without our body.[17]

Riemer Roukema doubts the authenticity of the attribution of this text to Marcion because Marcion, though docetic, was not a fan of allegory. In addition to this, according to Marcion, Christ came down from heaven to Capernaum in the fifteenth year of the emperor Tiberius. This does not align with what we have in this Syrian witness, which says the Lord appeared for the first time between Jerusalem and Jericho.[18] While I agree with Roukema in doubting the authenticity of the attribution, the docetic character of this text makes it likely that someone who shared Marcion's docetism must have been the author. That being said, this passage by an author I will call neo-Marcion identifies the victim with Jesus.

Irenaeus of Lyons in his interpretation which was mainly a rebuttal of Gnosticism, notes

> That the Lord commends to the holy Spirit his own man, who had fallen among robbers, whom he himself compassionated, and bound up his wounds, giving two royal denarii; so that we, receiving by the Spirit the image and inscription of the Father and the Son, might cause the denarius entrusted to us to be fruitful, counting out the increase of it to the Lord.[19]

According to Roukema,

> In this text Irenaeus apparently refers to the Good Samaritan, whom he interprets as the Lord, Jesus Christ. The wounded man is mankind fallen prey to the robbers, who stand for the devil. Irenaeus highlights that the Lord had mercy on man and entrusted him to the Spirit, who takes the place of the innkeeper of the gospel story.[20]

This is the first time we have an interpretation of the robbers. So, for Irenaeus, it is a relevant detail of the story.

Next is Clement of Alexandria, who is particularly relevant because Benedict XVI made a reference to his interpretation in *Africae Munus.* For Clement,

> And who else can this be but the Savior himself? Or who more than he has pitied us, who have been almost done to death by the world-rulers of the darkness with these many wounds—with fears, lusts, wraths, griefs, deceits and pleasures? Of these wounds Jesus is the only healer, by cutting out the passions absolutely and from the very root. He does not deal with the bare results, the fruits of bad plants, as the law did, but brings his axe to the roots of evil. This is he who poured over

> our wounded souls the wine, the blood of David's vine; this is he who has brought and is lavishing on us the oil, the oil of pity from the Father's heart; this is he who has shown us the unbreakable bands of health and salvation, love, faith and hope; this is he who has ordered angels and principalities and powers to serve us for great reward, because they too shall be freed from the vanity of the world at the revelation of the glory of the sons of God. Him therefore we must love equally with God.[21]

Clement therefore sees humankind as the victim, the world-rulers of darkness as the robbers, and Jesus as the Samaritan. Again, we have an interpretation of the robbers.[22] The difference noticeable between Clement and Irenaeus is that, whereas the former thinks that the robbers are the world-rulers of darkness, the latter sees them as the devil. Roukema notes that the designation of the evil powers of the world as robbers in this text is one interpretation we also find in gnostic texts.[23]

Origen's interpretation is unique in some ways as he writes that

> The man who was going down is Adam, Jerusalem is paradise, Jericho the world, the robbers are the hostile powers, the priest is the law, the Levite represents the prophets, the Samaritan is Christ, the wounds represent disobedience, the beast the Lord's body, the inn should be interpreted as the church, since it accepts all that wish to come in. Furthermore, the two denarii are to be understood as the Father and the Son, the innkeeper as the chair man of the church, who is in charge of its supervision. The Samaritan's promise to return points to the second coming of the Savior.[24]

Origen thinks the man is Adam (and in this way represents the human race) and gives some meaning to Jerusalem and Jericho.[25]

He also thinks the Samaritan is Christ and considers the return of the Samaritan as the second coming of Christ. However, they also interpreted the robbers. Two abiding features of these interpretations is the attention paid to the robbers and the identification of the Samaritan with Christ.

Ambrose of Milan expands on Origen's understanding and notes that Adam went down from the heavenly Jerusalem, or paradise, to the underworld because of his own fault. This descent for him is a change of conduct, not of location.[26] However, Ambrose still went ahead to see the robbers as angels of darkness whom Adam met after he had sinned. He would not have met them but for his change of conduct.[27] Augustine's interpretation reflects that of Ambrose, and his approach was a little more moralistic, calling everyone to behave like the Samaritan. He interprets the oil and wine as the sacrament of baptism which gives remission of all sins.[28]

Apart from the Church Fathers, an individual who valued this passage very much is Martin Luther. He dedicated at least ten sermons to this passage. According to I. Howard Marshall,

> The traditional allegorical interpretation suited his theology of God's compassion so well that he took his time when he returned to it—which was not his usual practice—and oriented it in a polemical way against each and every Roman Catholic theology of works. Luther refused in particular to interpret v. 35b in terms of works of supererogation (i.e., works that go beyond what is required).[29]

Many modern interpreters dwell more on the moralistic and linguistic interpretations and understanding of this passage, with little interest in an allegorical understanding of the passage. Marshall is a representative of modern scholarship in this regard as he notes (and also references another author),

> The story of the good Samaritan, as it is related in 10:30–35, is simple and conveys a clear lesson. It contrasts the

> lack of compassion shown by two members of the Jewish priesthood towards an unknown and unfortunate sufferer with the obedience to the law shown in practical compassion by—to Jewish eyes—the most unlikely of men, a Samaritan. The lesson is hardly the mere point that love appears in unlikely places; it is obvious that the Samaritan is presented as an example to be followed. (John Dominic Crossan has argued that the parable, taken on its own, is not primarily an example to follow but a means of showing that the coming of the kingdom of God demands the complete upturning of conventional opinions, such as the impossibility of a Jew bringing himself to talk of a *good* Samaritan. But this is quite unconvincing.)[30]

It is to be noted that allegorical interpretations were not made to undermine the moral or ethical value of this passage, but to undergird it. According to Roukema, "all the authors who offered an allegorical interpretation of this parable were convinced that the spiritual meaning with regard to salvation by Christ revealed the most profound and essential intention of this text.[31]

While I am not advocating for a return to allegorizing of the Scripture as the Fathers did it, there is something commendable in their desire to identify their world first with the characters in this passage. Luke Johnson therefore sees the Fathers as "appropriate conversation partners if we seek to restore the soul of biblical scholarship in, of, and by the Church as community of the faithful."[32] This does not mean we are blind to the errors of the Fathers, and in the same manner we should not be blind to ours too—but then a critical engagement with their style and method will have fruitful implication to the way we approach these texts since

> The most vibrant forms of interpretation in antiquity occur when the Scripture is *used* to explicate the Christian life. The way such uses bear within them an

> implicit understanding also of the biblical text requires careful analysis. Until contemporary scholars engage such readings of Scripture in the vast Christian literature of the patristic and medieval period (and of course, one should add as well, the riches of Reformation interpretation, much of which continues in the same vein), they cannot say that they have learned what that interpretation involves.[33]

We can therefore learn from them and still use our historical-critical method to advance a humane scholarship. If we can say that we have commentaries nowadays, we must be able to admit that the Fathers have the interpretation.[34] While we sometimes assume that commentary is where interpretation is found, Johnson argues (and I agree) that this is not the case.[35]

If Africa Is the Victim, Who Are the Robbers?

Following the allegorical interpretation of the synodal fathers and that of John Paul II and Benedict XVI, Africa today is the victim found on the road between Jerusalem and Jericho. But then who are the robbers?

As one trained in contemporary historical-critical tools, I will start with a linguistic understanding of the word robbers in the passage. The word for the robbers is λῃστής, and can mean 'robber,' 'brigand,' or 'bandits.' A particular usage was that of Josephus, who applied it to zealots.[36] As noted, at the level of the passage, nothing much can be noted, but then the Fathers have shown that at the level of interpretation, much more can be said. So, who could have been the robbers of Africa? Here I will be identifying two types of robbers who have left the African continent and Africans on the roadside half dead. One is the external robbers, and the other is the internal robbers.

For the external robbers, the documentation is quite extensive. Africa and Africans have been robbed by slavery, especially the trans-Atlantic slave trade perpetuated by Europeans (of course with the aid, help, and support of some Africans. Since the benefit of such robbery has ended up developing the West, however, they are the ring leaders of that operation).[37] Africans have been robbed by a colonialism that has deprived them of their humanity. This is not to say that colonialism is a totally bad regime, but the fact that someone who robbed me of my goods ended up painting my home does not remove the fact of the robbery. Africa and Africans are still being robbed by multinational companies who see the continent as up for grabs, they are everywhere in the continent returning proceeds of their loot back home in the form of capital flight. Africa is still being robbed by a worldwide economic system in which we are debtors to loans we may never be able to repay since the terms of repayment means we must sell our inheritance first. This is after our resources have been looted and used in part to develop the West. This is asking the victim of the robbers to pay the robbers so they can take him to the hospital or take a loan from them for his hospital expenses. There is always the refrain that African leaders are corrupted by the West, but the irony of this accusation is that the proceeds of corruption always find a safe haven in the West. So, while the West is not 'corrupt,' the West is still the best place for corrupt African leaders to keep their ill-gotten wealth.

Teresa Okure notes that "Africa's resources have been looted and exploited by colonial masters and would-be messiahs, in the past as well as in the present. For centuries Western countries have carved out the wealth of Africa, and now the Chinese and the Indians are following suit under the guise of helping Africa develop."[38] Okure further captures my sentiments in this regard when she writes,

> Africa is and has been martyred because of her God-given reality as a race distinct from other races (though in reality there is only one human race). Africa has been and is still being martyred because the languages, cultures, and skin color differ from those of other peoples. She has been martyred because of her God-given

> wealth in people, rich natural and mineral resources, fauna, forestry. She has been martyred for her history, sculpture, hospitality, religion, and a culture that in its rich diversity combines religion and politics (church and state, to use the traditional expression) as one integrated way of life. Africa was martyred in the past by slave traders, colonialists, neo-colonialists, apartheid lords who in diverse ways despoiled her of her multifaceted wealth. European countries used her as strategic locations for conducting their Cold War away from their borders and left her decimated by internal wars and strife, littered with broken tanks and explosive landmines. She has been martyred by technologically developed nations who see her as a ready-made source of cheap labor and raw materials for their industries and survival, and who continue to see her as a convenient market for dumping all kinds of used and outmoded commodities. Africa has been martyred by powerful Western nations who set up and support military despots all over Africa so they can freely loot her rich resources (gold, oil, silver, copper, diamond, etc.) in collaboration with their stooges.[39]

As we can see in some cases, this robbery is literal. Think about the mineral resources that were exploited. Many parts of the Western world make more (moneywise) on our natural resources than we Africans do. Also to be included are African precious artworks (for instance, the Benin Bronzes, some of which are here in the United States) which today has become an issue since Nigeria is calling for the return of some of these stolen goods.[40] How about human trafficking by organized gangs in West? The robbers in the interpretation of this passage are not hard to find, if only we will name them.

The Catholic Church cannot also absolve itself as not being a robber of Africa in the past. Not only were some of the evangelization efforts a gross misunderstanding of African values, but also the Church was complicit in the slave trade—if not a ringleader, at least a cheerleader. For instance, Portugal secured approval from successive popes for most of its activities at the start of the slave trade.[41] Therefore, in the identification of the robbers of Africa, the Catholic Church cannot absolve itself.[42]

However, it is not only external robbers we are dealing with. Sometimes the internal robbers are the worst, since they are really among us. There is a Yoruba proverb which says *"bí ikú ilé ò pani, ti òde kò lè pani."*[43] That is the case with many African politicians and leaders, both past and present. Many of them are looters, killers, and robbers. They collude with foreign powers to loot their own people. However, it is not just the leaders alone. We Africans are often our own worst enemies . While it is true that the economic conditions have been terrible and many are finding ways of leaving the continent, the extent of man's inhumanity to man on the continent is shameful and appalling. The kidnappings in present-day Nigeria for instance are insane and inhumane. People now take loans to pay ransom. As in the first case of the external robbers, this internal robbery is literal sometimes. The stealing and corruption for instance is not just allegorical or metaphorical, it is real. Sometimes too, it adds some sense of humor. How about the story that broke in Nigeria sometimes ago about a snake swallowing millions of Naira, the Nigerian currency? Daylight robbery in Nigeria is not allegory, it does happen. Politics and elections become a channel to siphon public funds.[44] This does not just involve the leaders but also the followers. Therefore, our leadership is a reflection of our current citizenry.

The saddest part of it all is when Church leaders in Africa lead these robbery schemes. The consistent use of religion in the name of prosperity gospel, for instance, is a robbery of the African mind. How about when Church leaders, bishops, and priests sometimes are known as friends and cronies of politicians? We also have religious leaders fanning the fires of ethnic hatred in the name of faith. A Nigerian writer once noted that the Church is now the spiritual arm of corruption. How sad! Once the Church loses its prophetic voice, it has chosen the side of the robbers, not the victim. A Church that fails to speak and call out the robbers cannot be a Church of the good Samaritan, but is instead a Church of the robbers.[45]

The worst of it all is the role of some Church leaders in Rwanda during the Rwandan genocide. While some Church leaders were the victims of this genocide, some were the robbers of the human bodies through the orchestrated killings. Unfortunately, in *Ecclesia in Africa* no mention was made of the Rwandan genocide, or even the word "genocide" at all. This is in spite of the fact that this document was published in September 1995, only a year after this tragedy. In a twist of irony to this glaring absence, Rwandan bishops were not able to attend the 1994 Synod because the Synod coincided with the events of the genocide. What surprises me most is that while John Paul II repeatedly condemned the genocide, there is no single mention of the word genocide in the post-synodal exhortation *Ecclesia in Africa*. For its part *Africae Munus* mentions the word genocide once (21), but no mention of the word Rwanda. That is unfortunate for a document that leans on the Church's gift of reconciliation. Andrew F. Wells correctly states that "African theology must not fail to deal with the genocide in Rwanda; and above all, how this happened in our own day in what, by most calculations, was one of the most Christian countries in Africa.[46]

The inability of *Africae Munus* to fully take advantage of the Parable of the Good Samaritan is a prophetic oversight. Pope Benedict XVI will agree with this assessment as he notes in the same document (21) that,

> If it is to be effective, this reconciliation has to be accompanied by a courageous and honest act: the pursuit of those responsible for these conflicts, those who committed crimes and who were involved in trafficking of all kinds, and the determination of their responsibility. Victims have a right to truth and justice. It is important for the present and for the future to purify memories, so as to build a better society where such tragedies are no longer repeated.[47]

My argument however is that a better biblical scholarship will be served if the allegorical understanding of this parable is complete.[48] The Church by then would have been able to completely fulfill her prophetic role, for the prophet is always the alien, the herald of change, and the challenger of existing order."[49]

Conclusion

It is my hope that in the future, when this parable is being applied and interpreted, the interpretation of the robbers will not be left out, since leaving it out raises the question of justice. Leaving out the robbers also promotes a moralization of the story that does not provoke, in a way that detaches and distances us from the story. The greatest question this parable poses in the light of recent history is this: Am I the robber in this story?

Chapter 2 Endnotes

1 This is not a case of fatalistic pessimism but an acknowledgement of our present state of affairs.

2 I must note that my criticism of these two documents' oversight of the interpretation and identification of the robbers should be seen as a suggestion that I think that both documents are far from helpful to the African world. That is far from the case. I have seen firsthand, the positive impact of these documents in ideas of Justice and Reconciliation in my home country Nigeria. Rather, I see this omission as a 'heaven-sent opportunity for the ordinary hack like myself to plunge in an express an opinion." See Dom Hubert Van Zeller, *We Die Standing Up* (New York: Sheed and Ward, 1949), 61.

3 Elizabeth Schüssler Fiorenza, "The Ethics of Biblical Interpretation: Decentering Biblical Scholarship." *JBL* 107 (1988): 3–17, here 10–11.

4 Luke Johnson, "Rejoining a Long Conversation" in Luke Timothy Johnson and William S. Kurz, S. J *The Future of Catholic Biblical Scholarship: A Constructive Conversation.* (Grand Rapids, Michigan: Eerdmans, 2002), 57.

5 Johnson, "Rejoining a Long Conversation." 39.

6 For this, see I Howard Marshall who writes that 'the identity of the bandits is irrelevant.' Cf. I Howard Marshall, *The Gospel of Luke: A Commentary on the Greek Text New International Greek Testament*

Commentary, (Exeter: Paternoster Press, 1978), 447–8. See also, François Bovon who writes that "the identity of these thieves is not important to the story." François Bovon *Luke 2: A Commentary on the Gospel of Luke 9:9 51–19: 27*ed. Helmut Koester, *Hermeneia—A Critical and Historical Commentary on the Bible*, (Minneapolis, MN: Fortress Press, 2013), 57.

7 οἳ καὶ **ἐκδύσαντες** αὐτὸν καὶ πληγὰς **ἐπιθέντες** ἀπῆλθον ἀφέντες ἡμιθαν (Robbers: 4 verbal actions); ἱερεύς τις κατέβαινεν ἐν τῇ ὁδῷ ἐκείνῃ, καὶ **ἰδὼν** αὐτὸν **ἀντιπαρῆλθεν** (Priest: 3 verbal actions); Λευίτης κατὰ τὸν τόπον ἐλθὼν καὶ **ἰδὼν ἀντιπαρῆλθεν** (Levite: 3 verbal actions); Σαμαρίτης δέ τις **ὁδεύων ἦλθεν** κατ' αὐτὸν καὶ **ἰδὼν ἐσπλαγχνίσθη**, καὶ **προσελθὼν κατέδησεν** τὰ τραύματα αὐτοῦ **ἐπιχέων** ἔλαιον καὶ οἶνον, **ἐπιβιβάσας** δὲ αὐτὸν ἐπὶ τὸ ἴδιον κτῆνος **ἤγαγεν** αὐτὸν εἰς πανδοχεῖον καὶ **ἐπεμελήθη** αὐτοῦ. καὶ ἐπὶ τὴν αὔριον **ἐκβαλὼν** δύο δηνάρια **ἔδωκεν** τῷ πανδοχεῖ καὶ **εἶπεν**· Ἐπιμελήθητι αὐτοῦ, καὶ ὅ τι ἂν προσδαπανήσῃς ἐγὼ ἐν τῷ ἐπανέρχεσθαί με ἀποδώσω σοι. (Samaritan: 13 verbal actions).

8 See No 4 of *Africae Munus* Benedict XVI notes, "I see no need to dwell at length on the various socio-political, ethnic, economic or ecological situations that Africans face daily and that cannot be ignored. Africans know better than anyone else how difficult, disturbing, and even tragic these situations can very often be. I pay tribute to Africans and to all the Christians of that continent who face these situations with courage and dignity. Rightly, they want this dignity to be recognized and respected. I can assure them that the Church loves and respects Africa."'

9 Fiorenza, "The Ethics of Biblical Interpretation." 14.

10 Fiorenza, "The Ethics of Biblical Interpretation." 14.

11 Fiorenza, "The Ethics of Biblical Interpretation." 15.

12 Andrew M. Mbuvi, "African Biblical Studies: An Introduction to an Emerging Discipline." *CBR* 15 (2017): 149–178, here 153.

13 Jean-Claude Loba-Mkole, "The New Testament and Intercultural Exegesis in Africa." *JSNT* 30 (2007): 7–28, here 8.

14 Mary Getui, "The Bible in African Theology" in Mary Getui, Knut Holter, and Victor Zinkuratire, *Interpreting the Old Testament in Africa: Papers from the International Symposium on Africa and the Old Testament in Nairobi, October 1999* (New York: Peter Lang, 2001), 181–88 (here, 182). James Ukpong notes that "In spite of this however, biblical scholars in Africa have been able to develop a parallel method of their own. The particular characteristic of this method is the concern to create an encounter between the biblical text and

the African context. This involves a variety of ways that link the biblical text to the African context such that the main focus of interpretation is on the communities that receive the text rather than on those that produced it or on the text itself, as is the case with the Western methods." Justin S. Ukpong "Developments in Biblical Interpretation in Africa: Historical and Hermeneutical Directions" in West, O. Gerald and Musa W. Dube, *The Bible in Africa: Translations, Trajectories and Trends* (Boston. Leiden: Brill, 2001), 11–28, here 11.

15 Johnson, "Rejoining a Long Conversation" 40.

16 Johnson, "Rejoining a Long Conversation" 40–41.

17 See Riemer Roukema, "The Good Samaritan in Ancient Christianity." *Vigiliae Christiane* 58 (2004):56–74, here 57.

18 Roukema, "The Good Samaritan in Ancient Christianity." 58.

19 Irenaeus of Lyons, *Adversus Haereses* III,17, 3.

20 Roukema, "The Good Samaritan in Ancient Christianity." 59.

21 Clement of Alexandria, *The Rich Man's Salvation* 28–9 (Butterworth, LCL); Cf. Roukema, "The Good Samaritan in Ancient Christianity," 61.

22 Roukema, "The Good Samaritan in Ancient Christianity." 61.

23 Roukema, "The Good Samaritan in Ancient Christianity." 61. Apocryphon of John, Nag Hammadi Codex II,21,11; III,26,22 (NHMS 33); Sophia of Jesus Christ, Nag Hammadi Codex III,101,15; 107,15 (NHS 27); Clement of Alexandria, Excerpta e Theodoto 53,1; 72,2 (SC 23). Ecclesiastical authors also used to represent demons as robbers; see G.J.M. Bartelink, 'Les démons comme brigands,' Vigiliae Christianae 21 (1967): 12–24.

24 Origen, *Hom. Luc.* 34,3; Cf. Roukema, "The Good Samaritan in Ancient Christianity." 61.

25 Elsewhere he notes that He identified the wounded man with Adam who has been driven away from paradise in order to live in exile in this world, and whose situation applies to 'us.' See Origen, *Comm. Cant.* I prol. 2,30, Origen, *Comm. Rom.* IX. 31; Roukema, "The Good Samaritan in Ancient Christianity." 65.

26 Roukema, "The Good Samaritan in Ancient Christianity." 69.

27 Roukema, "The Good Samaritan in Ancient Christianity." 69.

28 Roukema, "The Good Samaritan in Ancient Christianity." 70; Saint Augustine: Essential Expositions of the Psalms (Expositions and Psalms, translation, and notes by Maria Boulding, OSB, selected and introduced by Michael Cameron, New York: New City Press of the Focolare, 2015), Psalm 121:102.

29 Marshall, *The Gospel of Luke*, 63.

30 Marshall, *The Gospel of Luke*, 447–8. Another moral interpretation is even by An African Commentary. Paul John Isaak notes: "People from countries such as the United States of America, South Africa, Namibia, Rwanda, and Burundi and other countries wracked by racial and ethnic divisions have a special appreciation of this story of travelers. It deals with racial harmony and what it means to be human and humane, or to be someone with *ubuntu*, that is, someone who is welcoming, hospital, warm and generous, with a servant spirit that affirms others and says, 'I am because you are: you are because I am.'" Cf. 1225. Paul John Isaak 1203–1250 *African Bible Commentary* (Tokunboh Adeyemo General Editor, Word Alive Publishers, 2006), here 1225. See also, Luke Timothy Johnson, "The parable itself is intended to provoke. The violence done to the traveling Judean is overt: he is stripped, beaten, left half dead. This is not a sentimental tale. A deeper level of shock, however, is the recognition that Jews esteemed for their place in the people and dedicated to holiness before the Lord would allow considerations of personal safety or even concern for ritual purity (a corpse defiled) to justify their not even crossing the road to look. They "pass by on the other side." If love for neighbor meant anything, it meant to care for the "sons of your own people." But they cannot be bothered. A third shock is the discovery that a despised Samaritan, himself most at risk in this dangerous no man's land of deserted territory, takes the chance of stopping, looking, and—increasing his own vulnerability—leading the man on his beast to an inn. It is the hated enemy who is the hero with a human heart. More stunning still is the use to which Jesus turns the parable. The point, we learn, is not who deserves to be cared for, but rather the demand to become a person who treats everyone encountered—however frightening, alien, naked or defenseless—with compassion: "you go and do the same." Jesus does not clarify a point of law but transmutes law to gospel. One must take the same risks with one's life and possessions that the Samaritan did!" Cf. Luke Timothy Johnson, *The Gospel of Luke* ed. Daniel J. Harrington, Sacra Pagina Series, (Collegeville, MN: The Liturgical Press, 1991), 3:175.

31 Roukema, "The Good Samaritan in Ancient Christianity." 70

32 Johnson, "Rejoining a Long Conversation." 61.

33 Johnson, "Rejoining a Long Conversation." 45.

34 Johnson, "Rejoining a Long Conversation." 45.

35 Johnson, "Rejoining a Long Conversation." 45.

36 Marshall, *The Gospel of Luke*, 447–8. Cf. Jewish War 2.17.6 §425 (Thackeray, LCL).

37 I must note that not only were African elites implicated in the trans-Atlantic slave trade, they also perpetuated slavery at other levels within the continent.

38 Teresa Okure, "Jesus and the Samaritan Woman (John 4:1–42) in Africa." *Theological Studies* 70 (2009) 401–418, here 411.

39 Teresa Okure "Africa, a Martyred Continent: Seed of a New Humanity." *Rethinking Martyrdom* Edited by Teresa Okure, Jon Sobrino and Felix Wilfred. London, SCM Press. Concilium 2003/1: 38–46, here 39–40.

40 A Cambridge University college is handing over a bronze cockerel looted from Africa in the 19th century to Nigerian authorities: Cf. https://abcnews.go.com/Entertainment/wireStory/colonial-art-cambridge-hands-looted-bronze-nigeria-80813820. Some are in the Metropolitan Museum of Art in New York. Cf. https://www.nytimes.com/2020/01/23/arts/design/benin-bronzes.html

41 Hugh Thomas, *The Slave Trade: The Story of the Atlantic Slave Trade 1440–1870* (New York: Simon and Schuster, 1997), 64–5. My criticism of the role of the Catholic Church is part of my historical evaluation of the African experience. I am therefore not oblivious that in the last two centuries, the Catholic Church has been one of the largest (if not the largest) providers of social services on the continent. However, it is important to point out that the relationship of Africa with the Church is more complicated (and even complicated) than present realities. I hope that with this I have been able to balance out the complex relationship of the Church with Africa. Also, since the Church is a reality under Christ, every relationship of the Church needs to be evaluated in the Light of the Person and Mission of Christ and on this point, the Church has, at least in past (in part) have failed to live up to this standard. In the words of Joseph Ratzinger, "the linking of experience with faith, or the insight that faith provides the key to meaning of our human experience." See Joseph Ratzinger, "The Dignity of the Human Person" in H. Vorgimler (ed.) *Commentary on the Documents of the Documents of Vatican II: Pastoral Constitution on the Church in the Modern World* (Vol 5, New York: Herder and Herder, 1969), 115–163, here 126.

42 It can be easy to read from this statement an attack on the Catholic Church. That would be a gross misunderstanding of my point. I am aware that the Catholic Church is probably the largest provider of education, charity, and healthcare in Africa, and I will never deny that. My point here is historical, and it is good that this history is not erased from these pages so we should not have a jaundiced

notion of the Church down the years. Truth and honesty demand that I point this out just as I noted the good that the Church currently does. I also think pointing to this unfortunate picture of the Church's role in the laundering of Africa in the past will serve as a warning for the current Church.

43 If you are not killed by the 'death' in the house, you cannot be killed by the 'death' outside the house." Death here is personified.

44 As I type these pages, a terrorist attack took place some days ago at Saint Francis Xavier, Ọ̀wọ̀, Oǹdó State (June 5, 2022). This same night, the Nigerian President, Muhammadu Buhari had dinner with presidential aspirants of the ruling party All Peoples Congress (APC). Even the dead have not been buried, yet the leaders are dining.

45 I must point out that there are also Church leaders who are quite prophetic in the face of these atrocities. The Catholic Bishops Conference of Nigeria was a prophetic voice during the years of military rule in the country.

46 Andrew F. Walls "Christian Scholarship in Africa in the Twenty-First Century." *Transformation* (2002): 217–228, here, 225. I think that the story of the Rwandan genocide and the role Church leaders played in this heinous crime should be taught in all Catholic seminaries in Africa. Sometimes, we need to look at ourselves in the mirror in order to get better. I was in seminary formation for 9 years in Nigeria and never once did any of our professors talk about this genocide. We cannot continue to bypass history if we want to learn how to avoid repeating past errors.

47 The oddity here is why Pope Benedict XVI did not align this to the interpretation of the Parable. See also, "In her prophetic role, whenever peoples cry out to her: "Watchman, what of the night?" (Is 21:11), the Church wants to be ready to give a reason for the hope she bears within her (cf. 1 Peter 3:15), because a new dawn is breaking on the horizon (cf. Rev 22:5). Only by rejecting people's dehumanization and every compromise prompted by fear of suffering or martyrdom can the cause of the Gospel of truth be served." (No. 30) "Today, many decision makers, both political and economic, assume that they owe nothing to anyone other than themselves. (82).

48 I must suggest that Benedict XVI's decision not to put the Parable into full use might have come from his unease and disapproval of the Church's intervention in politics, an idea which is very dear to him. For instance, he writes at paragraph 17: "The task we have to set for ourselves is not an easy one, situated as it is somewhere

between immediate engagement in politics—which lies outside the Church's direct competence—and the potential for withdrawal or evasion present in a theological and spiritual speculation which could serve as an escape from concrete historical responsibility." However, as is evident from my analysis, the robbers are not only politicians.

49 Morris West *The Clowns of God* (Sydney: Allen and Unwin, 1981), 17.

Chapter 3
Benedict XVI and the Ecclesiology of Communion in Africae Munus

Maurice A. Agbaw-Ebai

The concept of communion is one of the constants that has marked the Ratzingerian theological edifice. Its presence in *Africae Munus* in terms of understanding the nature and mission of the Church in Africa is therefore predictable. The fractured history of Africa, marked by inter-tribal and regional conflicts, renders communion as an ecclesial model all the more urgent. This lecture will explore the basic historico-theological warrants that account for the significance that Ratzinger gives to ecclesial communion in his theological corpus. It will further examine the facets that come into play when examining the treatment of the theology of communion in *Africae Munus*. By making the argument that context is key to understanding Ratzinger, the lecture will provide the theological roots of Ratzinger's communion ecclesiology, all in a bid to make the case that situating *Africae Munus*' treatment of the ecclesiology of communion within the wider Ratzingerian framework has the potential of offering a richer engagement with *Africae Munus*, obviously beneficial in terms of comprehensibility and applicability.

As already indicated, to Ratzinger, communion is central to the DNA of the community called the Church. He takes as his starting point the decision of Christ to call the Twelve, which Ratzinger reads as the foundation of the New Israel, in the first signification, and the cosmic dimension, in a second signification:

> Twelve is this the symbolic number of the people of God; if Jesus calls twelve, then his symbolic gesture

> says that he himself is the new Jacob-Israel and that now, with these men, a new people of God are beginning. Mark expressed this very clearly in his gospel: 'He named twelve.' (3:4). In this connection, one knew that twelve was also a cosmic number, the number of the signs of the zodiac which divides the year, the time of man. The unity of history and cosmos, the cosmic character of salvation history, was thus underscored. The twelve are to be the new signs of the zodiac of the definitive history of the universe.[1]

In this light, Christ forms a community of disciples and apostles, and to this apostolic college he entrusts the mission of bringing the gospel message to the ends of the earth, the cosmos, hence fully opening up the mission of Israel as a people to its most sublime calling, purpose and destiny. Added to the choice of the Twelve lies the pathway thanks to which one becomes a Christian, namely, the sacraments of initiation. We are not baptized into solitary paths. By baptism, we enter into a community, the Body of Christ, united by stronger bonds of faith, hope and love. The communal nature of the sacraments is therefore, from the Ratzingerian perspective, a further testimony to the precedence of the concept of communion in Ratzinger's ecclesiology. Additionally, the spiritual treasury of the Church in terms of the message of the gospel of Jesus Christ (the Scripture) and the sacred gifts encountered in the celebration of the sacramental economy, mitigate against anti-communal theological understanding. Such is the case, because the content of the gospel of Jesus Christ is essentially communitarian, calling men and women into the mystical Body of Christ, saving them from nihilistic aloneness. In this light, it is certainly the case that one can see in the entire sacramental economy the foundational aspect of an ecclesiology of communion.

But it is with the event of the Second Vatican Council, especially in terms of its aftermath, its implementation, that Ratzinger's initial impulses for the primacy of an ecclesiology of communion find its most explicit expression. Unlike previous councils such as Trent, Vatican II did not provide an explicit systematic hermeneutical framework. It left no keys as to how the interpret its documents. This constituted a source of ecclesial upheaval, and the pontificates of Paul VI and John Paul II sought to provide hermeneutical keys to the interpretation of the letter and spirit of the Council. To Ratzinger, the proper hermeneutical principle regarding Vatican II is that of continuity and reform, not rupture, for a Church that is at war with its own past and that criminalizes what previous generations held sacred, is one that is destined for aridity, for it will be severing itself from its own roots. To ensure the practical applicability of such a hermeneutic, the model of the Church as communion is found central stage in the Ratzingerian theological scenery.

Following the Council, therefore, Ratzinger, together with von Balthasar, Congar, Bouyer, Medina, and Guillou, set about founding a theological journal, *Communio,* aimed at fostering a conversation within the Church centered around the common Christian faith of all. Such a move appeared necessary and urgent because of what they perceived to be a certain egalitarian understanding of the Church as the "people of God" that was being pushed by certain theological forces after Vatican II. While Vatican II's ecclesiology of the "people of God" was a genuinely new contribution to the Church's self-understanding, the *Communio* theologians did not see it as indicating an ecclesial revolution, in which one section of the Church, the laity, were now to view the hierarchy as adversaries hindering the establishment of an egalitarian Church that was called for by Vatican II. As Ratzinger notices,

> More and more, 'people of God' was understood in the sense of popular sovereignty, as a right to a common, democratic determination over everything that the Church is and over everything that she should do. God was taken to be the creator and sovereign of the people because the phrase contained the words 'of God,' but even with this awareness he was left out. He was amalgamated with the notion of a people who create and form themselves.[2]

To Ratzinger, therefore, it was necessary to approach the "people of God" ecclesiology of *Lumen Gentium* (particularly Chapter Two) in such a way that Vatican II is not perceived as ushering in a war-like revolution with the Church's own past, setting up a kind of class warfare in the internal life of the Church. After all, as he discovered in his doctoral dissertation on Augustine, which likewise included others Fathers of the West such as Tertullian and Cyprian, and of the East such as Chrysostom and Origen, the term "people of God," from the evidence of the New Testament, could only be applied to the Church through the medium of a Christological transformation. In other words, the Church is the "people of God" to the extent that the Church is the New Israel, for strictly speaking, "people of God" refers to the historical Israel. But it must be pointed out that even this designation of Israel as the "people of God" is not a sociological description, for that will make communion with God a kind of tribal descent, which would amount to blasphemy. Israel is the "people of God" only to the extent that Israel turns to the Lord and remains in a relationship with the Lord. Israel is the "people of God" to the extent that she transcends herself, becoming what, left to herself, she could never become. One could say that it is in the nature of Israel as a "people of God" to live in a permanent genitive and dative case, if one is permitted to employ a linguistic metaphor. The New Testament designation of the Church is *ecclesia,* which describes that gathering of the people that have responded to the proclamation of the word of God, a people called out by the word of God that is preached to a people that, before the proclamation of the word, were a non-people. If the expression "people of God" is applied to the Church, then one must place beside it "Church as sacrament" in a balancing act that points to the Christological foundation that makes possible the application of "people of God" to the Church. Such is the case as it is thanks to the sacraments that the living Christ opens the possibility of the Church to relate to the Father in the power of the Spirit.

But setting aside these biblical and patristic nuances, Ratzinger notices that adding "God" to "people" did not immediately resolve the horizontalization and immanentist understanding that was increasingly being pushed by certain theological circles that were eager, albeit imperceptibly, to construe Vatican II as a sharp break with all that had preceded it, as if the Church was only beginning in 1962. Such a mode of thinking and acting reveals an understanding that sees the Church as that which we can remake all over, according to our human ingenuity. But as Ratzinger rightly argues,

> One cannot make the Church but only receive it, that is receive it from where it already is and where it really is: from the sacramental community of Christ's body passing through history. . . . The Church is not something we make today but something we receive from the history of the faithful and something we pass on as unfinished, which will only be fulfilled at the coming of the Lord.[3]

By holding this position, Ratzinger is not denying the genuine contributions of the Second Vatican Council. If anything, he is providing a wider basis for engaging the Council by rooting the achievements of the Council in the long and rich history of the Church.

And to Ratzinger, further, not only was "people of God" being interpreted as a clarion call for a more democratic egalitarian Church that prioritizes the given local Church above all else, but even more, this understanding of "people of God" was being predicated on "Church as communion," so much so that "people of God" and "Church as communion" were deployed as revolutionary tools to usher in a new democratic Church, the only one capable of speaking to the needs of the hour. As Ratzinger explains, "According to this interpretation, Vatican II had abandoned the hierarchical ecclesiology of Vatican I and replaced it with an ecclesiology of *communio*. Thereby, *communio* was apparently understood in much the same way the 'people of God' had been understood, i.e., as an essentially horizontal notion."[4] But as Ratzinger upholds,

> It is simply out of the question to separate an earlier, unsuitable ecclesiology from a new and different one. Ideas like these not only confuse conciliar texts with party platforms and councils with political conventions, but they also reduce the Church to the level of a political party. After a while political parties can throw away an old platform and replace it with one which they regard as better, at least until yet another one appears on the scene.[5]

If this Ratzingerian reading is correct, then the problem of hermeneutics appears in all its brilliance as key or central to the appropriation and implementation of Vatican II. As Benedict would point out in his now famous 2005 Address to the Roman Curia, Vatican II was not meant to be a declaration of war with the Church's own past. Rather, the past which is present in the living tradition of the Church, must be seen as a precious resource from which we can draw energy for the present as we head towards the future. As Ratzinger maintains,

> The result is either an entirely sterile faith that has nothing to say to the present, or an arbitrary act that skips over two thousand years of history, throwing them into the waste bin of failures, and then concocting how Christianity—according to Scripture or according to Jesus—should really look. But what results can only be an artificial product of our own making in which there is no inherent permanence. True identity of the origin exists only where there is a living continuity that develops it and in so doing preserves it at the same time.[6]

It is thanks to this line of thinking that Ratzinger proposed the hermeneutic of reform and continuity over and against a hermeneutic of discontinuity or rupture, as the interpretive key to Vatican II.

With the hermeneutic of reform and continuity, the principal actor is the Holy Spirit that helps the Church of the present to better understand that which has been handed to her from the past, opening her to newer insights that are capable of giving life to present challenges. In other words, thanks to the presence of the Holy Spirit, the Church, in interpreting the signs of the times (*Gaudium et Spes*), studies, reflects, and pays attention to what God has said to the Church in her long history through the ages, and from that treasury of wisdom, gains insights that can provide a deeper and wider framework for engaging the present. In effect, a hermeneutic of discontinuity and rupture ends up shallow, depriving the Church of the present of a unique and unmatchable treasury of her history, lived through and by the prophets, apostles, Fathers, saints, and scholars. It might appear the only modus operandi that is capable of speaking to present times. It might appear as a quick-fix solution to present problems and challenges. But at what cost? And as has often been seen, quick-fix solutions do not eventually solve ecclesial problems. They often end up kicking the can down the road, and the problems end up growing new heads. I agree with this position by Ratzinger, that

> If the Second Vatican Council brought the notion of *communio* to the forefront of our attention, it did not do so in order to create a new ecclesiology or even a new Church. Rather, careful study and the spiritual discernment which comes from the experience of the faithful made it possible at this moment to express more completely and more comprehensively what the tradition states.[7]

Such a spiritual discernment is necessary because in the light of a long tradition, Christian communion is modelled after the communion of the Godhead. In other words, the communion between the Father, the Son, and the Spirit is the blueprint for what we mean by communion in the Church. Thanks to creation, the prehistorical or Immanent Trinity has revealed, in the singular event of the Incarnation and the sending of the Spirit, that is, the historical or Economic Trinity, what the hub of ecclesial communion is or ought to be—namely, God. As Ratzinger explains,

> Trinitarian faith and faith in the Incarnation guide the idea of communion with God away from the realm of philosophical concepts and locate it in the historical reality of our lives. . . . To put it in the form of a concrete statement: the communion of people with one another is possible because of God, who unites us through Christ in the Holy Spirit so that communion becomes a community, a 'church' in the genuine sense of the word.[8]

This suggests that communion is not a sociological category. It is a theological category, rooted and modeled after Trinitarian communion. We are not reinventing the wheel, starting from point zero, when we talk about communion as belonging to the DNA of Church.

This approach thus roots ecclesial communion in the solid ground of salvation history, preventing it from appearing as a kind of afterthought that is brought about by merely practical concerns. In this light, from the moment of creation, God, understood as Father, Son, and Spirit, has been forming human history in the pattern of communion. Scripture offers a testament to this, especially in Acts 2:42, which to Ratzinger captures the essential nature of the Church: "These remained faithful to the teaching of the apostles, to the brotherhood, and to the breaking of bread and to the prayers." To Ratzinger, this picture of the primitive Church remains the exemplar for the form of the Church for all ages.[9] Therefore, ecclesial communion, which in this text is captured by the term *koinonia,* notwithstanding all the nuances of the word, has been constitutive of the Church from its very inception.

Turning to the Lineamenta for the Second Synod for Africa, *The Church in Africa in Service to Reconciliation, Justice and Peace,* we read this expectation of the synod participants in terms of what they hoped to achieve regarding the fostering or nurturing of a spirit of culture of ecclesial communion in the Church that is in Africa:

> The Bible and Church Fathers provide the third aspect, namely, the communion of members in the one Body of Christ. We become Christians only through union with other Christians in the great communion of saints. This highlights the community dimension of freedom and commitment. No one is saved alone; Christ saves humanity as a whole so as to make it the family of God united in his Body and Blood. Communion refers to communication. This is possible on several levels: in work groups, meetings, moments of discussion and sharing, associations, the family, the workplace and circles of friends. A Christian is someone who knows how to work in a team, in collaboration and sincere friendship with others. Wherever a Christian is at work, he tries to create a family atmosphere. The family is always the basic place where this community aspect is expressed.[10]

The following aspects stand out in this vision of the Lineamenta:

Firstly, the framework for understanding ecclesial communion has to be Scripture and the Church Fathers. In other words, Sacred Scripture, its interpretation and the lived experiences of the Fathers are normative regarding what the Church in Africa must understand and be called to be, regarding ecclesial communion. The experience of living tradition, namely the Fathers, and the testimony of Scripture as the Word of God, provides the Church in Africa with a stable hermeneutical framework thanks to which she must come to a fuller appreciation, understanding, and living out of ecclesial communion.

The second aspect in terms of the vision of the Lineamenta delves into the lively question of the relationship between soteriology and ecclesial communion. When the Lineamenta says, "no one is saved alone; Christ saves humanity as a whole so as to make it the family of God united in his Body and Blood," it immediately raises our consciousness that ecclesial communion, properly understood, has a Christological foundation that is rooted in Soteriology. Such is the case, because the saving work of Christ, Soteriology, is always intrinsically linked, rooted, or more precisely, flows from the person of Christ, his nature as God and Man, Christology, as Chalcedon declared in AD 451.

The third aspect of the vision that is deduced from the Lineamenta points to the essentiality of communication in bringing about ecclesial communion. The Lineamenta envisages communication at all levels—family, friends, work places, various groups, et cetera. As the Lineamenta states, "A Christian is someone who knows how to work in a team, in collaboration and sincere friendship with others." (90) Evidently, the spirit of communion envisaged by the Lineamenta is one that is outgoing and engaging, one that comes about thanks to a conscious and an active reaching-out by Christians to all, neighbors and the distant alike.

The fourth and final feature that one notices in the Lineamenta sees the family as the privileged locus encountering and nurturing of the spirit of communion (90). This clearly places the vision of the Second Synod in continuity with the 1994 First Synod for Africa on the Church as Family. In an increasingly individualistic world, the Second Synod for Africa still nurtured the hope that the experience of communion in family life would help break down ever new barriers that continue to separate Africans along tribal, political, socio-economic, and even religious lines.

Given these four aspects of communion as deduced from paragraph 90 of the Lineamenta, the seed was readily planted for a profound consideration of ecclesial communion when the Synod met in Rome, in October of 2009. With the post-synodal exhortation, *Africae Munus*, Benedict XVI took up the expressed desire of the synod participants to foster an ecclesiology of communion in the Church in Africa. With an aerial view of two parts of the text, one can reasonably assert that *Africae Munus* is a document whose central nexus is ecclesial communion. Such is the case, because it is difficult, perhaps even impossible to imagine a

Church that is an instrument for justice, peace, and reconciliation in Africa if the Church herself is lacking in communion, for what is justice, if not the right ordering of society; what is peace, if not the harmony between peoples, as John XXIII expresses in *Pacem in Terris*; and what is reconciliation if not the return to harmony between ourselves, our neighbors and ultimately, God?

At the risk of oversimplification, one could make the observation that a fruitful actualization of the vision of *Africae Munus* in the light of its different aspects (namely: the Care for the Human Person (Part I, Chapter II), Living in Harmony in the Family comprising of the Elderly, Men, Women, the Young and Children (Part I Chapter II), the African Vision of Life (Part I Chapter III), Dialogue and Communion Among Believers (Part I Chapter IV), and the summons towards the Common Good in terms of the members of the Church and the ensuing apostolates, built and strengthened by and in the celebration of the sacraments (Part II, chapters I, II and III), would necessarily demand an ecclesiology of communion, without which the urgent desire for peace and reconciliation would prove unrealizable. How can the Church in Africa be an agent of reconciliation and peace in a continent that is no stranger to war and discord, if her inner life does not flow from communion, which is a testament to a reconciling and peaceful spirit? One is reminded of the exhortation of our Lord Jesus Christ: first remove the beam in your own eye, before removing that in your brother or sister's (Mt 7:5).

In my opinion, the foundational nature of communion to the ecclesial witness of justice, peace and reconciliation is what underlies Benedict's proposal for a spirituality of communion as the pathway for the Church's advocacy for genuine justice, peace, and reconciliation (*Africae Munus*, 34). In spelling out the concrete details of what this might mean, Benedict turns to the conditions that John Paul II had spelled out that would guarantee the spirituality of communion for the universal Church in *Novo Millennio Ineunte*: first, the ability to see the light of God in the face of the other; second, an attentiveness to the joys, sufferings, needs, and desires of our brothers and sisters in Christ, that is, those with whom we share the life of grace in the Mystical Body of Christ; third, the ability to recognize God's grace operating in the other who is different from me, a recognition that makes the other to become a channel of God's grace for me as well; and finally, the ability to make room for our brothers and sisters, bearing each other's burdens (Gal. 6, and eschewing the temptations that foster egoism, such as unhealthy competition, careerism, distrust, and jealousy. (*Africae Munus*, 35) Benedict appears to believe that a life of communion lived in and by the Church in Africa will offer a prophetic witness of courage, truth, and self-denial, necessary ingredients of communion, and ultimately, joy.

Though Benedict accedes to John Paul II in his explicit meaning of communion in terms of spirituality in *Africae Munus*, it is certainly the case that a profound understanding of the spirituality of communion shares an intrinsic link with an ecclesiology of communion. In effect, spirituality and ecclesiology, if set against each other, leave both sides impoverished. If this argument is true, then understanding Benedict's call for a spirituality of communion in *Africae Munus* must be grounded in, and stands to benefit from, a deeper engagement with Benedict's theology of ecclesial communion. Given the nature of a papal document such as *Africae Munus*, a comprehensive engagement of the theology of communion might have been too detailed an undertaking. But studying *Africae Munus* ten years later, and given the intent of the necessity of its ongoing implementation, it appears certainly necessary to further unpack the framework or theological contours of Benedict's theology of communion, which hopefully, will provide the hermeneutical framework especially for *Africae Munus'* call for ecclesial communion.

To unpack Benedict's *communio* ecclesiology, it is helpful to turn to an image that the young Ratzinger found in Augustine, in the course of his doctoral work on *The People and House of God in Augustine's Doctrine of the Church*. Ratzinger has remained a decided Augustinian thereon. The life of Augustine demonstrates why communion would occupy a significant space. As a bishop not shy of controversies, especially when he felt the very meaning of the Church and her teachings was at stake, Augustine battled

the entry into divinity of human nature, for the glory of God is a living man; and the life of man consists in beholding God.[20] This divine–human meeting in Christ embodies Irenaeus' doctrine of recapitulation, in which the whole of reality is gathered into Jesus Christ, who is *God's nearness*, to use a Ratzinger phrase.[21] As Ratzinger expounds,

> Communion means that the seemingly uncrossable frontier of my "I" is left wide open and can be so because Jesus has first allowed himself to be opened completely, has taken us all into himself and has put himself totally into our hands. Hence, Communion means the fusion of existences; just as in the taking of nourishment the body assimilates foreign matter to itself, and is thereby enabled to live, in the same way my "I" is "assimilated" to that of Jesus, it is made similar to him in an exchange that increasingly breaks through the lines of division.[22]

There is, therefore, a meeting of persons, resulting in an exchange in which I give up myself for Christ to take root in me, living, as Paul would say, no longer for myself, but Christ living in me (Gal. 2:20). If such is the state of things, then at the root of Benedict's theology of communion is spiritual conversion. Ecclesiology is never just about practical Church arrangements, important as these might be. If the link is severed from Spirituality, ecclesiology becomes another modern tower of Babel, so much effort at churching without the Spirit, planification guided by a technical mindset that ends up leaving out the soul of the Church, Jesus Christ, and the presence of the Holy Spirit from the Father and the Son, whom, together with the Father and the Son, is worshiped and glorified.

The consciousness of catholicity in understanding ecclesial communion; and the Christocentric character of ecclesial communion bring us to the third factor in the Ratzingerian understanding of ecclesial communion, namely, that the basis of it is prayer.[23] The celebration of the Eucharist thus becomes the heartbeat for *communio* ecclesiology. To quote St. Paul, "because it is one bread, we, though many, are one body" (1 Cor 10:16ff). In the calling of the Twelve and the celebration of the Last Supper, Israel's religious ritual is opened up to the nations, the new Twelve, whose origin, nature and destiny are no longer tied to ethnic or nationalistic bounds. Something new happens, and that explains why ritual must continue to be an invitation to overcome tribal barriers in our particular African ecclesial contexts. As Ratzinger elucidates:

> Just as the old Israel once revered the temple as its center and the guarantee of its unity, and by its common celebration of the Passover enacted this unity in its own life, in like manner this new meal is now the bond uniting a new people of God. There is no longer any need for a center localized in an outward temple. . . . The Body of the Lord, which is the center of the Lord's Supper, is the one new temple that joins Christians together into a much more real unity than a temple made of stone could ever do.[24]

In this light, African pastors must be continuously encouraged to say that investing in the formation of the Eucharistic faith of our people is a primary and very significant part of our ministry. The growing presence of chapels of Eucharistic Adoration, which is an extension of the Holy Mass, is a very encouraging phenomenon in the African Church. However, it is important to continue to emphasize and to catechize African Christians on the intrinsic bound between this prevailing Eucharistic ecclesiology and communio-ecclesiology, for as Ratzinger points out based on a study by Henri de Lubac, "the notion of the Church as the body of Christ was inseparably bound to the notion of the Eucharist in which the Lord is bodily present and gives us his body to eat."[25] Hence, in a continent that continues to be no stranger to conflicts and divisions, it is not permissible to drop the mic regarding the question of the relationship between Eucharist and the fostering of communion ad intra and ad extra.

By way of conclusion, this essay has done four things: First, it has unpacked the historical and theological warrants for Ratzinger's preference for an ecclesiology of communion as representative of an organic development and deepening of the Church's self-understanding of her nature and mission. Second, it has uncovered the vision of ecclesial communion that the Lineamenta put forth regarding the Second Synod for Africa. Third, we showed Benedict's engagement with that vision following the fruits of the Second Synod itself as spelled out in *Africae Munus*. And fourth, given the nature of the document as a reflection on the propositions handed to the Pope by the Synod Fathers, my contentment is that African scholarly engagement of the *communio* ecclesiology would benefit from a deeper engagement with the Ratzingerian framework of what Ratzinger understands ecclesial communion to be and not be. That explains the delving into the relationship between Augustine and Ratzinger, hoping that the lessons Ratzinger learnt from the Great North African Doctor of the Church could have something to say to us today, as we seek to build ecclesial communion. As Ratzinger says, "communion makes the Church by breaching an opening in the walls of subjectivity and gathering us into a deep communion of existence. It is the event of "gathering," in which the Lord joins us to one another."[26] Hence, while these four elements of our study, namely, the historical and theological warrants for an ecclesiology of communion as a course correction to a run-away misinterpreted understanding of Vatican II's model of the Church as the people of God; the vision of communion in the Lineamenta; the model of an ecclesiology of communion as spelt out in *Africae Munus*; and the understanding of ecclesial communion in Augustine and Ratzinger, while certainly not exhaustive of all that one could say about Ratzinger's theology of ecclesial communion, can hopefully contribute something to the study, understanding, and reception of the ecclesiology of communion as put forth in *Africae Munus*, and by so doing, help the Church in Africa to continue to find its place and its voice in the mystical Body of Christ that comprises peoples from all tribes, tongues and nations (fully conscious of the limitations of the theological metaphor of "Body of Christ" as designative of the Church).

Such a presence in the mystical Body of Christ that is derivative from an ecclesiology of communion is a pointer to the significant realization that, in the final analysis, what ecclesial communion brings about is the consciousness that ultimately, the Church is above all else, an inward experience. Guardini was right in his assessment that the Church was awakening in the souls of people. Ecclesial communion is a declaration that the Church is a living being, a living organism that grows in the hearts of believers, opening persons and communities to one another, gathered by the power of the Holy Spirit around the person of the Living Christ. While what we tend to encounter and what often takes up the space in our consciousness is the institutional dimension of the Church, when we approach the Church from a spirit of communion, sooner or later, the consciousness is born thanks to which we see that the thriving and sustaining locus of the Church is in hearts of believers. I should now conclude this presentation of Ratzinger's ecclesiology of communion in the light of *Africae Munus* by stating that Ratzinger's ecclesiology of communion is a constant reminder that the Church is not a mechanical device, merely organizational and bureaucratic, but, over and above all, the Church is living reality that is not made in its origin but born from faith, living in love, and sustained by hope, a hope that has a face, Jesus Christ the Lord, *Dominus Iesus*.

Chapter 3 Endnotes

1 David L. Schindler, (ed.) Joseph Ratzinger in Communio Vol. I, The Unity of the Church (Grand Rapids, MI: William B. Eerdmans Publishing Company, 2010), 71

2 Schindler, 123–124.

3 Schindler, 69–71.

4 Schindler, 124.

5 Schindler, 124.

6 Schindler, 65–66.
7 Schindler, 125.
8 Schindler, 126.
9 Joseph Ratzinger, *Pilgrim Fellowship of Faith, The Church as Communion,* trans. Henry Taylor (San Francisco: Ignatius Press, 2005), 63.
10 Second Synod for Africa, Lineamenta, The Church in Africa in Service to Reconciliation, Justice and Peace, 90.
11 Joseph Ratzinger, *Volk und Haus Gottes in Augustins Lehre von der Kierche,* 133–134.
12 Augustine, *Against Cresconius the Grammarian,* 3, 35, 39; PL 43, 517.
13 Joseph Ratzinger, *Called to Communion* (San Francisco: Ignatius Press, 1996), 86.
14 Ratzinger, *Volk und Haus Gottes in Augustins Lehre von der Kierche,* 170.
15 Augustine, *City of God,* XXIII, 6, 1.
16 Ratzinger, *Called to Communion,* 10.
17 Ratzinger, *Called to Communion,* 29.
18 Ratzinger, *Called to Communion,* 19.
19 Emery de Gaál, *The Theology of Pope Benedict XVI, The Christocentric Shift* (New York: NY: Palgrave MacMillan, 2010).
20 Irenaeus of Lyons, *Against Heresies,* (Washington, DC: Ex Fontibus Co., 2016), IV: XX, VII.
21 Ratzinger, *Called to Communion,* 23.
22 Ratzinger, *Called to Communion,* 37.
23 Ratzinger, *Called to Communion,* 24.
24 Ratzinger, *Das neue Volk Gottes* (Düsseldorf, 1969), 79.
25 Schindler, 66.
26 Ratzinger, *Called to Communion,* 37.

Chapter 4
Africae Munus *and African Cultural Values: Towards an African Liturgical Theology*

Mary-Reginald Ngozi Anibueze

I. Introduction

Africae Munus, the post-synodal document from the Second Synod of the African Bishops, written by Pope Benedict XVI, begins with a positive image of Africa: "a precious treasure is to be found in the soul of Africa, where I perceive a spiritual 'lung' for a humanity that appears to be in a crisis of faith and hope" (*Africae Munus*, 13). In five chapters, Pope Benedict XVI emphasizes the commitment of the Church in Africa to the service of reconciliation, justice, and peace, which culminates in an evangelization that promotes personal priority, theological developments, pastoral orientations, and social involvements.[1] The importance of African culture and values is duly highlighted in the document as it stresses "a commitment to transmit the values that the Creator has instilled in the hearts of Africans since the dawn of time. These have served as a matrix for fashioning societies marked by a degree of harmony, since they embody traditional formulae for peaceful coexistence" (AM, 38). These African values include inter alia: the family seen as the sanctuary of life, a cell of the African society and the church (a school of love, peace, respect, faith and reconciliation)[2] and the African concept of life such as a comprehension of the ancestors, the living, the unborn, the visible and invisible universe.[3] *Africae Munus* goes further to emphasize that "these positive elements therefore need to be emphasized, lit up from within (cf. John 8:12), so that Christians may truly receive the message of Christ, and in this way God's light may shine before the eyes of all" (AM, 38).

Despite the difficulties that countries and particular African churches have encountered, as the Synod fathers rightly expressed, the difficulties encountered by the countries and particular churches in Africa are not so much insurmountable obstacles, but challenges, prompting us to draw upon the best of ourselves: our imagination, our intelligence, our vocation to follow without compromise in the footsteps of Jesus Christ and to seek God, the "Eternal Love and Absolute Truth" (*Africae Munus,* 12).

Focusing on theological development, which will be the crux of this essay, *Africae Munus* encourages the African Church to embrace elements within its culture and challenges her leadership "to seek ways of inspiring in Christ's disciples in Africa the will to become effectively committed to living out the Gospel in their daily lives and in society" (*Africae Munus*, 32). The path towards reconciliation, justice, and peace highlights the urgent need for the inculturation of the gospel and the evangelization of culture. The Church in Africa, most importantly the bishops, has the task of identifying and promoting aspects of the culture which foster authentic witnessing and incarnation of the gospel message in the Church. The document further states:

> While remaining true to itself, in total fidelity to the gospel message and the Church's tradition, Christianity will thus adopt the face of the countless cultures and peoples among whom it has found a welcome and taken root. The Church will then become an icon of the future which the Spirit of God is preparing for us, an icon to which Africa has a contribution of her own to make. In this process of inculturation, it is important not to forget the equally essential task of evangelizing the world of contemporary African culture. (AM, 37)

Contemporary African culture needs a theology grounded in sound catechesis that integrates practical dimensions, "which is experienced at the liturgical, spiritual, ecclesial, cultural and charitable levels…" (AM, 165), a theology that will help African Christians encounter God in worship leading to a *metanoia* that will be translated to a reconciled and just society. Hence, the task of an African liturgical theology begins with the experiences of the people in the pews, the worshiping congregation, and then shows how these participants can integrate their encounter with God with their lifestyle and relationship with other people in society.

The focus of this essay is mainly to reemphasize the need for an African liturgical theology in a continent where worship and rituals are prevalent in every sphere of life. I do not claim in any way to give a detailed study of how all nations in Africa are theologizing, nor do I exhaust in these few pages all studies in African theology. Rather, my focus is on the general understanding of African Christian theology and some African liturgists who have championed the cause of African liturgical theology from a Catholic perspective through the years. An African liturgical theology will study the nature, content, purpose, and function of worship rendered to God, and how the resultant findings can be applied to the daily life of African Christians to create a connection with God, one another, and the world. In this way, African Christians and theologians will be able to understand and reconcile the God described in theology books with the God worshiped on Sunday by the Christian faithful. On the one hand, this renewed understanding will make liturgical theology a practical experience expressed by the worshiping community and, on the other hand, show the close connection between liturgy and theology. "If liturgical theology stems from an understanding of worship as the public act of the Church, then its final goal will be to clarify and explain the connection between this act and the Church, i.e. to explain how the Church expresses and fulfills herself in this act."[4]

II. Towards an African Liturgical Theology

The task of liturgical theology consists in giving a theological basis to the explanation of worship and the whole liturgical tradition of the Church. This means, first, to find and define the concepts and categories which are capable of expressing as fully as possible the essential nature of the liturgical experience of the Church; second, to connect these ideas with that system of concepts which theology uses to expound the faith and doctrine of the Church; and third, to present the sacred data of liturgical experience as a connected whole, as, in the last analysis, "the rule of prayer" dwelling within the Church and determining her "rule of faith."[5]

We speak of liturgical theology today thanks to Alexander Schmemann, who more than forty years ago observed the relationship between worship and theology, noting that liturgical theology requires its own special methods and tasks, distinct from all other theological disciplines.[6] Subsequent scholars like Aidan Kavanagh,[7] Edward Kilmartin,[8] Gordon Lathrop,[9] David Fagerberg,[10] Kevin Irwin,[11] and others have further developed the understanding of liturgical theology in various Christian traditions. Even though there is no agreed-upon definition for liturgical theology,[12] the phrase continues to be used, especially by liturgists, to explore the meaning derived from faith expressions and ritual action, and consider how these expressions inform the worshiping community. Foremost of these liturgists are Alexander Schmemann, Aidan Kavanagh, and David Fagerberg's masterful book, *Theologia Prima: What is Liturgical Theology?* describes a refined practical relationship between liturgy and theology.

Fagerberg first enlarges our understanding of a liturgist not as one who studies, writes books on liturgy, or directs liturgical activities, but rather as one who performs the action of entering into an encounter with God in worship.[13] This lays the foundation that liturgical theology derives from the liturgist's encounter with God, arising from lived faith expressions and not mere theoretical analysis.[14] The subject matter of liturgical theology is not liturgy or worship; it is God and the meaning of the experience encountered by the primary liturgist, the one who commits the action, and experiences its effect on humanity and the world.

> The method of liturgical theology differs from the theology of worship because the former does not seek to generalize. Liturgical theology seeks to observe the rite in motion, to notice detail, and the convenience of sameness does not blind it to structurally unique components. The subject matter of liturgical theology is not worship in general, but the theological meaning which derives from the symphony of structures called rite.[15]

Therefore, liturgical theology has a task of giving a theological basis to the elucidation of worship and the entire Church's liturgical tradition. Relying on Schmemann and Kavanagh, Fagerberg believes that liturgical theology seeks to explain how the Church expresses and fulfills itself in liturgical acts since it is the nature of liturgical theology to give voice to the *lex orandi* (law of praying—liturgy) which in turn enables the *lex credendi* (law of faith—theology) of the Church to be heard.[16] It is at worship that both the Church and world encounter God, making liturgy the *theologia prima,* since liturgical acts bring a change in participants as they enter into a profound encounter with God in word and sacrament.[17] Liturgy is simply the Church's faith in motion, upon which other forms of theology depend: ecclesiology, Christology, soteriology, and pneumatology.

Since we are dealing with a dynamic Church, made up of diverse cultures, the need to engage liturgical theology within a cultural context becomes imperative. The diversity of faith experiences that comes as a result of the unique way various cultures engage in worship and ritual practices in the Church have encouraged the fervent need for scholars to pay attention to, and engage in interpreting, liturgical expressions of various faith traditions. As Dionysius Bar Salibi rightly asserts:

> The fact that people of every country pray differently, and have something which singles them out from the rest, goes to their credit, first because it indicates the wealth of their devotions and spiritual vigor, and

> secondly because it is a sign of tl
> of God, who wishes to be glorifi
> different countries and towns.[18]

The need for a theological synthe
God applies to Christian theologians
well, since Africans exhibit unique fai
their tradition and culture. African Cl
to the pioneers,[19] have over the years
of inculturated theology from the Af
The areas include inter alia Liturgy,
Pneumatology, Biblical Hermeneuti
Feminism, Soteriology, and Ethics.[20]
ogy have helped African Christians, t
derstand the Christian faith. But what
will offer every Sunday church-goer a
contextualized faith that embodies th
the African Christian's daily life and e
connects the worshiping individual
standing of the relationship between

III. Liturgy and Theology: A

> *When we assemble to participate in an en*
> *so in order to worship God—not to please*
> *but to worship God. We also do so becau*
> *ourselves will be altered in some way, gu*
> *the everyday. . . . Indeed if the alteration*
> *hope for comes about, it does so as a conseq*
> *shiping God.*[21]

Liturgy, as the *culmen et fons* of t
Church,[22] recalls the divine presence o
fect the sanctification and edification
nity (encountered during worship) an
of God with a practical consequence
world and becoming what we celebr

> ones buried, and in many other ways no one can count or always account for. Their critical and reflective discourse is not merely about faith. It is the very way faith works itself out in the intricacies of human life both individually and in common. Its vocabulary is not precise, concise, or scientific. It is symbolic, aesthetic, ascetical, and sapiential. ... It is a sinuous discourse by which they and those innumerable millions like them, dead and born and yet unborn, work out the primary body of perceived data concerning what it really means when God pours himself out into humanity, into the world as a member of our race. Nowhere else can that primary body of perceived data be read so well as in the living tradition of Christian worship.[25]

According to Kavanagh, Mrs. Murphy is a theologian. Thus Fagerberg says that although various people have used her for diverse purposes, she is "someone who has been capacitated by liturgical rite in the language of primary theology."[26] Hence, the believer is a theologian who reflects upon his or her experience during worship and tries to turn these experiences into explicitly lived expressions. So, whereas the functioning of these lived expressions is liturgical theology, making *theologia prima* explicit is the task of liturgical theology:

> It is the liturgiologist that must again become a theologian and adopt a theological context and depth for his work. It is indeed the entire church—clergy and faithful alike—who, in spite of all 'pseudomorphosis,' still continue to live by the liturgy, who must in the *lex orandi* rediscover the *lex credendi*, must make their liturgical piety a way of theological knowledge and understanding.[27]

This premise of a connected reality between liturgy and theology notwithstanding, the relationship between liturgy and theology is not without limitations, as some liturgical scholars, like Maxwell Johnson, Paul Bradshaw, and Michael Aune have noted in their works. Maxwell Johnson maintains that there is an intimate relationship between liturgy and theology, a relationship between the prayer of the Church and the Church's faith and doctrine, but the precise nature of the relationship between liturgy and theology remains "elusive and obscure."[28] Paul Bradshaw points out the need for a careful and attentive historical approach towards the understanding and interpretation of the relationship between liturgy and theology, despite their connectedness and relationships. He also asserts that liturgical theology should take seriously the fruits of historical research by giving a positive evaluation of the multivalent patterns of liturgy.[29] Michael Aune suggests that liturgical theology should take seriously the fruits of liturgical-historical research of a particular tradition or a particular practice while developing "a theological concept of liturgy that takes its bearings from the self-communication of the Triune God."[30] However, Alexander Schmemann cautions about the notion of liturgy being reduced to history by historians who are not theologians:

> The same can be said of the historical reduction of mere liturgiology, its fixation on the historical interest and attention. Absolutely indispensable as it is, this historical aspect not only can never be an end in itself, but, in the last analysis, it is only from a theological perspective that it can receive its most important and proper questions. Very good and knowledgeable historians, because of their theological ignorance, have produced monuments of nonsense comparable to those produced by the theologians of liturgy ignorant of its history.[31]

Furthermore, some liturgical theologians have resorted to studying the connectedness of liturgy and theology that include a 'plurality of particularities.' This approach demands that liturgical theology engage and pay attention to particular liturgies in order to understand or interpret faith expressions manifested in the Christian liturgy.

Despite the limitations and cautions we have pointed out, scholars agree on the close connection between liturgy and theology, since the experience of faith in the Church is found in actual liturgical celebrations. Thus, for us to suggest a disconnect between liturgy and theology means that we do not understand the connectedness between what the worshiping community already knows through theological interpretation, text, or cultural context, and what they experience in every liturgical act.[32] Where we may find disconnects among liturgiologists is in the various ways this relationship is explained, interpreted, and applied. By making the Church's living faith its ultimate concern, and giving a theological basis to the explanation of worship and to the whole liturgical tradition of the Church, liturgical theology "must deal with liturgy and it must be theological in nature."[33] This "does not mean theology should have liturgy as its sole object of study, or that theological statements should be sprinkled with phrases from the sacramentary, or that doctrine is authenticated by footnoting rubrics."[34] How, then, can other cultures interpret and apply these tasks of liturgical theology in order that faith expressions are given meaning from their local context?

To address this question, we turn our attention to the cultural engagement of liturgical theology in the African continent where religion, worship, and liturgy thrive. We will begin by posing the following pertinent questions: What is liturgical theology for African Christians and theologians who have unique ways of worshiping and interpreting their liturgical experience, coupled with a well-developed contextual theology in the continent? How would liturgical theology respond to the current state of liturgical inculturation in the continent? How will the engagement of liturgical theology and culture help in fostering the connection between liturgical acts and lived experiences? The next section will be devoted to answering the aforementioned questions and, thus, reignite the conversation on African liturgical theology.

IV. African Christian Theology: A Catholic Perspective

Africans need to worship God in the way the Spirit prompts them. They need and want worship that is free from liturgical drabness. They want to worship with spontaneity. They want to worship God the way their hearts move them. And they want to enter deep in worship, not just nibbling at it, hanging around at the periphery or watching as onlookers while "experts" perform.[35]

The study of African theology in the continent began with a theology that addressed the cultural identity of Africans, their cultural heritage and their worldview. This new way of theologizing was not an easy task, as one can imagine, but, with years of rigorous studies and debates by African theologians on what African theology should be and should not be, we are proud of a theology that is not necessarily "re-cooked or re-warmed" but a theology that draws from the Christian faith and African culture.[36]

African Christian theology began from the dynamic interaction between faith, culture, and the church, by studying the "experience of a particular Christian community in relation to what God has done, is doing, and will do."[37] It is theology, in every shape and form that seeks "to translate the one faith of Jesus Christ to suit the tongue, style, genius, and character of African peoples."[38] African Christian theology, according to Paulinus Odozor, developed as a result of fostering ways of understanding the Christian faith by African Christians, who inherited the faith that was not theirs and now share the faith with so many other Christians around the world.[39] This local or contextualized theology emanates from a relationship between the church and the worshiping community, taking cognizance of the worship forms of the community and the interaction of faith and culture that goes on in worship and life. African theology, as a contextualized theology, has led to the deepening of the Christian faith in the continent for the obvious fact that it studies Africa's cultural, religious, and historical past. As a contextual theology, it leads to an understanding "that the African religious experience and heritage were not illusory and that they should have formed the vehicle for conveying the Gospel verities to Africa and that many of Africa's religious insights had real affinity with those of the Bible. In many respects, the African was much more on the wavelength of the Bible than the Occidental ever was."[40]

African theology, thus, is faith seeking understanding within a context, and in this case, it is the African context and reality. This it does by dialoguing with the gospel and the African worldview (religion and culture) and incorporating, when allowed, these cultural praxes into the African Christians' way of life, thereby producing a Christianity that is fully Christian and truly African. At present, African Christian theology is an all-encompassing theology that has developed not only to study the spiritual life of Africans, but also to study how socio-political and economic issues affect the practical living out of the Christian faith in the continent.

V. Liturgical Theology in the African Context

The very fact that liturgical expressions of faith are thought and spoken of theologically means that liturgical theology must take into account the shape of the faith as embodied in prayer and ritual actions of particular cultural faith expressions. Robert Taft agrees with studying faith as it originates in the worshiping assembly when he opines:

> The history of liturgy is the story of a people at prayer, expressing in worship its peculiar cultural incarnation of the common faith. For the forms of worship are the product of a religious culture and spirit, the unique way that a particular faith community perceives, lives, and celebrates its Christian life. If liturgy is the most perfect religious expression of the soul that animates each tradition, a proper understanding of the liturgy demands understanding and sympathy for the genius and temperaments, the excess from which the liturgy springs.[41]

Finding ways for Africans to worship God in their own style and genius has motivated African liturgiologists to seek the connection between theological thinking and liturgical expressions of faith in the continent. African liturgical theology pushes the agenda of African theology much further, so that it will include and focus on the real-life experiences and faith expressions of the African Christian faithful whose religious life is customarily tied in with the entire sphere of their living as humans in the world. Africans have a unique way of viewing and interpreting reality, which implies also an expression of universal ideas in ways that best suit circumstances and experiences in the African society. Indeed the African mind has never been *tabula rasa,* for the African people have always had religion and morals to guide their life and thought patterns. As William Robertson Smith argues:

> No positive religion that has moved [people] has been able to start with a *tabula rasa* to express itself as if religion was beginning for the first time; in form if not in substance, the new system must be in contact all along with the old ideas and practice which it finds in its possession. A new scheme of faith can find a hearing only by appealing to religious instincts and susceptibilities that already exist in its audience, and it cannot reach these without taking account of the traditional forms in which a religious feeling is embodied, and without speaking a language which [people] accustomed to these forms can understand.[42]

African Christianity therefore incorporates aspects of the African heritage into the Christian faith so as to help understand better the faith Africans have embraced, and also construct a theology that is authentic to their reality, worldview, and experience. This theology begins from the African understanding of the notion of God and worship. Just as *Africae Munus* rightly states, "to deprive the African continent of God would be to make it die a slow death, by taking away its very soul."[43]

When Africans worship, they show with their hearts, minds, bodies, souls, and in fact with their whole being, that they are attuned to God who is unfathomably great and beyond all comparison. God, in the African concept, is above all forms of existence, as various authors have rightly stated in their works on African religion and philosophy. In the words of P. Tempels, God is the "great powerful life force."[44] For J. Mbiti, God is the ultimate explanation of the genesis and sustenance of humans and all things alike.[45] The prominent position of God in African cosmology is stressed by L. Magesa when he argues that "it is because of the place that God occupies in the universal order of things that human beings can even speak of their existence let alone their tradition."[46] If God did not exist, B. Idowu argues, all things would have fallen apart.[47] Without doubt, God, who goes by different names[48] and whose revelation is apprehended as per local experiences, is real for African people. In essence, Africans have an identical way of speaking about God and rendering worship to God who is the source of all life, hence the need for emergent local liturgies in Africa that integrate the liturgical celebrations with African authentic expressions and everyday life experiences.

Harkening to the call of *Africae Munus*, the need for local liturgiologists to articulate Christian faith and worship for African Christians became very important and gave rise to African liturgical inculturation for African Catholic Christians. African liturgical inculturation, therefore, became the starting point for understanding and harnessing the connection between liturgy and theology in the African context. Generally, the Church in Africa has made tremendous accomplishments in the area of liturgical inculturation since the Second Vatican Council's call to a "full, conscious, and active participation in the liturgy."[49] In various African regions, liturgical inculturation has flourished in areas of the Eucharistic liturgy and the Sacraments. We see in various churches in Africa, the use of African proverbs and interpolations during the homily,[50] local liturgical hymnody, local instruments, rhythmical dancing and hand clapping, vestments and vessels from the local culture, vernacular language in the entire liturgy.[51] There are also other visible signs of liturgical inculturation in Africa evident in the use of local liturgical art and architecture, incorporation of traditional ritual ceremonies into the liturgy,[52] adaptation of gestures, veneration of ancestors, and composition of particular rites.[53]

Such theological thought on inculturation that resulted from liturgical expression has developed various themes that reflect African worship, worldview, and tradition. The pioneers of African liturgical theology used various themes to develop a liturgical theology that speaks to the "plurality of particularities" and "cultural diversity" that exists in catholic liturgies. Names like Elochuku Uzukwu,[54] Kabsele Lumbala,[55] Patrick Chibuko,[56] Bishop Austin Echema,[57] John Lukwata,[58] and Chris Egbulem[59] come to mind when speaking of developed African liturgical theology. Their studies are not only groundbreaking, but also methodologically focused on particularities by paying attention to liturgical themes of prayer, texts, sacraments, rituals, and music. We will only focus on the proposed African Eucharistic prayers as a perfect example of the ongoing effort of African liturgical theology *in concreto*.

VI. African Liturgical Theology: Proposed African Eucharistic Prayers

> Since worship is the most important element that unites the entire community, only a living and adapted form of worship can generate the indispensable deepening of the faith, which cannot be given through instruction alone. ... An elaborate study and critique of the religious customs as well as a living contact with the people will reveal the fundamental cultural needs and will furnish the necessary elements for the elaboration of a living African liturgy sensitive to the aspirations of the population.[60]

That the liturgy be celebrated in an African way was a cherished topic in the 1994 Synod of Bishops Special Assembly for Africa, which emphasized the need for the Church in Africa to inculturate the Christian faith in a way that encompasses the entire Christian life in its process. "The field of inculturation is vast; the Synod which has so strongly insisted on its spiritual dimension by the place it accords to witnessing demands that none of its dimensions, theological, liturgical, catechetical, pastoral, juridical, political, anthropological, and communicational be lost sight of. It is the entire Christian life that needs to be inculturated."[61] To this effect, African liturgists took up the task of composing prayers that would connect with daily life experiences of Africans as well as communicate authentic expression of prayer and worship the African way. The Church in Africa and African liturgists believe that:

> If the liturgical celebrations are not tuned to the people's cultural background, if they are not concurrent with their way of expression and mentality, then the liturgy will appear foreign and consequently the Church will be considered foreign and be vulnerable in its most visible form. If the liturgy, however, is a full expression of the life of the community, then Christianity will manifest itself as a truly indigenous and an effective presence within society and its transforming force.[62]

As a result, African Eucharistic prayers were composed to "produce a text that made use of the language and symbolism of African traditional prayers."[63] African bishops and liturgists sought ways to interpret, understand, and enhance liturgical expressions of faith embodied by Africans. An "All-Africa" Eucharistic prayer,[64] enriched with expression of African sentiments from various African religious traditions, was composed and the structures were as follows: 1) two initial addresses to God, both containing references to a festive and thankful communion meal; 2) litanic declaration of thanksgiving; 3) invocation of the Father to send the Spirit; 4) institution narrative; 5) acclamation; 6) anamnetic declaration (addressed to Christ); 7) intercessions and 8) closing address to Christ.[65] Despite the liturgical theological analysis of this Eucharistic prayer, and the popularity it gained in the African continent, it remained an experimental Eucharistic prayer for the whole African Catholics. Three other African Eucharistic prayers, a Tanzanian Eucharistic prayer, a Kenyan Eucharistic prayer, and a Ugandan Eucharistic prayer,[66] composed from texts taken from a collection of more than 300 published African prayers emerged in the continent. In addition, Elochukwu Uzukwu composed an Igbo (Nigerian) Eucharistic prayer that captures the dynamism of the Igbo people and the reverence for God by adopting prayers arising from the traditional Igbo setting. It is important to note that all these prayers maintained the "structures of the Eucharistic prayers as arranged in historic liturgies: thanksgiving, epiclesis, institution narrative, anamnesis, intercessions, and doxology."[67] Sadly, none of these Eucharistic prayers, though linked by striking characteristics to African way of worship, prayer, and life, have received formal approval by the Congregation for Divine worship. Setbacks on approval of these Eucharistic prayers notwithstanding, we shall study the Igbo (Nigerian) Eucharistic prayer as it demonstrates an African liturgical theology that focuses on prayer and the relationship between God and the African people in liturgical acts of Church life.

By analyzing and interpreting a particular part of the liturgy, and also by paying attention to how worshippers reflect and articulate this liturgical act, the renowned African liturgist, Elochukwu Uzukwu,[68] shows the undeniable connection between liturgy, faith, and theology. Uzukwu attempts to develop a Eucharistic celebration that uses the Igbo (Nigerian) language and worldview, as the faithful praise and thank God for the wonder of their being. He employs the salvation-history approach: how God's action in the Igbo world is brought to fulfillment in Christ, and he uses various cultural influences in the evolution of the Eucharistic prayer. Uzukwu further explains the position of prayer in Igbo life, which includes the position of *Chukwu* or

Chi (God), morning prayers, sacrificial prayers directed to *Chukwu*, prayers for breaking the kolanut, the position of Spirits (*Ala* – Earth Spirit, *Ifejioku* – Yam spirit, *Amadioha* – spirit of lightning, and spirits who are sources of oracle), and the role of the ancestors. In Uzukwu's own words, findings from the study revealed that:

> African people praise, give thanks, and make petitions to *Chukwu* just as the Jews and Christians do. Similarly, the narration of divine favors is converted into an instrument of praise. There are, however, Igbo peculiarities: concrete symbols are preferred while praising and petitioning *Chukwu* and the other spirits; desire for communion with the deity is felt at the beginning of each prayer—*bia welu oji* (come and take kolanut—the kolanut is a symbol of commensality); life and progeny are overriding motives for prayers of petition and thanksgiving; the closeness and providence of *Chukwu* or *Chi* in relation to each individual Igbo, and in relation to the collectivity (directly or through agents) is strongly emphasized; spiritualization or fullness of life is a value the Igbo strive for in this world, and they hope to possess it firmly after death (ancestral status).[69]

It is from the historical, liturgical, and theological study of the evolution of the Christian Eucharistic prayer that the Igbo Eucharistic prayer, replete with Jewish-Christian-Igbo sentiments, emerged. The hope is that this prayer will foster the active participation of Igbo Christians during worship and also strengthen their relationship with *Chukwu* through Christ. The following proposed *Eucharistia Africana* by Uzukwu[70] focuses on explaining a particular liturgical act that enhances the deeper understanding and transformation of the faith expressions through lived experiences by African Christians. Divided into six sections, the prayer reads:

Introductory Dialogue	*Introductory Dialogue*
Onyenwe-anyị nọnyere ụnụ. **R/ Nọnyekwara gị.** Welitenụ obi elu. **R/ Anyị ewelite ha na ebe Dinwenụ nọ.** K'anyị nyenụ Dinwenụ Chukwu anyị ekele. **R/ Okwesịrị, bụrụ ihe ziri ezi.**	The Lord be with you.[71] **R/ And also with you.** Lift up your hearts **R/We lift them up to the Lord.** Let us give thanks to the Lord our God. **R/ It is right and just.**
Praise and Thanksgiving to God for Creation and Redemption	*Praise and Thanksgiving for Creation and Redemption*
Osebulu-ụwa, Chukwu ji ike nile, ekele! Eke kere ụwa, Chi nwe ndụ, ekele! Nna anyị, Nna ndi nna anyị ha, Anyị agbakọọ iji aja anyị kele Gị. Ụmụ Gị kwụ na-ihu Gị n'ekele , n'anụrị na Gị: N'ihi na ịbụ ndụ anyị, N'ihi na Ngi na-edu,na-echekweba anyị n'otu, n'otu, N'ihị na Ngị nyere anyị ndụ, na-eme ka anyị bawanye n'ụwa. Ike Gị na otito Gị na egosị onwe ya n'igwe na ala. Anyawụ, ọnwa, na kpakpando jupụtara igwe na-ek-	*Osebulu-uwa* (Lord), *Chukwu* (God), the all-powerful, we thank you! Creator of the world, *Chi* (God), the owner of life, we praise you! Our Father, Father of our ancestors, We gather together to praise and thank you with our sacrifice. Your children stand before You, thanking, praising, and rejoicing in you: Because You are our life, Because You lead and protect us one by one, Because You gave us life and cause us to increase in the world.

wupụta ebube Gị. Ala ọma nkea anyị bi n ime ya bụ aka ọrụ Gị. Nri nile anyị ji adị ndụ nke si n'ala pụta, bụ ihe ngozị Gị.	Your power and glory is manifest in the heavens and the earth. The sun, the moon, and the stars, which fills the heavens proclaim your glory. This goodly land in which we live, is the work of your hands. The food which gives us life, produce of the land, is your blessing.
R/ Nna dị ebube, ekele! Chi nke ndụ, onye ndụ anyị, ekele!	R/ Father, full of glory and majesty, we thank you! God of life, our leader, we thank you!
Nna dị ebube, Anyị amarala na anyị etosigh ịgbakowa n ihu Gị: ọbu mmehie anyị tinyere ajọ ihe n'ụwa Mana ihụnanya Gị na ebere Gị gbara anyị gburu-gburu. Ị gosịrị uche Gị n ebe ndị mmadụ nọ Ngị na agbaziri na akuziri ndi nna anyị ha na mmadụ nile ụzọ Gị; N'ihi na ọbụ uche Gị ka ụwa nile ghọta ka mma Gị di. Ka uwa nile nweta ndụ n uju n ime Gị	Majestic Father, We acknowledge that we are not worthy to gather before You: It is our sins that brought evil in the world. But Your love and Your mercy surround us. You made your will manifest among [people], You were directing and teaching our ancestors and all [people] your ways: Because it is your will that the whole world understand Your goodness, That the whole world experience fullness of life in you.

R/ Ekele dịrị Gị , Dinwenụ, onye ndu nke nna anyị ha! **Obi ọma Gị n'ebeanyị nọ,ọkarịka!** **Ihụnaya Gị n'ebeanyị nọ,ọkarịka!**	**R/ We thank you, Lord, the leader of our fathers!** **Your kindness to us is limitless!** **Your love towards us is limitless!**
Chukwu onye okike anyị, Anyị ji anụrị kwụrụ n ihu Gi, N'eto Gị, n'egori na oru nke kacha ọrụ Gị nile n'ụwa: Izite-ere anyị otu Nwa Gị ihụrụnanya, Jesu, nwanne anyị, onye ihe ya n'asọ Gị ; Ya bu mmeju nkwa Gị n'ebe ụmụ mmadụ nọ, O gosịrị anyị ka afọ-ọma Gị dị. Mee ka anyị ghọta na Ị bụ Chi-na-azọ anyị, Ya bụ anya anyị na ntị anyi n'ebe Ị nọ, Ya gosịrị anyị etu esi ahụ ụzọ, etu esi anụ ihe , na ụzọ anyị ga esi efe Gị, Ka anyị wee nweta ndụ n uju.	God, our Creator, We stand before You with joy, Praising, and rejoicing in Your greatest work in the world: You sent Your only beloved Son to us, Jesus, our brother, who is pleasing to you: He is the fulfilment of your promises to all peoples, He showed to us Your loving-kindness, and made us understand that You are the God who saves us, He is our eyes and our ears in your presence, He showed us how to see, how to hear, and how to worship You, That we may have life to the full.
R/ Ekele dịrị Gị Nna! **Ekele dịrị Gị maka onye nzọpụta anyị Jesu Christi!**	**R/ We thank You Father!** **We thank You for our Saviour Jesus Christ!**
Institution Narrative and Anamnesis	*Institution Narrative and Anamnesis*

Mgbe Ọrụsịrị ọrụ Ị ji zite Ya, Mgbe Ọkwadoro iwere ndụ ya nye maka anyị, Na anyasị na-eso mbọsi ọtara ahụhụ, Ka ha na eri nri, Owere achịcha, too Gị, nye ya ndị ụmụazụ ya sị: Naranụ, rienụ, ọ bụ Ahụ M! Ihe aja maka ụnụ! Mgbe ha richa-ara oriri ahụ, Owere mmanya nke otito, kene-e Gị maka ọrụ ọma Gị nile, nyekwa ndị ụmụazụ ya sị: Naranụ, ńụọnụ, ọ bụ Ọbara M! Ihe ọgbụgba ndụ, Nke na-ekpochapụ njọ, Nke na-ejikọ mụ na ụnụ na mmadụ nile, n'otu ezi-na-ụlọ nke Chukwu ga adị ebebe. N'eme nụ ya na ncheta nke M!	When he completed the work for which You sent him, When he was ready to give his life for us, On the night before he suffered, While they were eating, He took bread, gave praise to you, and gave the bread to his disciples, saying: Take, all of you, and eat; it is my body! The victim sacrificed for you! At the end of the festival meal, He took the cup of blessing, thanked You for all your wonderful works, and gave it to his disciples saying: Take, all of you, and drink; it is my blood! The covenantal bond, which wipes away sin, which binds me to you and to all [people], in the one everlasting family of God. Do this in memory of me!
Nna anyị na-ekwupụta ọnwụ Christi! **R/ Ọnwụ ya n'enu obe!** Anyị n'egori na mbilite na-ọnwụ ya! **R/ Mbilite na-ọnwụ ya di itụnanya!** Anyị na atu anya maka mbiaghachi ya na mbọsi ikpeazụ!	Father, we proclaim the death of Christ! **R/ His death on the cross!** We rejoice at his resurrection! **R/ His marvellous resurrection!** We look forward to his return on the last day!

R/Mgbe anyị ga abanye na oriri nke ndụ ebebe!	**R/ When we shall enter into the feast of life everlasting!**
Prayer of Offering and Epiclesis	*Prayer of Offering and Epiclesis*
N'obi ọma Gị, nekwasa anya na aja nke a, Nara ya n'ihi Christi Nwa Gị na nwanne anyị , Nara ya n'ihi obi ọma Gị n'ebe anyi nọ. Zitere anyị Mụọ Gị, Mụọ nke Nwa Gị, Mụọ nke ndụ, Onye nkuzi nke ndi kwelụnụ, Onye ndu nke nna anyị ha. Mee ka ọdakwasi na aja anyị: K'anyị were jupụta na ndụ na n'ezi-okwu, Ka oriri Ahụ na Ọbara Christi wetara anyị ndụ na nzọpụta, Ka oriri Ahụ na Ọbara Christi jidesie anyị ike n'otu ezi-na-ụlọ Gị.	In your loving-kindness, look upon the sacrifice, Accept it because of Christ your son and our brother, Accept it because of your kindness towards us, Send us Your Spirit, The Spirit of your Son, The spirit of life, Teacher of those who believe, Guide of our fathers. May he rest on our sacrifice: So that we may be filled with life and truth, May this feast of the body and blood of Christ bring us life as salvation, May this feast of the body and blood of Christ hold us firmly together in Your one family.
Intercessions	Intercessions
Nna gọzie ezi-na-ụlọ Gị nke a Ị doro nsọ site na Ọbara Christi. **R/ Nna nụlụ onu anyị.**	Father, bless this your family which you sanctified in the blood of Christ. **R/ Father hear our voice.**
Lota ụmụ-nne anyị, ụmụ Gị ,	Remember our brothers and

ndi na anọghị n'ezi-na-ụlọ ọhụrụ nke a, Site na ihe nke Mụọ Gị, mee ka ha hụ na Christi mmeju ekpere nke nna anyị ha. **R/ Nna nụlụ onu anyị.**	sisters, your children, who are not yet within this new family. By the light of Your Spirit, enlighten them to see in Christ the fulfilment of the prayer of our ancestors. **R/ Father hear our voice.**
Jikọọ ndi nile na akpọku Gị site na Christi n ụwa nile, Mee ka ha jisie ike na otu okwukwe. **R/ Nna nụlụ onu anyị.**	Gather all, throughout the world, who call upon you through Christ, grant that they be strengthened in one faith. **R/ Father hear our voice.**
Bụrụ ike ndị ịhọpụtara ka ha na-achị nzukọ Gị, nye ha amamihe na nghọta. **R/ Nna nụlụ onu anyị.**	Be the strength of those you have chosen to be the guides of your church, Give them wisdom and understanding. **R/ Father hear our voice.**
Gọzie obodo nile dị n'ụwa, Nye ha ihụnaya, ịdịkọ n'otu, na udo. **R/ Nna nụlụ onu anyị.**	Bless all the countries of the world, give them love, unity, and peace. **R/ Father hear our voice.**
Gọzie ala ọma nke a anyị bi n'ime ya, Nye ya ụba na mmadụ na n'ihe oriri. **R/ Nna nụlụ onu anyị.**	Bless this goodly land in which we live, Give it increase in people and in food. **R/ Father hear our voice.**
Gwọọ ndi ọya, tasie ndi nọ na ahụhụ obi, nye ndi agụrụ na agụ nrị.	Heal the sick, comfort the suffering, give food to the hungry.

R/ Nna nụlụ onu anyị.	**R/ Father hear our voice.**
Me-ere ụmụ-nne anyị ndi nwụrụ anwụ ebere, Nye ha ndụ n'ụjụ. Mee ka anyi na ndi nke Gị nile bụrụ otu, ọkacha ndi nna anyị ha mere uche Gị, Maria nne Nwa Gị, Jesu, ndi Ozi, na ndinile omume ha sọrọ Gị. **R/ Nna nụlụ onu anyị.**	Have mercy on our departed brethren, grant them the fullness of life. Grant that we may be one with all your people, especially our ancestors who did your will, Mary, mother of your Son Jesus, the Apostles, and all those whose lives were pleasing to you. **R/ Father hear our voice.**
Conclusion Anyị etinye onu anyị na nke ha, Soro ha n'ekele, n'akpọku Gị , Nna di nsọ, Site na Christi Nwa Gị, N'ime nke Mụọ nke ndụ , Ka ekpere anyị ruo Gị ahụ, Ka anyị banye na ndụ ebebe. Amen.	*Conclusion* We join our voices to theirs, In praising (thanking) and invoking you, O Holy Father, Through Christ your Son, In the Spirit of life, May our prayers reach you, so that we may enter into life unending. Amen.

Faithful to the structure of the Roman Catholic Eucharistic prayer, the Igbo Eucharistic prayer is punctuated with congregational responses, giving this prayer an African flair. Each section contains a response to praise and thanksgiving for creation, providence, and redemption which sums up the main thoughts of individual segments. The introductory dialogue, as presented above, remains the same in order to preserve the history and sentiments evident in the Judeo-Christian tradition. In explaining the praise and thanksgiving section, Uzukwu employs a historical, liturgical, and theological analysis of the Eucharistic prayer in the

Jewish and Christian tradition and shows the similarity of these two traditions with the Igbo traditional prayer patterns. He models this praise and thanksgiving section according to how Igbo Christians experience and understand the marvelous deeds of God. The prayer invites the community to praise and thank God for creation, the gift of Christ (presented as the peak of divine benevolence—salvation-history approach), the experience of God in Igbo life, the celebrating community and their ancestors. There is also an acknowledgment of human failure and an assertion that the community's gathering is likewise for a sacrifice of atonement, in this section of the Igbo Eucharistic prayer.

The institution narrative and anamnesis are the climax of the Christological memorial, containing an explication of Christ's redemptive events and acknowledgments of the covenantal bond between the Igbo community and God through Christ. This covenant not only strengthens the bond already existing between individuals, families, village groups, and *Chukwu,* but it also transcends this bond to include all those who are bound to Christ.[72] The bond between *Chukwu* and the Igbo community is further expounded in the prayer of offering and epiclesis as the Trinity is evoked to accept the sacrifice of praise and thanksgiving of the Christian community. This prayer implores God:

> To accept the community's sacrifice because it is that of Christ who is the concrete manifestation of God's loving kindness towards the community; it is a prayer which asks God to declare that the sacrifice is acceptable to him and complete, by sending the Holy Spirit—the Spirit of Christ who brings fullness of life and teaches the Church, the Spirit who has been the guide of the community's ancestors, making it possible for them to make a profession of faith in Christ.[73]

That the faithful effect of the Eucharist celebrated be expressed by the community and in the world is highlighted in the intercessions (prayer for the Church universal, conversion, Christian unity, Church leaders, and all those suffering) with a congregational response, which emphasizes participation in, and agreement with, the petitions made. The concluding section goes back to the central motive of praise, thanksgiving, and petition directed to the Father, through Christ, and in the Spirit of Life with a full eschatological reality that summarizes the experience of the community.

Uzukwu's proposed Igbo Eucharistic prayer is a perfect example of a methodological focus on a particularity in liturgical theology. He focuses on a prayer that helps us understand that in worship "faith is known, fed and lives,"[74] and he proposes a prayer that is 1) Biblical—a description of the greatness of God as creator of the world and owner of life, salvation-history, covenantal bonds, personal and communal demand of response to God's love; 2) Eucharistic—giving thanks and praise for the gift of life and the gift of Christ who showed believers how to worship; 3) Christological—expounding the full Christ event; 4) Trinitarian—a worship in which believers encounter the Father, Son, and the Holy Spirit; 5) Ethical and Existential—Christ making worshippers understand who God is and how to live as faithful believers in order to have life in full; 6) Anthropological—applying the worshippers' understanding, thought patterns, and experience as unique to their worship of God; 7) Ecclesiological—the place of gathering is the Church, which makes worshiper the people of God and the body of Christ; 8) Eschatological—a worship of what the community is and will experience in the fullness of time.
In Uzukwu's own words, the Igbo Eucharistic prayer "allows the Igbo to express gratitude to *Chukwu* for his marvelous works climaxing in the Christ-event; it makes it easier for the community to understand and intensify its relations with God in Christ."[75] A unique text like this will lead to an authentic faith building, communal engagement, commonality, and strengthened solidarity, since worshippers will understand the implications and demand of the Eucharistic celebration: their *lex vivendi*. As beautiful as this proposed Igbo Eucharistic prayer and other African Eucharistic prayers are, one wonders why there has not been a possible

studying, restructuring, approval or use of these prayers in the Church in Africa. What are the barriers?

African Liturgical Theology: Hiccups or Setbacks?

The task of liturgists is to interpret or analyze the liturgical acts that accrue from celebrating the Christian life in the liturgy. With inculturation setting the stage for an incarnated theology in the African context, African liturgical theology will be dependent on expounding meanings in already contextualized African texts of worship that need to be "dusted off the shelves" and used in an actual liturgical celebration. The problem is the practical use of the theological findings which some liturgiologists and theologians have studied in the continent. How can our liturgical theologizing transcend from "written literature to living literatures"? I cannot claim to have the answers to this question, but I believe that first and foremost, it is time that the efforts of African liturgists who are studying ways to enhance the liturgical life of the Christians in the continent, is recognized, and proposed texts that can enhance worship studied and approved for use in the continent. We cannot speak of an African liturgical theology when efforts to propose, enhance, and explain the theological meaning of liturgical acts do not see the light of day, since they are either suppressed or actively discouraged.

African Bishops hold the key to making liturgical studies flourish in the continent. Unfortunately, "many bishops have placed obstacles to harmless practices, many have refused permission for experimentation and many more have ignored the whole issue."[76] A change of attitude towards liturgical inculturation on the part of some bishops would help promote more fruitful studies in liturgical theology, so that African liturgy will be an avenue for deepening the understanding of liturgical experience or expressions foremost to the transformation of lives, from liturgical experience to liturgical fulfillment. If we wish to see Christian faith lived out by believers in the continent, we need to make the efforts of theologians worthwhile in the continent. Proposals on inculturation by liturgiologists should be examined before they are rendered to shelves where they sit and accumulate dust for centuries.

The way forward for African liturgical theology rests with African liturgists and theologians going back to resurrect, from libraries and archives, proposals about liturgical inculturation and experimentation and possible implementation of innovations.[77] This will mean reigniting the zeal of the founding fathers of African liturgical inculturation, accepting the need of an inculturated way of worship in the continent, and a change of attitude, and an open mind. Our academic theology should be in touch with, respond to, and facilitate, popular theology through a range of creative approaches, all for the equipping and maturation of the Church.[78] For some African bishops and theologians, those who do not feel the need to enhance worship to conform to African Christian life experience and world, need to understand and value the gifts the African Church brings to the Church universal. We really need to "emancipate [ourselves] from mental slavery; none but ourselves can free our own minds."[79] African liturgical theology should not end in writing theological books or articles; rather, our degrees and theological training and writings should encourage true discipleship in practically living out the faith in the African way. The Church recognizes and appreciates the efforts of theologians in advancing dialogue with the world of cultures but still urges theologians not to be content with a desk-bound theology in evangelizing.[80]

There has to be more openness of the Church universal. Better put, we should become a listening Church on those issues which pertain to the creation of particular rites and prayers for the incarnation of the faith in given cultures. Yes, we need to retain the heritage that the liturgy preserves, but this should not impede authentic evangelization based on people's cultural heritages, experiences, and world view. Finally, we must not fail to establish a close connection with African liturgical theology and ecclesiology in theologizing. "Mission is much more comprehensive than bringing people to an initial commitment of their lives to Christ. The Church must become the center of theological instruction and discussion."[81] To achieve this, our perception of the Church should portray an understanding of the Church "as the entire People of God which evangelizes"[82] and "take the Church seriously as the social and historical embodiment of the Christian way of life."[83]

In summary, the task of any liturgical theology is to foster the close connection between liturgy and theology, and cease from making liturgy a ceremony and theology an intellectual discipline that remains unattainable by the faithful. Schmemann alludes to the danger of separating liturgy, theology, and even piety, which are supposed to bond together to make a Christian:

> It deprived liturgy of its proper understanding by the people, who began to see in it beautiful and mysterious ceremonies in which, while attending them, they take no real part. It deprived theology of its living source and made it into an intellectual exercise for intellectuals. It deprived piety of the living content and term of reference. . . . To understand liturgy from inside, to discover and experience that "epiphany" of God, world, and life which the liturgy contains and communicates, to relate this vision and this power to our own existence, to all our problems: such is the purpose of liturgical theology.[84]

VII. Conclusion

Liturgical theology, as we have studied it in theory and practice, aims at giving expression to the theological foundations discovered in worship. Thus, we understand what we celebrate, and in understanding, we become what we celebrate, and in becoming what we celebrate, we practically live out the fruits and demands of Eucharistic celebration. "The liturgy, which is celebrated at certain moments but lived at every moment, is the one mystery of Christ who gives life to human beings. . . . The Christ whom we celebrate is the identical Christ by whom we live; his mystery permeates both celebration and life."[85]

African liturgical theology, using the African Christians' experience, worldview and life, offers a deeper meaning and understanding of worship in the continent and speaks to the enrichment and evangelization of contemporary African culture as demanded by *Africae Munus* (AM, 37). Paying attention to interpreting particular parts of liturgical acts, while doing liturgical theology, reveals for worshippers a better understanding of God, his relatedness to us, and our relatedness to each other and the world. It is truly a way "of inspiring in Christ's disciples in Africa the will to become effectively committed to living out the Gospel in their daily lives and in society" (AM, 32). We come to know that "in the end, liturgy is primarily about what God has done among us and for us. All that we do in the liturgy is but a response to the overarching, grace-filled initiative of God. . . . There is a delicate balance in liturgy: divine initiative and human response, the action of God and the sanctification of humanity. . . . Even then it is not about what we achieve but what God works among us and through us."[86]

Therefore, liturgical theology, African liturgical theology included, must accept the task of theologizing in ways that the "God-talk" can reach our audience who are the churchgoers who sit in pews every Sunday hoping for a transformative and informative liturgical experience lived out in the "Kingdom of God on earth." For what theology teaches, liturgy celebrates. Thus, we speak of theology in liturgical celebrations knowing that theology finds full expression, vigor, and practicality in the worship forms of the Church. Evidently, in doing liturgical theology, we see vividly the interdependence of theology and liturgy where liturgy becomes the *"locus theologicus"* and theology the *"locus liturgicus."* An African liturgical theology responds to *Africae Munus'* call to theologians to "continue to probe the depths of the trinitarian mystery and its meaning for everyday African life." (AM, 172)

Chapter 4 Endnotes

1 Peter Henriot, "*Africae Munus* and Priestly Formation," *Journal of Hekima College* (May 2012): 128–135.

2 See *Africae Munus*, 42–68.
3 Ibid., 69–72.
4 Alexander Schmemann, *Introduction to Liturgical Theology* (New York: St. Vladimir's Seminary Press, 1975), 14.
5 Schmemann, *Introduction to Liturgical Theology*, 14.
6 Alexander Schmemann, "Liturgical Theology: Its Task and Method," St Vladimir's Theological Quarterly 1:4 (1957):16–27; *Introduction to Liturgical Theology* (New York: St. Vladimir's Seminary Press, 1975).
7 Aidan Kavanagh, *On Liturgical Theology* (New York: Pueblo Press, 1984).
8 Edward Kilmartin, *Christian Liturgy: Theology and Practice* (Kansas City, MO: Sheed & Ward, 1988).
9 Gordon Lathrop, *Holy Things: A Liturgical Theology* (Minneapolis: Augsburg Fortress, 1993).
10 David Fagerberg, *What is Liturgical Theology? A Study in Methodology* (Minnesota: The Liturgical Press, 1992).
11 Kevin W. Irwin, *Context and Text: Method in Liturgical Theology* (Minnesota: The Liturgical Press, 1994); *Liturgical Theology: A Primer* (Minnesota: The Liturgical Press, 1990).
12 Kevin W. Irwin, "Liturgical Theology," *The New Dictionary of Sacramental Worship*, ed. Peter Fink (Minnesota: The Liturgical Press, 1990), 722.
13 David Fagerberg, *Theologia Prima*, 7–8.
14 Ibid., 9.
15 Ibid, 51.
16 Ibid, 100.
17 Aidan Kavanagh, *On Liturgical Theology*, 77.
18 Dionysius Bar Salibi, "Against the Melchites." Cited in Baby Varghese, *West Syrian Liturgical Theology* (Burlington, VT: Ashgate Publishing, 2004), 3.
19 These pioneers of African Theology include inter alia: Vincent Mulago, Engelbert Mveng, Msgr. Tharceisse Tshibangu, Alphose N. Mushete, Sidbe Sempore, Oscar Bimwenyi, Benezet Bujo, Barthelemy Adoukonou, Elochukwu Uzukwu, Laurenti Magesa, Francois- Marie Lufuluabo Mizeka, Alexus Kagame, Meinrad Pierre Hebga, Laurent Mpongo, Ikenga Metu, Bolaji Idowu, John Mary Waliggo, Justin Ukpong, Charles Nymiti, Jean-Marc Ela, Patrick Kalilombe, Mercy Amba Oduyoye, Theresa Okure, Kwame Bediako, Kwesi A. Dickson, and Partick Chibuko. C.f Benezet Bujo and Juvenal Muya, ed., *African Theology: The Contribution of Pioneers Vol I&II* (Nairobi: Paulines Publications Africa, 2002).

20 For more details on these topics, see Rosino Gibellini, ed., *Paths of African Theology* (MaryKnoll, NY: Orbis Books,1994); Kofi Appiah-Kubi and Sergio Torres, eds., *African Theology en Route* (MaryKnoll, NY: Orbis Books,1979); Miguel A. De La Torre, ed., *Introducing Liberative Theologies* (MaryKnoll, NY: Orbis Books,2015); Paulinus Odozor, *Morality Truly Christian, Truly African* (Notre Dame: University of Notre Dame Press, 2014), J.N.K. Mugambi and Laurenti Magesa, ed., *Jesus in African Christianity: Experimentation and Diversity in African Christology* (Kenya: Initiative Ltd, 1989); Mercy Amba Oduyoye, *Introducing African Women's Theology* (Sheffield, England: Sheffield Academic Press, 2001); Mercy Amba Oduyoye, ed., *The State of Christian Theology in Nigeria, 1980 81* (Ibadan, Nigeria: Day star Press, 1986);Stan Chu Ilo, Joseph Ogbonnaya, Alex Ojacor, eds., The Church as Salt and Light: Path to an African Ecclesiology of Abundant Life (Cambridge: James Clarke & Co, 2012); Ferdinand Nwaigbo, *Mary—Mother of the African Church: A Theological Inculturation of Mariology* (Frankfurt am Main ; New York: P. Lang, 2001); Agbonkhianmeghe E. Orobator, ed., *Practising Reconciliation, Doing Justice, Building Peace: Conversations on Catholic Theological Ethics in Africa* (Nairobi, Kenya: Paulines Publications of Africa, 2013); G, Wakuraya Wanjohi, ed., *African Ethics: Gĩkũyũ Traditional Morality* (Amsterdam; New York: Rodopi, 2010).

21 Nicholas Wolterstorff, *The God We Worship: An Exploration of Liturgical Theology* (Michigan: William B. Eerdmans Publishing Company, 2015), 23.

22 *Sacrosanctum Concilium*, 9–10

23 Helene L. Lenval, *The Whole Man at Worship* (New York: Desclee Company, 1961), 65.

24 Nicholas Wolterstorff, *The God We Worship: An Exploration of Liturgical Theology*, 24.

25 Kavanagh, *On Liturgical Theology*, 146–147.

26 David Fagerberg, *Theologia Prima*, 133

27 Alexander Schmemann, *Church, World, Mission: Reflections on Orthodoxy in the West* (St. Vladimir's Seminary Press, 1979), 145.

28 Maxwell Johnson, "Liturgy and Theology," in *Liturgy in Dialogue: Essays in Memory of Ronald Jasper*, Paul Bradshaw and Bryan Spinks, eds. (Collegeville, MN: Liturgical Press, 1993), 224.

29 Paul Bradshaw, "Difficulties in Doing Liturgical Theology," *Pacifica* 11 (1998): 181–194.

30 Michael Aune, "The Current State of Liturgical Theology: A Plurality of Particularities," *St. Vladimir's Theological Quarterly* 53(2009): 210–213.

31 Ibid.
32 Michael Aune, 54.
33 Dwight Vogel, 13.
34 David Fagerberg, *Theologia Prima*, 98.
35 Paul Ajah, *An Approach to Africa Theology* (Nigeria: Truth and Life Publications), 92.
36 See Paulinus Odozor, *Morality Truly Christian, Truly African* (Notre Dame: University of Notre Dame Press, 2014), 9–47; John Parratt, *A Reader in African Christian Theology* (Great Britain: SPCK, 1987),1–46; Some scholars, like Tite Tienou have also expressed concern about the way African theology is perceived, "When we think of theologians, most of us do not automatically think of people of non-European stock. Theology as we experience it in Africa is basically of European origin; may best have been re-cooked in Africa, or maybe only re-warmed." Cf. Tite Tienou, "The Theological Task of the Church in Africa," in *Issues in African Christian Theology*, Samuel Ngewa, Mark Shaw, and Tite Tienou, eds. (Nairobi: East African Educational Publishers, 1998), 4.
37 Walbert Buhlmann, *The Coming of the Third Church: An Analysis of the Present and Future of the Church* (Slough, UK: St. Paul Publications, 1976), 20.
38 Andrew Walls, *The Missionary Movement in Christian History: Studies in the Transformation of Faith* (Mary Knoll, NY: Orbis books, 1996), 149.
39 Paulinus Odozor, *Morality Truly Christian, Truly African* (Notre Dame: University of Notre Dame Press, 2014), 9.
40 Desmond Tutu, "Whiter African Theology?" in *Christianity in Independent Africa*, ed., Edward Fasole-Luke, Richard Gray, Adrian Hastings, and Godwin Tasie (Bloomington: Indiana University Press, 1979), 368.
41 Robert Taft, *The Great Entrance: A History of the Transfer of Gifts and Other Pre-Anaphoral Rites of the Liturgy of St. John Chrysostom* (Rome: Pont.Institutum Studiorum Orientaliun, 1978), vii.
42 William Robertson Smith, *Lectures on the Religion of the Semites* (London: A&C Black Ltd, 1923), 2.
43 See *Africae Munus*, 7.
44 P. Tempels, *Bantu Philosophy* (Paris: ET, 1959), 28.
45 J.S Mbiti, *African Religions and Philosophy* (London: Heinemann, 1969), 16.
46 Laurent Megaesa, *African Religion: The Moral Traditions of Abundant Life* (MaryKnoll: Orbis Books, 1997), 40.
47 Bolaji Idowu, *African Traditional Religion: A Definition* (London: SCM Press, 1973), 104.

48 Proper names for God like "Yamba that occurs in parts of Nigeria similar to the *Yambe, Yembe,*or *Ndyambi* in Cameroon and Congo, and as *Onyame* or *Nyame* among the Akan of Ghana and the Nilotic peoples of the greater Sudan." Cf. Idowu, African Traditional Religion, 103ff; also see Edwin W. Smith who acknowledges that the name of God appears in various forms in very large area of Western Equatorial Africa, *African Ideas of God* (London: Edinburg House Press, 1950), 156–157.

49 *Sacrosanctum Concilium,* 14.

50 See Mary Reginald Anibueze, "Immigrants and Cultural Continuance in the Liturgy: Celebrating the Nigerian Igbo Mass in the United States," The *Journal Of the Black Catholic Theological Symposium* 8 (2014) :61–67.

51 Paulinus Odozor, *Morality Truly Christian, Truly African: Fundamental, Methodological, and Theological Considerations* (Notre Dame: University of Notre Dame, 2014), 38–39. Also see Elochukwu Uzukwu, *Worship as Body Language* (Minnesota: The Liturgical Press, 1997), 2–10.

52 Seen in Ordination rites, religious rites and consecration of virgins, baptism, rites of reconciliation, marriage, anointing of the sick, initiation rites, and rituals of blessing and consecration. Cf. Kabasele Lumbala, *Celebrating Jesus Christ in Africa: Liturgy & Inculturation* (New York: Orbis Books), 58–103.Patrick Chibuko, *Paschal Mystery of Christ: Foundation for Liturgical Inculturation in Africa* (Frankfurt: Peter Lang GmbH, 1999), 186–252.

53 Some Catholic dioceses in Burkina Faso have incorporated the traditional initiation rites into the Christian initiation rite in the liturgy known as the Moore Ritual; Christianization of the traditional naming ceremony in Yoruba culture, Nigeria; The Cameroonian Mass; The Eucharistic Prayers of East Africa, and the Consecration of Virgins in Zaire. Cf. Elochukwu Uzukwu, *Worship as Body Language,* 272–316; Nwaka Chris Egbulem, *The Power of Africentric Celebrations: Inspirations from the Zairean Liturgy* (New York: Crossroad Herder Book, 1996).Patrick Chibuko, *Paschal mystery of Christ: Foundation for Liturgical Inculturation in Africa* (Frankfurt: Peter Lang, 1999), 111–136 & 161–184.

54 Elochukwu E. Uzukwu, A *Listening Church: Autonomy and Communion in African Churches* (New York: Orbis Books, 1996); Evangelization *in Southeastern Nigeria 1885–1985: Reflections on the Past, Prospects for the Future* (Enugu: Spiritan Booklets, 1985); *Inculturation: A Nigerian Perspective* (Enugu: Spiritan Press, 1988); "African Symbols and Christian Liturgical Celebration." *Worship 65* (1991):

98–112; *Church and Culture* (Obosi: Pacific College Press, 1985); "Food and Drink in Africa and the Christian Eucharist." *AFER 22* (1980): 370–385; "Igbo World and Ultimate Reality and Meaning." *URAM 5* (1982): 188–209; "Inculturation of Eucharistic Celebration in Africa." *CHIEA: African Christian Studies* (1985); *Liturgy: Truly Christian, Truly African* (Kenya: GABA Publications, 1982); *Inculturation A Nigerian Perspective* (Enugu: Spiritan Press, 1988); *Worship as Body Language* (Minnesota: Liturgical Press, 1997).

55 Kabasele Lumbala, *Celebrating Jesus Christ in Africa: Liturgy and Inculturation* (New York: Orbis Books, 1998); "Nouveaux Rites, Foi naissante," in *Lumiere et Vie* 158 (1983); 61–73; "L'Inculturation Sacramentelle au Zaire," Lumen Vitae XLII(1987); 75–84; *Alliances avec le Christ en Afrique: inculturation des rites religieux au Zäire* (Paris:Karthala, 1994); *Le christianisme et l'Afrique: une chance réciproque* (Paris: Karthala, 1993); *Symbolique bantu et symbolique chrétienne: Rencontre dans la liturgie* (Kinshasa, Zäire: Editions Filles de St Paul, 1990); and *Liturgies africaines: l'enjeu culturel, ecclésial et théologique* (Kinshasa: Facultés catholiques de Kinshasa, 1996); "Comparison Between Syriac Eucharistic Prayers and Actual African Eucharistic Prayers," *The Harp* 4 (1991) 225–234.

56 Patrick Chibuko, *Paschal Mystery of Christ* (Frankfurt: Peter Lang, 1999); "Alternative Order of Eucharistic Celebration: A Case for Local Churches in Nigeria." *Journal of Inculturation Theology 10* (2008): 51–71; *Liturgical Inculturation: An Authentic African Response* (Frankfurt am Main: IKO-Verlag, 2002); *Church Wedding and Traditional Marriage in one Ceremony* (Enugu: Snaap Press, 1999); *Igbo Christian Rite of Marriage* (Frankfurt: Peter Lang Gmbh, 1999); "Inculturation as a Method of Evangelization in the Light of the African Synod." *Journal of Inculturation Theology* 3 (1996): 31–44; *The Undying Hope of the Church* (Enugu: Black Belt Konzult Ltd, 2004); "Liturgical Theology of Church Architecture: Challenges to the Nigerian Church Today" in *Theology and Liturgy in the Life of the Church: Proceedings of the 26th Annual Conference of the Catholic Theological Association of Nigeria, Luke E. Ijezie, Stephen Audu & Agnes I. Acha, ed.(Nigeria: CATHAN, 2012).*

57 Austin Echema, *Anointing of the Sick and Healing Ministry* (Frankfurt: Verlang fur Interkulturelle Kommunikation, 2006); *Corporate Personality in Traditional Igbo Society and the Sacrament of Reconciliation* (Frankfurt am Main: P. Lang, 1995); *Igbo Funeral Rites Today: Anthropological and Theological Perspectives* (Berlin: LIT Verlag, 2010).

58 John Lukwata, Integrated African Liturgy (Kemya: AMECEA Gaba Publications, 2003).

59 Nwaka Chris Egbulem, *The Power of Afrocentric Celebrations: Inspirations from the Zairean Liturgy* (New York: Crossroad Herder Book, 1996); "Mission and Inculturation: Africa," in *The Oxford History of Christian Worship*, ed. Geoffrey Wainwright and Karen B. Westerfield Tucker (Oxford: University Press, 2006), 678–695.

60 Conference Episcopale du Congo, "Apostolat Liturgique – Adaptation du culte," in *Actes de la Assemblee Pleniere de l' Episcopat du Congo* (Leopoldville: Secretariat General de l' Episcopat, 1961), 362–63.

61 Message of the Synod, 18; Browne, "The African Synod," 75.

62 D.R.K Nkurunzinza, "Liturgy: The Privileged Arena for Inculturation" AFER 27(1985):n212.

63 Alward Shorter, "Three More African Eucharistic Prayers," *AFER* 15 (1973):152.

64 The All-African Eucharistic prayer marked the beginning of Africans' attempt to have a liturgical prayer that is true to the language, style, mentality, and symbolism in African traditional religion. For a complete text of the All-African Eucharistic prayer, see Alward Shorter, "An African Eucharistic Prayer," *AFER* 12 (1970): 143–148.

65 Elochukwu Uzukwu, "The All-African Eucharistic Prayer: A Critique" AFER 21(1979): 340–341.

66 For the three African Eucharistic prayer texts see Aylward Shorter, "Three More African Eucharistic Prayers," *AFER* 15 (1973):155–160; Aylward Shorter, *African Culture and the Christian Church* (Mary-Knoll, NY: Orbis Books 1974), 114–116. The Gaba Pastoral Institute, Eldoret, Kenya, composed four African Eucharistic prayers between 1969 and 1973. These prayers are either on paper or used in experimental centers in East Africa.

67 Aylward Shorter, *African Culture and the Christian Church*, 114; Elochukwu Uzukwu, "Inculturation and Liturgy," 105.

68 Fr. Elochukwu Uzukwu, a Spiritan and Catholic priest, is a renowned African theologian whose researches in African theology and liturgy have impacted the Church in Africa. As a versed scholar and theologian, his research interests are in the areas of liturgy-sacraments, ritual studies, ecclesiology, missiology, and contextual theology, with particular focus on continental Africa and Africa in the diaspora. He has authored various books and published numerous articles. Fr. Uzukwu has taught graduate and undergraduate courses in seminaries and universities in the United States, Nigeria, France, Congo, India, and Ireland. He is currently a professor of theology and the Father Pierre Schouver C.S.Sp., Endowed Chair in Mission at Duquesne University Pittsburgh. Uzukwu proposed an

Igbo Eucharistic Prayer in his unpublished doctoral dissertation, "Blessing and Thanksgiving Among the Igbo: Towards a *Eucharistia Africana.*" University of St. Michael's College (Canada), Th.D. 1979.

69 Elochukwu Uzukwu, "Blessing and Thanksgiving Among the Igbo: Towards an African Eucharist" *AFER* 22 (1980): 18.

70 Elochukwu Uzukwu, "Blessing and Thanksgiving Among the Igbo: Towards a *Eucharistia Africana.*" University of St. Michael's College (Canada), Th.D. 1979.

71 The author has modified the English translation to give a better translation of the Igbo version.

72 Uzukwu, "Blessing and Thanksgiving Among the Igbo: Towards a *Eucharistia Africana,*" 325–326.

73 Ibid., 330.

74 Taft, "Christ in the Byzantine Duvine Office," 71.

75 Uzukwu, "Blessing and Thanksgiving Among the Igbo: Towards a *Eucharistia Africana,*" 334.

76 Uzukwu, *Worship Body Language*, 30.

77 John Lukwata, *Integrated Liturgy*, 70.

78 Tienou, "The Theological Task of the Church in Africa," 11.

79 Bob Marley, Music Track "Redemption song."

80 *Evangelium Gaudium*, 134.

81 Tienou, "The Theological Task of the Church in Africa," 8.

82 *Evangelium Gaudium* , 17.

83 Emmanuel Katangole, *A Future for Africa: Critical Essays in Christian Social Imagination* (Scranton, PA: University of Scranton Press, 2005), 154.

84 Alexander Schmemann, "Liturgical Theology, Theology of Liturgy and Liturgical Reform," in Thomas Fisch, ed., *Liturgy and Tradition: Theological Reflections of Alexander Schmemann* (Crestwood, NY: St. Vladimir's Seminary Press, 1990), 217.

85 David Fagerberg, *Consecrating the World: On Mundane Liturgical Theology* (Kettering, OH: Angelico Press, 2016), 97.

86 Kevin Irwin, " A Spirited Community Encounters Christ: Liturgical and Sacramental Theology and Practice," in *Catholic Theology Facing the Future: Historical Perspective*, Dermot A. Lane, ed.(New York: Paulist Press, 2003), 119–120.

Chapter 5
Ratzinger's Only African Doctoral Student: Bishop Barthélemy Adoukonou (1942–) – A Brief Portrait

Emery de Gaál

A Christocentric Valorization of Family Life, Culture, and Religion

As the Church commemorates the tenth anniversary of Pope Benedict XVI signing his third apostolic exhortation *Africae Munus* on November 19, 2011, it is fitting to turn one's attention to a man who had first acquainted the young professor of theology Ratzinger with African Catholicism: Barthélmemy Adoukonou. *Africae Munus* echoes powerfully the concern of Adoukonou for all of sub-Saharan Africa's focus on family life as *the* core element of human life and as "the sanctuary of life."[1] *Africae Munus* continues: "The family is the best setting for learning and applying the culture of forgiveness, peace and reconciliation."[2] Paraphrasing St. John Paul II's 1982 apostolic exhortation *Familiaris Consortio* 39, it describes "the educational mission of the Christian family'" and its

> true ministry through which the Gospel is transmitted and radiated, so that family life itself becomes an itinerary of faith and in some way a Christian initiation and a school of following Christ. In the family conscious of this gift, as Pope Paul VI noted, "all the members evangelize and are evangelized." By virtue of their

> ministry of educating, parents are, through the witness of their lives, the first heralds of the Gospel for their children ... they become fully parents, in that they are begetters not only of bodily life but also of the life that through the Spirit's renewal flows from the Cross and Resurrection of Christ.[3]

Africae Munus invites us to a deeper understanding of family life based on the incarnation of the second person of the Blessed Trinity. It powerfully echoes the Vatican II's pastoral constitution *Gaudium et Spes*:

> The truth is that only in the mystery of the incarnate Word does the mystery of man take on light. For Adam, the first man, was a figure of Him Who was to come, namely Christ the Lord. Christ, the final Adam, by the revelation of the mystery of the Father and His love, fully reveals man to man himself and makes his supreme calling clear. It is not surprising, then, that in Him all the aforementioned truths find their root and attain their crown.[4]

Neither accidentally nor *en passant* does the document observe that "the Church remembers that Africa offered a place of refuge for the Holy Family when they were fleeing the murderous political power of Herod...."[5] It is perhaps an indication that Benedict XVI divines a particular calling for the Church in Africa to forcefully remind the global Church and the present age as a whole of the beauty and irreplaceable role of family life in God's plan for humankind. This the theologian Adoukonou does repeatedly and on numerous occasions.

1.0 Introduction

The name Barthélemy Adoukonou is intriguing in numerous regards. The bearer of this name is a high-ranking Catholic intellectual.

He is a bishop who served both in his home country of the West African nation of Benin, formerly known as Dahomey, and the African continent at large. In addition, he served the universal Catholic Church by working in prominent positions at the Roman curia. Relevant for our purposes is especially the circumstance that Adoukonou is the only sub-Saharan theologian who earned his doctorate under the direction of then Professor Joseph Ratzinger. Thus, he belongs to the closely knit *Ratzinger Schülerkreis* of originally fifty three doctoral students.[6] In all probability Adoukonou contributed in central ways to *Africae Munus*.

Barthélemy Adoukonou, was born on August 24, 1942 in Abomey. He is a Catholic bishop from francophone Benin, who had been appointed secretary of the Pontifical Council for Culture.[7] A descendant of the royal family of Abomey, Barthélemy Adoukonou was born in that kingdom's former capital Abomey in 1942 and ordained a priest in 1966 in Rome by the Armenian Cardinal Grégoire-Pierre XV Agagianian (1895–1971). Abomey is the capital of the Zou Département in Benin. The town of Abomey houses the Royal Palaces of Abomey, a collection of small traditional residences that were inhabited by the kings of Dahomey from ca. 1600 until 1900. They consist of earthen structures built by the Fon people.[8] They are considered one of the major cultural landmarks in Western Africa. These buildings were designated a World Heritage Site by UNESCO in 1985.[9]

From 1971 to 1977 Adoukonou studied sociology of religion in Paris at the venerable Sorbonne. Thereupon he pursued theological studies in Regensburg (Ratisbone), Germany, where he obtained in 1977 a doctorate under the direction of Ratzinger.[10] The doctoral thesis (*thèse d'état*) submitted in France is titled *Grammaire et sémantique de la violence: le cas du Vodun béninois*. The massive *Jalons pour une théologie africaine, Essai hérmeneutique chrétienne du vodun dahoméen* (Road Marks toward an African Theology. A Christian Hermeneutics of Dahomian Voodooism) is published in two volumes. The two volumes encompass 347 and 245 pages respectively, with over 500 titles processed from different disciplines: theology, philosophy, psychology, anthropology and ethnology. The intellectual vigor of his disciplined exposition is oftentimes not easy to follow. He introduces new French terms in order to give expression to the richness of his thoughts, such as *univociste* and *intersociétable*. From 1984 to 1988, he prepared his hugely difficult state doctorate in sociology at the University of Paris-Descartes in the French capital. He was successively professor at the minor seminary of Sainte-Jeanne d'Arc in Ouidah (1967–68), chaplain and professor at the P. Aupiais Collège in Benin's port city Cotonou (1968–70) and vicar of the parish of Saint-François d'Assise in Bohicon, Abomey (1970–71), Benin.

From 1977 to 1984, he served as rector of the minor seminary of Saint Paul de Djimé, Abomey, then as missionary professor at the Catholic University of West Africa, in the sprawling metropolis of Abidjan, the economic and cultural capital of Ivory Coast, thereupon as professor of research methodology in human and social sciences at the State University of Abomey-Calavi and finally at the Major Seminary of Saint-Gall in Ouidah. From 1988 to 1999 he served as rector of the propaedeutic seminary of Benin, in Misséreté (Porto Novo). In addition to these diverse obligations, he had been general secretary of both the *Regional Episcopal Conference of French-speaking West Africa* (CERAO), and of the *Association of Episcopal Conferences of Anglophone West Africa* (AECAWA).

He succeeded the French scholar Bernard Ardura O.Praem. (1948–) as consultor at the Congregation for the Causes of Saints. There he was particularly responsible for the postulation for the cause of canonization of several French Catholic figures, such as Robert Schuman (1886–1963) and Claire de Castelbajac (1953–1975).

Barthélémy Adoukonou served also as a consultor to the Pontifical Council for Promoting Christian Unity and had been a member of the prestigious International Theological Commission. There he served in the Fourth Quinquennium (1986–92) with Hans Urs von Balthasar, and in the Fifth Quinquennium (1992–97) with Avery Dulles, Joachim Gnilka, Servais Pinckaers and Christoph von Schönborn.

He was appointed secretary of the Pontifical Council for Culture on December 3, 2009, the first African to hold this post, and was appointed Titular Bishop of Zama Minor on September 10, 2011. He was consecrated on Saturday, October 8, 2011, by Cardinal Tarcisio Bertone, Vatican Secretary, in the Basilica of St Peter in Rome.[11] The sober and beautiful celebration lasted about two hours and was presided over by Cardinal Bertone. He was accompanied, as is customary on such occasions, by two co-consecrators, Cardinal Gianfranco Ravasi, president of the Pontifical Council for Culture, and Archbishop Giuseppe Bertello, president of the Pontifical Commission for the Vatican City State and president of the *Governato* of the Vatican City State.[12]

2.0 Advocating *Négritude* in the Catholic Church

Adoukonou is a spirited and enlightened advocate of a current called *Négritude. Nègritude* had been popularized by the noted Senegalese poet and statesman Leopold Sédar Senghor (1906–2001) in contradistinction to the colonialists' *francité*. The Martinique poet and politician Aimé Césaire (1913–2008) had actually coined the term earlier in more bellicose terms.[13]

Barthélemy Adoukonou is a fervent defender of a place among equals of a uniquely African charism within the Catholic Church. He is the founder of the *Mewihwendo / Sillon Noir* (Black Furrow, 1970), a movement promoting reflection on inculturation of both foreign cultures and of the Christian faith into the sub-Saharan context. It relies on a "community of intellectuals." Already in 1970, he affirmed his desire to collaborate in the process of inculturation by discovering the need to recover all that is precious and holy in African cultures prior to the advent of Christianity, for some provocatively including Voodooism in this enterprise. At first misunderstood, he managed to rally scholars and university professors around his ambitions concerning inculturation, notably thanks to the translation of the first week of the *Spiritual Exercises* of Saint Ignatius of Loyola into the local language of 'Fon,' for African Christians. He defends the idea that a genuine

African Christian theology must also emanate from its authentic anthropology.[14]

His appointment, the fifth appointment of an African to the Roman Curia by Pope Benedict XVI, illustrates the pontiff's desire, as expressed by Cardinal Bertone at a Synod on Africa in 2009, for a better representation of the African continent in the heart of the Catholic Church. In an interview with Gianluca Buccini, published in *L'Osservatore Romano* on February 26, 2010, Adoukonou observes:

"The black man, like any other, is capable of the Gospel because he has within him that expression of the dynamism of nature called culture in the deepest sense. With my appointment, a step forward has been taken in the recognition of African theology as an expression of [Christian] faith that becomes culture."[15]

As mentioned above, Adoukonou had been a doctoral student of Professor Joseph Ratzinger in Regensburg in the 1970's, now Pope em. Benedict XVI. Adoukonou describes Ratzinger as a "brilliant theologian, who did not read the lecture he had prepared from his desk, but seemed to read it from heaven. He had a deep historical and synthetic panoramic vision as befits a German and as clear as a Roman. The Christocentrism of his thinking appealed to me."[16]

The academic congeniality explains Adoukonou working on the *International Theological Commission* whilst the prefect of the Congregation for Doctrine and Faith was the future Pope Benedict XVI.[17]

3.0 Anthropology as Created Orientation

The point of departure for evangelization is always the core of a pre-Christian culture, i.e. its religion. To Adoukonou, the Enlightenment errs when it denies that religion is the indispensable core of every culture. Mindful of the fateful, pervasive and unchecked influence of Rousseau's subscription to the idea of an artificial divorce of faith and culture in *Emile* (published 1762), Paul VI does register in *Evangelii Nuntiandi* for his own age an unprecedented split between religion and culture, but exhorts Catholics to labor for "a full evangelization of culture or more correctly of cultures" (EN 20).[18]

The encounter with Christianity entails invariably a crisis for every culture and religion. Interestingly, Adoukonou states that overcoming such a crisis defines successful evangelization and the inculturation of the gospel. Christianity accepts the positive values of every culture and religion and purifies these, bringing them yet better to shine. "The seed of the good" meets "the seed of the incarnate Word."[19] For Adoukonou there is deeply engrained in principle "an eschatological orientation" in all religions and cultures towards the one Word. On this basis, Adoukonou proposed in *Jalons pour une théologie africaine* the taking up of novel African forms of celebrating the Passion of the Lord, Holy Thursday, the funeral rite, consecration of virgins, blessing by ancestral fathers, and ordination to the priesthood. For this purpose the *Centre de Recherche et de Spiritualité Notre Dame de l'Inculturation* had been founded in Cotonou, Bénin. Inculturation is perceived as a challenge towards holiness and "as logical outgrowth of an ecclesiology of the Church as the family of God."[20]

This statement is the result of reflections on the International Theological Commission's first ever document *The Unity of Faith and Theological Pluralism*, published in 1972. Tellingly, in Adoukonou's later *Doktorvater*, Joseph Ratzinger had composed the introduction, and parts A and C of the first section of this text. Alas, the full document is available in print only in German[21] and Italian.[22] This document is historic as it is the first official pronouncement of the ITC ever. Notably, it contextualizes the encounter of cultures and religions with Christianity in Christological categories.

Adoukonou utilized the French anthropologist and ethnologist Claude Lévy-Strauss' (1908–2009) language-subject discourse and French philosopher Paul Ricoeur's (1913–2005)[23] critique of structuralism to develop a phenomenology of Voodooism. But ultimately, it was Thomistic metaphysics and its emphasis on participation and the act of being in the context of the *analogia entis* that proved decisive for his project. He is careful to note that

Dahomenian Voodoo does not know that much of magic and witchcraft as its Caribbean offshoot in Haiti.[24]

In Voodoo (or Vodun, Wudu or Wodu, meaning "spirit" or "divinity") Adoukonou sees an expression of a heightened sense of the universal restlessness for Jesus Christ, à la Augustine's "Fecisti nos ad **te,** domine**, et inquietum est** cor **nostrum donec requiescat in te.**"[25] Voodoo belief is deliberately undogmatic as it continuously searches for the greater religious truth.

Voodoo is the *Fon* word for "spirit." Voodoo belongs now to the Yoruba and Ewe traditions, encountered as early as 500 to 200 BC in the *Nok* culture. Over its two millennia spanning existence, Voodoo is a syncretistic religion with African, Moslem, Berber and Catholic elements, and is practiced by around 50 million people.[26] "Since pre-colonial times, Beninois *Vodún* has exhibited ongoing amalgamations of deities introduced from neighboring peoples."[27] This hybrid religion originates in its present form in the Kingdom of Dahomey (1620–1892). It professes one God, called *Bondieu* (good god). As *Bondieu* is fearsomely almighty and inaccessible, the spirit *Loa* is his mediator who can alter the course of events. He is complemented by Mawu, a supreme goddess who is beyond representation. Mawu is used by Christian Ewes and Fons to designate the Christian God.[28] Jesus is equated with *vodún Lisà* by some practitioners.[29] African Voodoo knows neither paradise nor hell.[30] Adoukonou considers the manipulative elements of Caribbean and Haitian Voodooism alien to its West African origins. This religion does practice animal sacrifices for the spiritual nourishment of Loa and the benefit of its faithful.[31] For Adoukonou, it is important to note that Vodún, as almost all indigenous religions, is not diabolical but *praeparatio evangelica*.

There exists to his mind a valorization and enhancement of the subject in all religion and culture. The speaker of the language of the culture in question "becomes its people." On this basis he developed an ethnographic overview comparing Fon and French terms. All of the Fon language undergoes a Christological interpretation on three planes: lexicographical, logical and socio-historical. Adoukonou undertook a yeoman's work. The sovereignty of the speaker is such that the person expresses a primordial truth beyond his control or making. This insight is initially indebted to French philosopher Michel Foucault (1926–84), but apprehends in language, that is in both the individual speaker and the collective people, something primordial, but universally true, as it is something like an echo of the eternal Word's creative uttering into the universe; thereby bringing humankind into being. Obviously Adoukonou moves well beyond Foucault's postmodern delimitations of human society to the isolated individual: "one must permit the matter to express itself" Adoukonou observes.[32] *Pace* Foucault, Adoukonou argues passionately that one cannot create artificially a world without God and intergenerational solidarity of humankind.

In the experience of the death of a father, the child formulates "a loving memory" (*To xwiyo* in Fon) that expresses this chain of meaning that ultimately predates every known person, and is primordial and at the same time present and concrete for a living person. This is the power of naming every human being in Voodoo. While it does not make of the speaker a creator, it does enable a symbolic link for the speaker: "*Me we no ylo do Vodun b'e no nyi Vodun*" (in English: "It requires the human power of naming, in order for the Voodoo to come about").[33] Such loving remembrance entails entry into a broad religious mindset. It connects for the believer the present to the past. The speaker himself becomes a voodoo, connecting him to his forebears, honoring what his forebear, father or mother had honored (*nu e to xwiyo be No xwiye e*).[34] That this *memoria* is not merely an insular, cultural phenomenon particular to the people of Benin, but a manifestation of a global facticity indebted to Christ as its ultimate trigger, which Adoukonou discovered by reading Ratzinger. In fact, Voodooism begs for a Christocentric interpretation or recasting through the sacrament of baptism. Self-sacrificing missionaries from Europe have unearthed this.

This is the seeming paradox: The one origin Christ permits for a rich pluralism that does not devolve into sectarianism or eclecticism. Significantly, Ratzinger's understanding of inculturation/interculturality[35] enabled Adoukonou to apprehend the African Church not as a passive object of evangelization from different cultures and a distant continent, but therein importantly the discovery of itself as *a theological subject* in its own right within the process of inculturating the mystery of the ongoing incarnation of Jesus Christ.

This occurred ironically first in a process of rejection of and defense over and against Christianity. The altar of King Agadja in the royal palace of Abomey is a case in point. On top of a vertical iron rod there is depicted a chapel, governed by a cross. There a cord connects the cross to a calabash. The whole is cast in bronze. Shortly before Beninians began converting to Christianity, in this calabash is contained already for ages the Christ mystery, hidden from the beginning of the universe. The Christ mystery is intrinsic to every culture. This is the unifying theme of the ITC document *The Unity of Faith and theological Pluralism* (1972), Cardinal Ratzinger's talk in Hong Kong *Christ, Faith and the Challenge of Cultures* (1993)[36] and Pope Benedict XVI's post-synodal exhortation *Africae Munus* (Africa's Commitment, 2011). Adoukonou argues that no artificial, extrinsic transplantation of faith can succeed à la Neo-Scholasticism's concept of a self-sufficient *natura pura*. Ever again there need be a conversion from one's respective culture to the historic events of the passion, crucifixion and resurrection of Jesus of Nazareth. But this conversion is not something imposed externally unto the neophyte. Rather, echoing Bernard Lonergan's (1904–84) "conversion as transformation," Christian baptism is actually the fulfillment of that hope contained somehow in every religion and culture from its respective beginning.

"It is right, then, to 'maintain a living connection between memorized catechism and lived catechesis, which leads to a profound and permanent conversion of life.' Conversion is experienced in a unique way through the sacrament of Reconciliation, which calls for particular attention so that it can serve as a genuine 'school of the heart.'"[37]

This universal yearning for meaning and reconciliation finds its fulfillment in the person of Jesus of Nazareth.[38]

In a qualified sense, Adoukonou argues that just as the Old Testament prophetically anticipates Jesus Christ, every religion does so, while, *nota bene,* not becoming already part of positive revelation. All religion intends a fullness it cannot express unaided by positive Christian revelation. For this the Old and New Testaments are indispensable. Christianity is a monotheism that wishes not to leave behind an understanding of God as the richest of realities, which polytheism had successfully given expression to. To this dynamic vivacity the Christological and trinitarian monotheism of Christianity actually does full justice to it. The indwelling dynamics proper to every religion find their proper theological articulation in the Scholastic concept of *"perceptio veritatis divinae tendens in ipsam"*—(the natural perception of divine truth tends towards it).[39] The 1972 ITC text interprets this Thomistic axiom in this sense. To the mind of Adoukonou, ultimately every reality "tends" to transcend itself towards Jesus Christ. This he sees well-articulated in Bernard Lonergan's understanding of conversion as a convergence of intellectual, ethical and religious dimensions (i.e., "transformation").[40] Conversion means embarking into the tension of the crucified and risen Lord, who unites and opens all localities of faith.[41]

In keeping with this understanding *Africae Munus* uses the words "transform" and "transformation" seven times:

> ... It should also be constantly kept in mind that no medium can nor should replace personal contact, verbal proclamation and the witness of an authentic Christian life. Such personal contact and verbal proclamation need to express a living faith which engages and transforms one's life, as well as the love of God which reaches and touches everyone just as he or she is.[42]

As Ratzinger wrote in 1972: Christian "Faith is not bound to a level of differentiation of consciousness, but is bound to conversion. In this faith context of conversion to the risen Lord lies what unites complicated and simple minds. The *tendere in ipsum* (going towards him, Jesus Christ) is, as it were, the common 'time' of faith that 'synchronizes' people [and peoples] across the differences of times."[43] Herein Christian faith evidences itself as anamnetic, i.e., as a form of "remembering" that does no violence unto the Word. This Word is God's ultimate and definitive creative utterance. Thus enriched, the message in its integrity remains fresh for every generation anew. No cultural or historical form can exhaustively contain it. "Pluralism is also diachronous."[44] Christian faith enters the trinitarian mystery in a tension that replicates the *tendere in ipsum* of the Son himself to the Father. Thus, the Son becomes the truth, our truth, on the way to the Father. With inimitable precision Ratzinger continues: "The Trinitarian character of the Christian faith cannot therefore mean a coexistence of different forms of truth, but means the process of remembering through [human] history in the strength of the Holy Spirit, which leads [humankind] into the one Word of Jesus and therein to the knowledge of the Father."[45] Echoing Bonaventure,[46] Ratzinger reminds one that the unifying point of faith is not found in a particular age, but in the uniqueness of the living subject of faith called the Church, which includes all temporality. Every Christian believes with the totality of history and thus both synchronously and diachronously.

4.0 Adoukonou's Views

It is difficult to assess the role Bishop Adoukonou played in the composition of the post-apostolic exhortation *Africae Munus*. Probably it was significant. It is telling that the document was signed by Pope Benedict XVI in the basilica of Ouidah, Benin, in the home country of Bishop Adoukonou, celebrating 150 years of Christianity in that country. In it Benedict XVI mentions the Church as "God's family," echoing a central thought of Adoukonou and of *Ecclesia in Africa* as well.[47] *Africae Munus* dedicates one section to the social category "family."[48]

In the wake of the 2015 Synod on the Family, African prelates and theologians wrote reflections on the centrality of the natural family in the order of God's creative wisdom. One of the contributors had been Adoukonou. He registers several points of concern regarding the synod's *Instrumentarium laboris.* It uncritically "utilizes the resources of almost all the human and social sciences to put into context the topic of the family today without bringing to light the most important background, namely the historical choices that led to this disaster," i.e. the collapse of family life in Western societies.[49] A deliberately godless society "invented different socio-anthropological, cultural economic, and political paradigms that, becoming global, are gradually leading to the active destruction of the family."[50] He underscores the obligation for Christians and Africans outside the postmodern context to register protest against such chic nonchalance to reinvent the human being and society. One must "call into question fundamentally the exclusion of God"[51] so much currently *en vogue* in the societies of the former colonizers of Africa. With regret he registers the *Instrumentarium laboris'* reluctance to spell this out. It seems to favor something akin to the norm-forming force of facts. However, there is a need to name sins. "These are the wounds that make up the extreme malaise of which the families of the world can be healed only by conversion from precisely the sort of sin that is at the origins of postmodernity." He concludes: "This movement ... wishes to kill mercy itself and the Holy Spirit...."[52] A view detrimental to matrimony and family alike is equally scandalous to Christians, pagans and atheists.

No inculturation of the Gospel can be successful without a call to conversion, which receives thereupon a singular, life-transforming strength from the "glorious Cross" of Jesus Christ.[53] He laments the "chiaroscuro" of the West in these areas.[54] Such atheist premises must be exposed by the Church. He goes into detail exposing the faulty reinterpretations Western sociologists give to African customs. In no way do pagan African customs past or present condone Western redefinitions of matrimony, Adoukonou argues. In fact, from time immemorial pre-Christian African traditions strongly resembled Jewish traditions. Never is cohabitation accepted. Marriage is understood to be "unique and indissoluble."[55] The true strength to live up to these already pre-Christian ideals comes ultimately from "the mystery of the cross, which, itself discerns spirits (cf. 1 John 4; 2 Cor 3:17)."[56] Only a radical Christocentric shift can effect a real conversion and genuine realization of human values: "'For I decided to know nothing among you except Jesus Christ and him crucified' (1 Cor 2:1–2)" as Adoukonou quotes Paul.[57]

Africae Munus states unambiguously in 2011:

> It is imperative therefore to make a commitment to transmit the values that the Creator has instilled in the hearts of Africans *since the dawn of time*. These have served as a matrix for fashioning societies marked by a degree of harmony, since they embody *traditional* formulae for peaceful coexistence. These positive elements therefore need to be emphasized, lit up from within (cf. *Jn* 8:12), so that Christians may truly receive the message of Christ, and in this way God's light may shine before the eyes of all. Then, seeing the good deeds of Christians, men and women will be able to give glory to 'the Father who is in heaven' (*Matthew* 5:16).[58]

The document emphasizes the role of elders in transmitting wisdom and—albeit only implicitly—to connect people with natural revelation and, once Christianized, with the life of grace.[59] "In Africa, the elderly are held in particular veneration. They are not banished from families or marginalized as in other cultures. On the contrary, they are esteemed and perfectly integrated within their families, of which they are indeed the pinnacle."[60]

The document assesses positively the role of ancestors in traditional African religions. "With their reference to *ancestors* and to a form of mediation between man and Immanence, these religions are the cultural and spiritual soil from which most Christian converts spring and with which they continue to have daily contact."[61]

5.0 Conclusion

There does exist something like a vision of the integrity of the human person and coherence of the human race well prior to the advent of Christianity. Not only is religion a constitutive dimension of every culture, but it contains already something positive, as it is already undeniably Christ-oriented and yearning for the incarnation of a truth that is both personal and universal. The world contains also in its postlapsarian state *logoi spermatikoi,* to speak with Justin Martyr (+165)[62] and Augustine (354–430).[63]

A primordially Christ-oriented disposition profoundly unites all races and peoples "right across all the cultures,"[64] as Ratzinger argues in a *Festschrift* for Karl Rahner SJ (1904–84) in 1964. In fact, human culture can be defined universally as implicit openness to and longing for such truth. The duty to seek and bind oneself to such truth is deeply connected to the essential core of being human and is the prerequisite for genuine human freedom. Having found such transcendental reality, humankind is capable of enjoying real happiness, and living to a greater degree in peace and harmony in the manner the Creator had originally intended.[65] Thus, Ratzinger and Adoukonou make out the human capacity for truth as one primordially, though inchoately, oriented ultimately towards Christ, a divine person and the all-encompassing truth. Ergo, to assume a dichotomy between divine and human realms, a disjuncture between culture and religion is a feature of an extreme, unnatural postlapsarian state (which is only an acquired and secondary perspective—wholly unimaginable prior to the Renaissance one might add—but also having a Catholic variant in Neo-Scholasticism's extrinsicism). Paradoxical and incomprehensible to the non-believer, in the particularity of his first century Palestinian Jewishness, Jesus Christ is the *universale concretum et personale* (cf. Irenaeus of Lyon).[66] Importantly, Adoukonou enriches the more isolated views of Ratzinger and the Second Vatican Council by a robustly communitarian perspective: *l'Eglise comme la famille de Dieu.*

Adoukonou proposes that while St. John Paul II reconciled the Catholic Church with the sciences after the fateful Galileo Galilei debacle of the 17th century, Pope Benedict XVI reconciled the Catholic Church with non-Christian religions and cultures. Culture and religion cannot be divorced. Christianity is not the denial of the good and precious found in other religions but, far from it, their only intellectually viable affirmation. More recent evidence of his sweeping Christocentric vision is his dialogue with the German neo-Marxist philosopher Jürgen Habermas (1929–) in Munich in 2004,[67] his speech at the *Collège des Bernardins* in Paris in 2008,[68] and the institution of the *Courtyard of the Gentiles*[69] as an open-ended forum of dialogue with non-Christians and secularists alike. Such a holistic Christocentric view of religion and culture is the very antidote to totalitarian exclusivism. It eliminates all forms of neocolonial suppression and opens universal intercultural dialogue without succumbing to secularizing manipulations. In the final analysis, neither Saints Paul nor Francis Xavier overcome the walls separating Christians and non-Christians, but in every epoch and people again only grace, only Jesus Christ himself and only he achieves this. In Jesus Christ the new Adam appears.

Referencing the encyclical *Caritas in Veritate*,[70] and echoing the insight of *Gaudium et Spes* 22 (cf. above the introduction), *Africae Munus* states along lines that may sum up the present essay:

> Christians who draw nourishment from the authentic source, Christ, are transformed by him into 'the light of the world' (*Matthew* 5:14), and they transmit the one who is himself 'the Light of the world' (*Jn* 8:12). Their knowledge must be shaped by charity. Knowledge, in fact, 'if it aspires to be wisdom capable of directing man in the light of his first beginnings and his final ends ... must be 'seasoned' with the 'salt' of charity.[71]

Chapter 5 Endnotes

1 *Africae Munus* 42. Accessed 12/30/2021 https://www.vatican.va/content/benedict-xvi/en/apost_exhortations/documents/hf_ben-xvi_exh_20111119_africae-munus.html.

2 *Africae Munus* 43. Accessed 12/30/2021 https://www.vatican.va/content/benedict-xvi/en/apost_exhortations/documents/hf_ben-xvi_exh_20111119_africae-munus.html.
3 *Africae Munus* 46. Accessed 12/30/2021 https://www.vatican.va/content/benedict-xvi/en/apost_exhortations/documents/hf_ben-xvi_exh_20111119_africae-munus.html.
4 *Gaudium et Spes* 22, accessed 12/31/2021 https://www.vatican.va/archive/hist_councils/ii_vatican_council/documents/vat-ii_const_19651207_gaudium-et-spes_en.html.
5 *Africae Munus* 85.
6 Accessed 8, 23,2021: https://ratzinger-papst-benedikt-stiftung.de/. Cf. Schülerkreis Joseph Kardinal Ratzinger, *Vom Wiederauffinden der Mitte. Grundorientierungen* (Freiburg i.Br.: Herder, 1997), p. 316.
7 This and subsequent biographical information was obtained from https://fr.wikipedia.org/wiki/Barth%C3%A9lemy_Adoukonou accessed 8/18/2021.
8 Stuart Butler, *Bradt Travel Guide - Benin*, (Chesham, Buckinghamshire: Bradt Travel Guides, 2019) pp. 135–45. In general for religion in Benin see: Douglas J. Falen, "Vodún, Spiritual Insecurity, and Religious Importation in Benin," in *Journal of Religion in Africa* 46 (2016), pp. 453–483. Still seminal: Melville J. Herkovits, *Dahomey. An Ancient West African Kingdom*, 2 vols. (Evanston, IL: Northwestern University Press, 1969), reprint of the 1938 edition.
9 Cf. https://whc.unesco.org/en/list/323/ accessed 9/12/2021.
10 His bibliography contains three books: Barthélemy Adoukonou, *Pour une problématique anthropologique et religieuse de la mort dans la pensée Adja-Fon*, in *La mort dans la vie africaine,* (Paris: Présence africaine UNESCO, 1979), pp. 119–332. This section is preceded by Chanoine Y. K. Bamunoba, *La conception de la mort dans la vie africaine*, pp. 9–118. Barthélemy Adoukonou, *Jalons pour une théologie africaine*, I-II,: volume I *Critique théologique* (Paris: Lethielleux, 1980), volume II *Étude éthnologique*,(Paris: Dessain et Tolra, 1980) as *Thèse d'État* in Paris in the series "Le Sycomore": ibid., *Grammaire et sémantique de la violence: le cas du Vodun béninois* (unpublished?). His list of published articles includes at least twelve titles: ibid., "Vodún, Démocratie et Pluralisme Religieux," in *Les Publications du Sillon Noir* (1993), pp. 9–93. Ibid. "L'Eucharistie: une approche africaine du débat interculturel", in *Communio,* X, 3 – nº 59, mai-juin 1985, pp. 65–78. Ibid., "Mariage et famille en Afrique," in *Communio*, XI, 6 nº 68 novembre-décembre, 1986, pp. 84–97. Ibid., "Le Sillon Noir. La théologie africaine comme œuvre de l'intellectuel communautaire," in *Communio,* XI, 5 nº 67, septembre-octobre 1986, pp. 86–101. Ibid., "Zur Aktualität der Inkul-

turation bei Joseph Ratzinger," in Maximilian Heim, Justinus C. Pech (eds.), *Zur Mitte der Theologie im Werk von Joseph Ratzinger/Benedikt XVI* (Regensburg: Pustet, 2013), pp. 195–208. Ibid. "Relecture du Concile Vatican II" in *Revue de l'Institut catholique de l'Afrique de l'Ouest*, n° 4/1993, pp. 99–108. Ibid., "Théologie de l'Église-Famille de Dieu: 10 ans après dans l'espace CERAO," in *Revue de l'Université catholique de l'Afrique de l'Ouest*, n° 20/ 2004, pp. 171–193. Ibid., "La problématique théologique pour une dialogue interreligieux au cœur de 'La Route de l'Escalve," in *Bulletin* 7 (1996), pp. 214–221. Ibid., "Cristianismo y las Culturas: Diálogo intercultural e interreligioso," in *Revista Española de teología* 60 (2000), pp. 413–433. Ibid., "Inculturazione della Fede in Africa," in Rino Fisichella ed., *Il Concilio Vaticano II recezione e attualità alla luce del giubileo* (Milano: Cinisella, 2000), pp. 598–611. Ibid., "Esperienza mistica in Africa," in no ed., *Sentieri illuminati dallo Spirito atti del congresso internazionale di mistica, Abbazia di Münsterschwarznach* (Roma: Morena, 2006), pp. 469–496. See also Joseph Babatounde, and Barthélemy Adoukonou "Historique du Sillon Noir," in *Une Expérience Africaine d'Inculturation*, vol. 1 (Cotonou: Centre de Recherche et d'Inculturation, 1991), pp. 3–18. Bishop Barthélemy Adoukonou, "Start from Living Faith: An African Take on the *Instrumentarium laboris*," in *Christ's New Homeland – Africa. Contribution to the Synod on the Family by African Pastors*, trans. by Michael J. Miller (San Francisco: Ignatius Press, 2015), pp. 34–53.

11 Members of the International Theological Commission (vatican.va) accessed 8/18/2021.

12 https://africa.la-croix.com/portrait-mgr-barthelemy-adoukonou-un-apotre-de-linculturation-en-afrique/ accessed 9/12/2021.

13 Gary Wilder, *The French Imperial Nation-State. Negritude & Colonial Humanism Between the Two World Wars* (Chicago: University of Chicago Press, 2005).

14 https://africa.la-croix.com/portrait-mgr-barthelemy-adoukonou-un-apotre-de-linculturation-en-afrique/ accessed 9/12/2021.

15 Cf. https://fr.wikipedia.org/wiki/Barth%C3%A9lemy_Adoukonou accessed 8/18/2021.

16 Cf. https://fr.wikipedia.org/wiki/Barth%C3%A9lemy_Adoukonou accessed 8/18/2021. … "théologien brillant, qui ne lisait pas la leçon qu'il avait préparée, de son bureau, mais qui paraissait la lire dans le ciel. Il avait une vision panoramique historique et synthétique profonde comme il sied à un Allemand et aussi claire, propre à un Latin. Le christocentrisme de sa pensée m'enchantait."

17 https://africa.la-croix.com/portrait-mgr-barthelemy-adoukonou-un-apotre-de-linculturation-en-afrique/ accessed 9/12/2021.

18 Accessed 8, 27, 2019: http://w2.vatican.va/content/paul-vi/en/apost_exhortations/documents/hf_p-vi_exh_19751208_evangelii-nuntiandi.html.
19 Adoukonou, "Zur Aktualität der Inkulturation bei Joseph Ratzinger," p. 195.
20 Adoukonou, "Zur Aktualität der Inkulturation bei Joseph Ratzinger," p. 196.
21 Internationale Theologische Kommission, *Die Einheit des Glaubens und der theologische Pluralismus,* in *Sammlung Horizonte,* Neue Folge 7, (Einsiedeln: Johannes Verlag, 1973), pp. 220.
22 Commissione Teologica Internazionale, *Pluralismo. Unità della fede e pluralismo teologico* (Bologna: Edizioni Dehoniane, 1974), pp. 250. This document is partially reproduced on the commission's official website in German, Italian and Spanish. Cf. https://www.vatican.va/roman_curia/congregations/cfaith/cti_documents/rc_cti_index-documentazione_en.html accessed 8/19/2021.
23 In this context he refers to Paul Ricoeur, *The Rule of Metaphor, The Creation of Meaning in Language,* (London?: Routledge, 2015).
24 Adoukonou, "Zur Aktualität der Inkulturation bei Joseph Ratzinger," p. 197.
25 Augustine, *Confessions,* 1,1.
26 For this salient feature see especially Dana Rush, *Vodún in Coastal Bénin: Unfinished, Open-Ended, Global* (Nashville, TN: Vanderbilt University Press, 2013).
27 Falon, "Vodún, Spiritual Insecurity, and Religious Importation in Benin," p. 453.
28 Olabiyi Yai, "From Vodún to Mawu: Monotheism and History in the Fon cultural Aras," in Jean-Pierre Chrétien (ed.), *L'Invention Religieuse en Afrique. Histoire et Religion en Afrique Noire* (Paris: Karthala, 1993), pp. 241–265.
29 Falon, "Vodún, Spiritual Insecurity and Religious Importation in Benin," p. 462.
30 Cf. Suzanne Preston Blier, *African Vodun: Art, Psychology, and Power* (Chicago: University of Chicago, 1995).
31 Cf. Christoph Henning, Klaus E. Müller, Ute Ritz-Müller, *Soul of Africa – Magie eines Kontinents* (Köhl: Konemann, 1999). Gert Chesi, *Voodoo in Afrika* (Innsbruck: Haymon, 2003).
32 Adoukonou, "Zur Aktualität der Inkulturation bei Joseph Ratzinger," p. 199.
33 Adoukonou, "Zur Aktualität der Inkulturation bei Joseph Ratzinger," p. 199.

34 Adoukonou, "Zur Aktualität der Inkulturation bei Joseph Ratzinger," p. 199.

35 Cf. Emery de Gaál, "Mission, inculturation and 'Interculturality' in the Thinking of Joseph Ratzinger/Benedict XVI in Relation to Arica," in Maurice Ashley Agbaw-Ebai and Matthew Levering eds., *Joseph Ratzinger and the Future of African Theology* (Eugene, OR: Pickwick Publications, 2021), pp. 183–213.

36 Joseph Card. Ratzinger, *Christ, Faith and the Challenge of Cultures*, Meeting with the Doctrinal Commissions in Asia, (Hong Kong, 3 March 1993) https://www.vatican.va/roman_curia/congregations/cfaith/incontri/rc_con_cfaith_19930303_hong-kong-ratzinger_en.html accessed 8/19/2021.

37 Benedict XVI, *Post-Synodal Apostolic Exhortation Africae Munus* 32 https://www.vatican.va/content/benedict-xvi/en/apost_exhortations/documents/hf_ben-xvi_exh_20111119_africae-munus.html accessed 11/7/2021.

38 Cf. Joseph Ratzinger/Benedict XVI, *Jesus of Nazareth*, 3 vols. (New York/San Francisco/New York: Doubleday/Ignatius/Image, 2007/2011/2012).

39 Adoukonou, "Zur Aktualität der Inkulturation bei Joseph Ratzinger," p. 204. Cf. Thomas Aquinas, *Summa Theologiae* 2–2, q. 1, a. 6, *sed contra*.

40 Cf. Bernard Lonergan, '"Self-transcendence: Intellectual, Moral, Religious," in ibid., *Philosophical and Theological Papers 1965–1980*, ed. Robert M. Doran and Robert C. Croken (Toronto: University of Toronto Press, 2005) pp. xx–xxx.

41 This is a paraphrase of a line found in Internationale Theologische Kommission, *Die Einheit des Glaubens und der theologische Pluralismus*, p. 19, and cited by Adoukonou, "Zur Aktualität der Inkulturation bei Joseph Ratzinger," p. 204.

42 Benedict XVI, *Post-Synodal Apostolic Exhortation Africae Munus* 166, accessed 11/8/2021 https://www.vatican.va/content/benedict-xvi/en/apost_exhortations/documents/hf_ben-xvi_exh_20111119_africae-munus.html.

43 "Der Glaube ist nicht an eine Differenzierungsstufe des Bewusstseins, wohl aber an Bekehrung gebunden. In diesem Glaubenszusammenhang der Bekehrung zum auferstandenen Herrn liegt das, was komplizierte und einfache Geister verbindet. Das tendere in ipsum (das Zugehen auf ihn hin) ist gleichsam die gemeinsame 'Zeit' des Glaubens, die Menschen quer durch die Unterschiede der Zeiten 'synchronisiert.'" Internationale Theologische Kommission, *Die*

Einheit des Glaubens und der theologische Pluralismus, p. 20, as cited by Adoukonou, "Zur Aktualität der Inkulturation bei Joseph Ratzinger," pp. 204f.

44 Adoukonou, "Zur Aktualität der Inkulturation bei Joseph Ratzinger," p. 205.

45 "Der trinitarische Charakter des christlichen Glaubens kann demgemäß nicht ein Nebeneinander verschiedener Wahrheitsgestalten besagen, sondern meint den die Geschichte hindurch währenden Prozess des Erinnerns durch den Heiligen Geist, der in das eine Wort Jesu hinein und darin zur Erkenntnis des Vaters führt." Internationale Theologische Kommission, *Die Einheit des Glaubens und der theologische Pluralismus*, p. 22, as cited by Adoukonou, "Zur Aktualität der Inkulturation bei Joseph Ratzinger," p. 205.

46 Joseph Ratzinger, *Theology of History in St. Bonaventure*, (Chicago, IL: Franciscan Press, 1971).

47 Catholic News Agency, November 19, 2011, https://www.catholicnewsagency.com/news/23811/pope-signs-apostolic-exhortation-africae-munus accessed 8/20/2021. In *Ecclesia in Africa* the term is mentioned eleven times https://www.vatican.va/content/john-paul-ii/en/apost_exhortations/documents/hf_jp-ii_exh_14091995_ecclesia-in-africa.html accessed 8/20/2021.

48 Cf. Benedict XVI, *Post-Synodal Apostolic Exhortation Africae Munus* 42–46 https://www.vatican.va/content/benedict-xvi/en/apost_exhortations/documents/hf_ben-xvi_exh_20111119_africae-munus.html.

49 Adoukonou, "Start from Living Faith: An African Take on the *Instrumentarium laboris*," in *Christ's New Homeland – Africa. Contribution to the Synod on the Family by African Pastors*, p. 37.

50 Adoukonou, "Start from Living Faith: An African Take on the *Instrumentarium laboris*," p. 38.

51 Adoukonou, "Start from Living Faith: An African Take on the *Instrumentarium laboris*," p. 40.

52 Adoukonou, "Start from Living Faith: An African Take on the *Instrumentarium laboris*," p. 41.

53 Adoukonou, "Start from Living Faith: An African Take on the *Instrumentarium laboris*," p. 43.

54 Adoukonou, "Start from Living Faith: An African Take on the *Instrumentarium laboris*," p. 44.

55 Adoukonou, "Start from Living Faith: An African Take on the *Instrumentarium laboris*," p. 50.

56 Adoukonou, "Start from Living Faith: An African Take on the *Instrumentarium laboris*," p. 53.

57 Adoukonou, "Start from Living Faith: An African Take on the *Instrumentarium laboris,*" p. 43.

58 Benedict XVI, *Post-Synodal Apostolic Exhortation Africae Munus* 38 https://www.vatican.va/content/benedict-xvi/en/apost_exhortations/documents/hf_ben-xvi_exh_20111119_africae-munus.html accessed 8/20/2021. Emphases added.

59 Benedict XVI, *Post-Synodal Apostolic Exhortation Africae Munus* 47–50 https://www.vatican.va/content/benedict-xvi/en/apost_exhortations/documents/hf_ben-xvi_exh_20111119_africae-munus.html accessed 8/20/2021. Cf. especially ibid. no. 49: "In Africa, stability and social order are still frequently entrusted to a council of elders or traditional chiefs. Through this structure, the elderly can contribute effectively to the building of a more just society which evolves, not on the basis of whatever experiences happen to come its way, but gradually and with a prudent equilibrium. The elderly are thus able to participate in the reconciliation of individuals and communities through their wisdom and experience."

60 Benedict XVI, *Post-Synodal Apostolic Exhortation Africae Munus* 47 https://www.vatican.va/content/benedict-xvi/en/apost_exhortations/documents/hf_ben-xvi_exh_20111119_africae-munus.html accessed 8/20/2021.

61 Benedict XVI, *Post-Synodal Apostolic Exhortation Africae Munus* 92f, here at 92 https://www.vatican.va/content/benedict-xvi/en/apost_exhortations/documents/hf_ben-xvi_exh_20111119_africae-munus.html accessed 8/20/2021. Emphasis added.

62 Leslie William Barnard, *St. Justin Martyr: The First and Second Apologies* (Mahwah, NJ: Paulist Press, 1997), pp. 196–200.

63 Augustine's *Confessions,* Book VII, Chapter IX, Section 13, Maria Boulding trans., (Hyde Park, NY: New City, 2006). Marian Hillar, *From Logos to Trinity: The Evolution of Religious Beliefs from Pythagoras to Tertullian,* (Cambridge: Cambridge University Press, 2012). Cf. Augustine, *Retractions.*

64 Joseph Ratzinger, *Truth and Tolerance: Christian Belief and World Religions,* trans. by Henry Taylor (San Francisco: Ignatius Press, 2004), p. 79. In general see: Joseph Ratzinger, "Natura e Finalità del Catechismo della Chiesa Cattolica e Inculturazione della Fede," in: *Un Dono per Oggi. Il Catechismo della Chiesa Cattolica. Riflessioni per l'Accoglienza,* ed. Tommaso Stenico et al., (Milano: Edizione Paoline, 1992), pp. 29–39. Joseph Ratzinger, "L'Inculturation de la Foi," in: Congrégation pour l'Évangélisation des Peuples, *Vie et Ministère de l'Évêque. Actes du Séminaire pour les Évêques dans les Territoires de Mis-*

sion (Rome, September 5–8, 2004), (Città del Vaticano: Editrice Vaticana, 2005), pp. 165ff.

65 Joseph Ratzinger, *Truth and Tolerance: Christian Belief and World Religions*, p. 72.

66 Leo the Great captures this with brilliant succinctness: "Totus in suis et totus in nostris" *Epistola 28 ad Flavianum* 3–4 ("complete in what is his [Christ's] own, complete in what is ours"). Cf. Hans Urs von Balthasar, *Theologie der Geschichte* (Einsiedeln: Johannes Verlag, 2004, 6th ed.), pp. 15, 64 and 69. Benedikt Harkyu Cho, *Universale Concretum. Die Bestimmung des unterscheidend Christlichen in den Gesammelten Werken Joseph Ratzingers* (St. Ottilien: EOS, 2015). Cf. Joseph, Ratzinger, *Volk und Haus Gottes in Augustins Lehre von der Kirche*, Diss. University of Munich, 1951 (München: Karl Zink, 1954) in: *Münchener Theologische Studien*, vol. 7 (reprint: St. Ottilien: Eos 1992) at ch. 7. Critically edited ibid., *Volk und Haus Gottes in Augustins Lehre von der Kirche, Die Dissertation und weitere Studien zu Augustinus und zur Theologie der Kirchenväter*, in *Joseph Ratzinger Gesammelte Schriften*, Band I (Freiburg i. Br.: Herder, 2011).

67 Joseph Ratzinger and Jürgen Habermas, *The Dialectics of Secularization, On Reason and Religion* (San Francisco: Ignatius, 2007).

68 Benedict XVI, "Meeting with Representatives from the World of Culture" in Paris, https://www.vatican.va/content/benedict-xvi/en/speeches/2008/september/documents/hf_ben-xvi_spe_20080912_parigi-cultura.html accessed 9/12/2021.

69 Cf. Pontifical Council for Culture, http://www.cultura.va/content/cultura/en/dipartimenti/ateismo-e-non-credenza/che-cos-e-il-cortile-dei-gentili—.html accessed 9/12/2021.

70 Cf. Benedict XVI, Encyclical Letter *Caritas in Veritate* (29 June 2009), 30: *AAS* 101 (2009), p. 665.

71 Benedict XVI, *Post-Synodal Apostolic Exhortation Africae Munus* 95 https://www.vatican.va/content/benedict-xvi/en/apost_exhortations/documents/hf_ben-xvi_exh_20111119_africae-munus.html accessed 11/7/2021.

Chapter 6
Augustinus Afer:
Preaching in Service to Reconciliation, Justice, and Peace

Andrew Hofer, O.P.

Pope Benedict XVI's post-synodal apostolic exhortation *Africae Munus* (2011) has much to offer the Church in Africa and throughout the world ten years after its promulgation and for many years more.[1] Its subtitle expresses pointedly its most enduring contribution: "On the Church in Africa in Service to Reconciliation, Justice and Peace." Benedict XVI wants the Church in Africa to show the world the truth about reconciliation, justice, and peace. Accepting the full title found in the 2006 *Lineamenta* and the 2009 *Instrumentum Laboris*, with its quotation of "You are the salt of the earth.... You are the light of the world" (Matt 5:13–14), he applies to Africa that preaching from Christ's Sermon on the Mount. He challenges Africa always to live out what Christ wants his disciples to be. We see the realization of those words of Christ in many ways as Africans proclaim the Gospel by word and deed on their continent and go throughout the other continents. African missionaries are re-evangelizing lands that sent missionaries to Africa. Christians throughout the world rightly look to the light of Christ carried by the faithful from this bright continent so full of life, Africa.

The present rise of Africa for the global Church can remind us of the continent's witness in early Christianity. Pope Benedict XVI's *Africae Munus* privileges the witnesses of the early Christians on the continent. Benedict names Clement of Alexandria (no.

9), and quotes the Alexandrian Origen (no. 54). He names Tertullian of Carthage, the first Latin theologian, once (no. 113), and names St. Cyprian, like Tertullian from the greatest city of North Africa and rival to Rome, twice (nos. 101 and 108). St. Augustine of Hippo's name appears twice in the text, and he is quoted without name elsewhere (nos. 88 and 106; no. 24). St. Fulgentius of Ruspe, the greatest theologian from North Africa living after Augustine, appears once (no. 52). The other patristic and scholastic authorities cited or named are St. Ignatius of Antioch (once), St. Irenaeus of Lyons (once), and St. Thomas Aquinas (twice). Is it merely coincidental that six of the nine authorities are not from Scripture, the recent Magisterium, or the synodal process, but are from early Christians who lived on the African continent? I do not think so.

Yet, these authorities seem so natural to this magisterial document that one may not realize that Benedict is using traditional voices from Africa for his twenty-first century teaching on the Church in Africa. Kenyan Anglican priest John Mbiti, often called the "father of modern African theology," writes, "Christianity in Africa is so old that it can rightly be described as an indigenous, traditional, and African religion.... It was a dynamic form of Christianity, producing great scholars and theologians like Tertullian, Origen, Clement of Alexandria, and Augustine."[2] Certainly, *Africae Munus* returns to Africa's own heritage so that the Church may hear again the faith of Christian ancestors. It is for the benefit of the entire Church, as *Africae Munus* no. 137 quotes Benedict XVI's earlier address for this desire: "Perhaps this century will permit, by God's grace, the rebirth on your continent, albeit surely in a new and different form, of the prestigious School of Alexandria. Why should we not hope that it could furnish today's Africans and the universal Church with great theologians and spiritual masters who could contribute to the sanctification of the inhabitants of this continent and of the whole Church?"[3]

This chapter deepens and broadens our appreciation for the teaching of *Africae Munus* through attention to one of these early African figures: St. Augustine of Hippo.[4] The saint has a special connection to the Second Special Assembly for Africa of the Synod of Bishops, which met October 4–25, 2009. The announcement for this second Synod of Bishops for Africa, after the 1994 Synod of Bishops for Africa, came on November 13, 2004, on the 1650th anniversary of the birth of St. Augustine.[5] St. John Paul II announced his intention for the synod when meeting with a group of African and European bishops at a symposium titled *Communion and Solidarity between Africa and Europe*. On June 22, 2005, less than three months after his election to the see of St. Peter, Benedict XVI confirmed his predecessor's intention for the special synod devoted to the Church in Africa.[6] The African Doctor is the favorite theologian of Benedict XVI and of many.[7] Playing on the adage that all roads lead to Rome, Benedict proclaimed in beginning a five-part series of addresses on Augustine: "It could be said on the one hand that all the roads of Latin Christian literature led to Hippo (today Annaba, on the coast of Algeria), the place where he was Bishop from 395 to his death in 430, and, on the other, that from this city of Roman Africa, many other roads of later Christianity and of Western culture itself branched out."[8] But one should not think that such stature was due to mere worldly success. Preaching on the feast of St. Augustine some decades before becoming pope, Joseph Ratzinger conceded to Nietzsche that our African Doctor seems so plebeian and ordinary. Ratzinger proclaims, "For the sake of Christ, who was not ashamed to lay aside his divine glory and become a man like us, Augustine relinquished all his higher education and learned to speak God's Word ever more simply and plainly to his people."[9]

This study considers the holy Bishop of Hippo under the aspect of *Augustine the African* for the Church's theology and pastoral practice as taught in *Africae Munus*. We will focus on his sermons.[10] Augustine's lengthy preaching—so instructive, delightful, and convincing—can especially speak to the people of Africa and elsewhere today. After exploring the significance of Augustine's preaching, we will consider Augustine's preaching in the three interrelated contemporary needs identified in *Africae Munus*: reconciliation, justice, and peace. By hearing the preaching of Augustine on reconciliation, justice, and peace, we will be in a better position today to be "transforming theology into pastoral care," as Benedict XVI envisions, for the Church in Africa and for the world.[11] In Augustine's preaching, we find an extraordinary theology communicated for pastoral care. A conclusion summarizes the chapter's argument and allows us to listen to Augustine's preaching to Africans of his day on the Gospel text of "light of the world" and "salt of the earth" featured in *Africae Munus*.

Augustinus Afer: Augustine the African's Preaching

Although *Augustinus Afer*, or Augustine the African, may sound strange to some ears, it is an apt description of the man. An international conference in 2001 on the African continent was devoted to the theme of Augustine's Africanness and universality. About three dozen essays on that theme were published in two volumes as *Augustinus Afer*.[12] Our understanding of early African Christianity and of Augustine are mutually enriched when we see him as Augustine the African.[13] Unfortunately, some theologians dismiss Augustine as irrelevant or even detrimental to the Church in Africa today. David E. Wilhite names E. Bolaji Idowu, A. J. Omoyajowo, Mercy Amba Oduyoye, and André Karamaga as scholars who construe Augustine's thought to represent colonialist Christianity in Africa.[14] Many theologians recognize Augustine's positive contributions in developing African Christian theologies with varying degrees of engagement, and here we briefly consider two exemplary theologians: Paulinus Odozor and Kolawole Chabi.

Father Paulinus Odozor belongs to the Province of Nigeria–Southeast of the Spiritans. He was an expert assistant at the 2009 Synod of Bishops for Africa and is Professor at the University of Notre Dame. In his *Morality Truly Christian, Truly African*, Father Odozor adduces Augustine to help Africans today think about evil. Odozor writes, "Augustine's view has sometimes been criticized for underestimating the power of evil. But for the African imagination, in which evil is certainly alive and well, this view is certainly what is needed." Odozor borrows from Augustine the teaching that evil is not a metaphysically independent force. Evil "is nothing ultimately to be afraid of." Odozor continues, "To put it more theologically, for Augustine Christ has triumphed over evil, over the temptation to stare at incoherence and the tendency to fragmentation as though they were ultimate." Only God can bring good out of evil, and we can participate in God's "victory over evil through our faith in Christ, our configuration to his sacrifice in the Eucharist. It is a eucharistically configured victory, proleptic of the final Wedding Supper of the Lamb."[15] Augustine thus provides a great resource for Africans today to praise God for his final triumph over every evil, celebrated now in the Sacrament of Charity.

Father Kolawole Chabi, a priest from the Province of Nigeria of the Order of Saint Augustine and scholar at the Augustinianum in Rome, writes that some dismiss Augustine's relevance to Black Africa because of Augustine's belonging to Roman Africa. "Sometimes they also tend to ignore the taunts of some of his opponents such as Julian of Eclanum, who would insult him about his African origin and mock his Punic dialectic," Chabi states. He continues: "For a specialist of Augustine who is also conversant with the African cultures, to see his African-ness reflected in his work is not difficult."[16] Chabi writes of many similarities in Augustine's use of language and African oral literature. "For example," Chabi proposes, "the use of proverbs in Augustine's homiletic production is markedly African in outlook and makes him seem an African elder in the midst of those to whom he is transmitting wisdom." Chabi proceeds to connect this preaching to community formation in Africa. After his conversion, Augustine "opted for a communal life style following the example of the first Christian community in Jerusalem. He founded communities to which he also wrote a Rule of life. This love for life in common, inspired as it is by the gospel, reflects an aspect of the 'Igwebuike' as a modality of being in African thought."[17] Chabi then develops Augustine's teaching in conjunction with the Igbo word Igwebuike, and he demonstrates how fruitful drawing from

Augustine can be to enrich a form of community life elsewhere on the African continent.

Given these examples of Odozor and Chabi for their reliance on Augustine, we are in a better position to consider Augustine's preaching for explicating the principal themes of *Africae Munus*. Whereas some minimize the role of preaching in the liturgy, many Africans want lengthy, substantive preaching to benefit their lives. Their desire matches the desire of Augustine's people long ago. The implementation of *Africae Munus*, and any other ecclesial documents that communicate scriptural teaching for our salvation for that matter, belongs in a special way to preachers among their people. As Augustine famously said to an African congregation, "We are your books."[18]

One of the most eloquent Latin orators in the Roman Empire before he was baptized, in his long episcopal ministry Augustine preached after praying and meditating on the Scriptures, and he delivered his sermons without notes. We have about 900 sermons extant because secretaries took down what they heard him preach to his people. Many of these sermons were in his cathedral named the Basilica of Peace in Hippo. Their orality, directness, and attention to the Word of God is a great treasure for theology and pastoral practice, and they give witness to what was the very core of his life. "St. Augustine was, above all," Brian Daley comments, "a preacher."[19] Edmund Hill observes that Augustine "wasn't just making speeches, but talking of what he had most at heart to his own people, and it is clear that he loved them and they loved him."[20] In one sermon, he complains that their keenness or "violence" in wanting him to preach caused his sermon to be long, which he concluded from the stench that was now in the Church because the people had spent so much time there![21]

Augustine's most important teaching on preaching lies within his *On Christian Doctrine*. In Book 4, which communicates the way of delivering what was discovered in Sacred Scripture, Augustine speaks of three styles or modes of rhetoric to match the three Ciceronian duties of rhetoric: teaching or arguing, delighting, and swaying.[22] The first is the low style for teaching, the second is the moderate style for delighting, and the third is the grand style to win the victory of persuading people to action. Augustine gives an example from his own preaching about a time of swaying hearers to stop the habit of cruel violence. Augustine writes:

> The grand manner, however, by its very weight frequently makes the voices hush, makes the tears gush. Well anyway, I was once in Caesarea of Mauritania, trying to dissuade the people from their local civil war, or rather something more than civil, which they called "the mob"—for it is not only citizens but also neighbors, brothers, indeed parents and sons, divided into two parties, ritually fighting each other with stones at a certain time of the year, and each of them killing anyone he could; and I did indeed speak and act in the grand manner, to the best of my ability, in order to root out such a cruel and inveterate evil from their hearts and habits and rid them of it by my speaking.[23]

Augustine continues that he noted that the people's applause gave witness to their instruction and delight, but it was their weeping that showed the victory of swaying them. Writing about eight years after that preaching, he says that the monstrous custom had not returned to those people.

Augustine's Africa was a place of terrible social and theological conflicts in need of reconciliation, justice, and peace. Donatists separated themselves from Catholics and did not consider them their brethren. The radical Donatist group known as the Circumcellions even sought to kill Augustine. His companion and biographer Possidius tells the story that once the Circumcellions failed to capture Augustine because his guide made an erroneous decision about what road to take.[24] By God's providence, Augustine did not take the road leading to the Circumcellions, and so his life was spared. When Augustine was dying, Vandals had swept across much of northern Africa to the gates of Hippo. Augustine died on August 28, 430, prepared for the possibility of martyrdom;

his city fell to the Vandals the following year. The great city of Carthage fell to the Vandals in 439.

Augustine wanted his people to be nourished in the church so that they could face the difficulties of division and violence in the world. He provides ample resources for what Benedict XVI teaches in *Africae Munus*: "The most effective means for building a reconciled, just and peaceful society is a life of profound communion with God and with others. The table of the Lord gathers together men and women of different origins, cultures, races, languages and ethnic groups." The document continues, "Thanks to the Body and Blood of Christ, they become truly one. In the eucharistic Christ, they become blood relations and thus true brothers and sisters, thanks to the word and to the Body and Blood of the same Jesus Christ. This bond of fraternity is stronger than that of human families, than that of our tribes" (no. 152). Eloquent preacher of the *Totus Christus,* that all Christians are one Body with their Head as the one Christ, Augustine can be heard in full support of Benedict's teaching.[25]

We now consider brief aspects of the themes of reconciliation, justice, and peace in *Africae Munus* and in Augustine the African, and find that his preaching most beautifully supports and amplifies the teaching of this apostolic exhortation.

Africae Munus and Augustine's Preaching on Reconciliation

In his apostolic exhortation, Benedict XVI gives many insightful teachings on reconciliation. Of overarching importance is the pattern that God reconciles us to himself through his incarnate Son, the Word who became flesh. Moreover, by being reconciled to God through Christ, who suffered, died, and rose for us, we can become reconciled to one another. Benedict writes, "Listening to and meditating upon the word of God means letting it penetrate and shape our lives so as to reconcile us with God, allowing God to lead us towards reconciliation with our neighbor: a necessary path for building a community of individuals and peoples. On our faces and in our lives, may the word of God truly take flesh! (no. 15)."[26] We see this same pattern repeated: "It is God's grace that gives us a new heart and reconciles us with him and with one another. Christ re-established humanity in the Father's love. Reconciliation thus springs from this love; it is born of the Father's initiative in restoring his relationship with humanity, a relationship broken by human sin" (no. 20). Benedict continues by quoting the synodal general relator's *Report before the Discussion*:

> In Jesus Christ, "in his life and ministry, but especially in his death and resurrection, the Apostle Paul saw God the Father reconciling the world (all things in heaven and on earth) to himself, discounting the sins of humanity (cf. 2 Cor 5:19; Rom 5:10; Col 1:21–22). Paul saw God the Father reconciling Jews and Gentiles to himself, creating one new man through the Cross (cf. Eph 2:15; 3:6). Thus, the experience of reconciliation establishes communion on two levels: communion between God and humanity; and—since the experience of reconciliation also makes us (as a reconciled humanity) 'ambassadors of reconciliation'—communion among men." (no. 20)[27]

Augustine, who had special concern for the separation caused by the Donatist schism, repeatedly preached this twin emphasis of reconciliation with God and with one another. He preached incessantly to heal the division, including urging Catholics to consider the Donatists as their brothers and sisters who likewise pray, "Our Father." The Donatists denied Catholic baptism, and so they denied even the commonality of being brethren together by the Spirit of adoption in Christ. While preaching on 1 John, Augustine shows the primacy of our reconciliation with God, who offers unity in the Church:

> *I am writing to you, little children, because your sins are forgiven through his name* (2:12). Therefore, little children,

> you are born through the forgiveness of your sins. But through whose name are your sins forgiven? Through that of Augustine? Then not through the name of Donatus either. You see who Augustine is and who Donatus is. Nor through Paul's name or Peter's name either. For, to those who are dividing the Church and attempting to fracture its unity, the childbearing mother charity in the Apostle manifests her heart, in a certain sense rends her womb with her words, beseeches the children whom she sees being carried away, recalls to the one name those desirous of making many names for themselves, turns them away from loving her so that they may love Christ, and says, *Was Paul crucified for you? Or were you baptized in Paul's name?* (1 Cor 1:13)[28]

Attentive to the mystery of the Trinity as the saving revelation found in the giving of the Son and the Holy Spirit, Augustine relates in *Sermon* 71, "So by what is common to them, both the Father and the Son wished us to have communion both with them and among ourselves; by this gift which they both possess as one they wished to gather us together and make us one, that is to say, by the Holy Spirit who is God and the gift of God." Augustine continues, "By this gift we are reconciled to the godhead, and by this gift we enjoy the godhead. After all, what use would it be to us to know any kind of good if we didn't also love it?"[29] In another sermon, Augustine preaches, "This is the grace which the apostle particularly commends to Christians when he says, *For the one God and one mediator between God and men*—and he doesn't just add *Christ Jesus,* in case you should suppose it was said about the Word, but he added *the man*: *mediator between God and men, the man Christ Jesus* (1 Tm 2:5)." Augustine asks, "What's a mediator?" He answers, "One by whom we would be joined together, through whom we would be reconciled, because we were lying there isolated by our own sins, we were in death, we had utterly perished. Christ wasn't man when man was created. To stop man perishing, he became man."[30]

In his preaching on reconciliation, Augustine shows how love makes us into what we love. Unbelievers, he explains, are called "the world," since they got the name from what they love. "By loving God," he continues, "we are made into gods. So by loving the world we are called 'the world.'" Then Augustine quotes the Apostle Paul: "But God was in Christ, reconciling the world to himself" (2 Cor 5:19).[31] God reconciles "the world," unbelievers, not because of their love, but because of his love in Christ, redirecting their love to himself.

This universality, preached by Augustine based on who God is, Love, and shown in the reconciliation offered in Christ and the Spirit, can help implement Benedict's teaching in *Africae Munus*:

> Within the Church's living tradition and following the desire expressed in the Exhortation *Ecclesia in Africa,* to see the Church as a family and a fraternity is to recover one aspect of her heritage. In this community where Jesus Christ, "the first-born among many brethren" (*Rom* 8:29), reconciled all people with God the Father (cf. *Eph* 2:14–18) and bestowed the Holy Spirit (cf. *Jn* 20:22), the Church for her part becomes the bearer of the Good News that every human person is a child of God. She is called to transmit this message to all humanity by proclaiming the salvation won for us by Christ, by celebrating our communion with God and by living in fraternal solidarity. (no. 8)

Africae Munus and Augustine's Preaching on Justice

Pope Benedict's apostolic exhortation gives conditions for justice worthy of its name. Benedict writes, "Love of truth—'the whole truth,' to which the Spirit alone can lead us (cf. Jn 16:13)—is what marks out the path that all human justice must follow if it is to succeed in restoring the bonds of fraternity within the 'human family, a community of peace,' reconciled with God through Christ. Justice is never disembodied. It needs to be anchored in consistent human decisions. A charity which fails to respect justice and the rights of all is false. I therefore encourage Christians to become exemplary in the area of justice and charity" (no. 18). From the insight that "Justice is never disembodied," we find the incarnational view of justice preached by Augustine.

Preaching on a psalm, Augustine uses the occasion of his sermon to offer a prayer to God that we too can offer: "Help me to do what you ordain, give me what you command. *In your justice give me life,* because what I had in myself is enough to kill me. Only in you do I find my hope of life. Your justice is Christ, *who has been made for us by God wisdom, and justice, and sanctification, and redemption. As it is written, Let anyone who boasts, boast in the Lord* (1 Cor 1:30–31)." Augustine continues in this striking first-person witness, "In him I find your commandments, for which I have longed, so that in your justice—in your Christ, I mean—you may give me life. He is God, the Word, but the Word was made flesh, that he might also be my neighbor."[32] For Augustine, we must care for Christ as the neighbor in need and render justice, such as in giving food for the hungry, for that is how the nations will be judged on Judgment Day, according to Augustine' favorite passage of Matthew 25:31–46 that frequently recurs in his preaching on the Psalms.[33]

Augustine emphasizes that Christ himself is justice in delightful food imagery in *Sermon* 28 to underscore the reward of a beatitude: "Now if you are seeking food, because you have been fasting, *Blessed are those who hunger and thirst for justice* (Matt. 5:6). But it is said of the Lord Jesus Christ himself that he has become for us justice and wisdom. There you have the banquet that has been provided. Christ is justice, nowhere is he in short supply; he is not provided for us by cooks, nor is he imported by merchants from overseas, like exotic fruits."[34] Later in this sermon, Augustine identifies Christ as the Living Bread who came down from heaven (Jn. 6:51), the food that does not perish. He then tells those gathered at the church's altar: "When you depart from here to your own tables, you won't eat anything like that. So because you have come together to this banquet, take care that you eat well.

And when you go away, mind you digest it well. You eat well and digest badly if you hear the word of God and don't do it. In that case you don't derive any useful energy from it, but belch it out in the raw discomfort of indigestion."[35]

Augustine makes clear that the justice experienced in the church should be lived out in Christian life. He compares proper Christian justice with the Roman Empire's justice, which calls a sacrilege someone harming an image of the emperor. Augustine preaches, "If, therefore, you would be guilty of sacrilege, or rather would be said to be so by civil law, if you insulted an image of the emperor, what will you be guilty of if you insult, or do injustice to, the image of God? Which is worse? To throw a stone at the image of a man, or to make the image of God into a stone?"[36] If we commit injustice, we make our souls, made to the image of God, into stones.

Pope Benedict writes in *Africae Munus*: "As reconciled men and women, the faithful will . . . promote justice everywhere, especially in African societies divided and threatened by violence and war, yet hungering and thirsting for true justice" (no. 170). With Augustine as preacher, the faithful can learn that justice at the feast of Christ our justice in the Church and practice that justice in accord with the dignity of being an image of God: "Justice is never disembodied."

Africae Munus and Augustine's Preaching on Peace

Pope Benedict declares, "True peace comes from Christ (cf. Jn. 14:27). It cannot be compared with the peace that the world gives. It is not the fruit of negotiations and diplomatic agreements based on particular interests. It is the peace of a humanity reconciled with itself in God, a peace of which the Church is the sacrament" (no. 30). Clearly, for Benedict, there can be no peace without reconciliation and justice, and that peace comes from Christ and is made manifest in Christ's Body, the Church.

The Latin word for peace, *pax*, appears in its various grammatical forms more than 2,500 times in Augustine's writings.[37]

Augustine most firmly communicates that the true peace is not of this world, and now is the time to turn to the peace that only God can give.[38] For example, on John 14, Augustine preaches, "But when the Lord proceeded to say, 'Not as the world gives, do I give unto you,' what else does he mean but, 'Not as those give who love the world, do I give unto you'? For their aim in giving themselves peace is that, exempt from the annoyance of lawsuits and wars, they may find enjoyment, not in God, but in the friendship of the world."[39] Evidently, the peace that Christ gives is not from the world, but it is meant for our anxious hearts now in the world.[40] It also has its fulfillment only in heaven, where we can at last know what Christ calls "my peace."[41]

Preaching on the beatitudes, Augustine recalls Christ's words, "Blessed are the peacemakers, for they shall be called sons of God" (Matt. 5:9). The preacher asks, "Who are the peacemakers? Those who make peace. Do you see two people quarreling?" He continues, "Be a promoter of peace between them. Say nice things about this one to that one, and about that one to this one." Augustine speaks clearly and directly. He says, "Do you hear one of them, apparently in anger, saying nasty things about the other? Don't repeat them; suppress the abuse uttered by an angry individual, give honest thought to the business of reconciliation." He emphasizes that peace must begin within one's own heart: "What's more, if you want to be a peacemaker between two quarreling friends of yours, begin the work of making peace with yourself; you should first pacify yourself inside, where perhaps you are wrangling and brawling with yourself every day."[42] In this same sermon, Augustine shows how each of us can have peace within: "Now the better part of you is the one where the image of God is to be found. This is called mind, it's called intelligence; that's where faith glows, hope takes courage, charity is kindled. Does your mind want to be capable of conquering your lusts? Let it submit to one greater than itself, and it will conquer one lower than itself, and you will have in yourself a peace that is genuine, stable, and supremely well ordered." Augustine proclaims the order necessary for peace: "What is the order of this peace? God controls the mind, the mind controls the flesh; nothing could be better ordered."[43] This gives one expression to Augustine's famous definition of peace as "the tranquility of order."[44]

Ultimately, the peace we are meant to experience comes only in heaven. Every day we must wage a battle for peace within our hearts. Augustine preaches in this same sermon, "All this fighting, though, which tires us out in our weakness—even when we don't give in to evil desires, we are still somehow or other engrossed in the combat, we are not yet safe—all this fighting will be over then, when death is swallowed up in victory." He evokes the authority ofPaul: "Listen how it will be over and done with: *The perishable body*—this is what the apostle says—*has to put on imperishability, and this mortal thing put on immortality. But when this mortal thing has put on immortality, then shall come about the saying that is written: Death has been swallowed up in victory* (1 Cor. 15:53–54)." The preacher then states clearly, "War is at an end, and eliminated by peace. Listen to the victory celebrations: *Where, O death, is your striving? Where, O death, is your sting?* (1 Cor. 15:55). That's now the tone of victory celebrations. No enemies at all will be left, no contender within, no tempter without. So, *blessed are the peacemakers, for they shall be called the sons of God.*"[45]

Pope Benedict writes in *Africae Munus*, "Heaven is promised to all who are simple, like children, to all who, like them, are filled with a spirit of trusting abandonment, pure and rich in goodness. They alone can find in God a Father and become, through Jesus, children of God. Sons and daughters of our parents, God wants us all to become his adopted children by grace!" (no. 68). Peace, the wondrous divine gift following reconciliation and justice that can begin here and now by grace, has the eschatological horizon of unending happiness of heaven for the children of God.

Conclusion

Introducing his apostolic exhortation, Benedict XVI writes, "It was my intention that Christ's words: 'You are the salt of the earth

. . . you are the light of the world,' would be the unifying theme of the Synod and also of the post-synod period" (no. 6). In its conclusion, he writes, "Dear brothers and sisters, through the Second Special Assembly for Africa of the Synod of Bishops, the Lord in his goodness and mercy urgently reminds you that 'you are the salt of the earth . . . the light of the world' (Matt. 5:13–14). May these words remind you of the dignity of your calling as children of God and members of the one, holy, catholic and apostolic Church!" (no. 176).

The dignity of being children of God is immense. Preaching helps the people gathered at the altar to know what God calls them to be. Many of the lay faithful have not and will not read *Africae Munus*, but they have preachers. Preachers are meant to translate what is written by life and speech for the lives of the faithful. Reflecting on the two apostolic exhortations on the Church in Africa and the social question that lingers on the continent, Valentine Ugochukwa Iheanacho writes, "When all is said and done, it is through the faithful that the Catholic Church in Africa can make its presence felt. It is by means of their witness that the Church can contribute to the spiritual and material well-being of Africans if it must fulfill its missionary mandate as the leaven of progress and social transformation in Africa."[46]

This study has contributed to the call in *Africae Munus* for reconciliation, justice, and peace by attending to Augustine the African's preaching for those gathered at the altar. In each of the apostolic exhortation's concerns of reconciliation, justice, and peace, we heard Augustine's fervent preaching for his African people about sixteen centuries ago. For our final consideration, we listen to excerpts of two sermons. Both stress Augustine's signature mark of humility in living the Christian life, for only in humility will the Church of Africa shine out and give season for the salvation of the world. His preaching remains powerful for those gathered at the altar in Africa and throughout the world.

In the first sermon, Augustine reminds his congregation that many people are humiliated and brought low for all sorts of reasons. Some endure the distress of lowliness in order to get money, win worldly honors, or acquire the good things of life in this world. "Why not do it for God's sake? Why not for Christ?" Augustine questions. He continues with a play on the Latin word *sapientia*, which means "wisdom," but also reminds Latin speakers of *sapor*, "taste" or "flavor": "Why not for the sake of the taste of salt? Or is this saying unknown to you: *you are the salt of the earth*? And that *once salt has become insipid, it is no good for anything, except to be thrown away* (Matt. 5:13)? Therefore it is good to be brought low in tasty wisdom (*Bonum est ergo sapienter humilari.*)"[47]

In the second sermon, Augustine preaches on his people as light, but he does not want them to jump up and down in pride, which would blow a little flame out. He wants them to shine. So how can they shine? On a lampstand. Augustine proclaims, "The cross of Christ is a great lampstand. Whoever wishes to shine, mustn't be ashamed of this wooden lampstand." Quoting Matthew 5:14–16, which shows that the light would allow others to see the good works and glorify the Father in heaven, Augustine makes clear: "Through your good works, may they glorify your Father. You were not able to light yourselves in order to be lamps, not able to put yourselves on the lampstand; let him be glorified, who did all this for you."[48]

For these reasons, and for many more, we do well to listen to the preaching of *Augustinus Afer* for understanding better what is contained in *Africae Munus* ten years after its promulgation and well afterwards. By doing so, we ask God in humble prayer that we ourselves may be more and more transformed to be the light of the world and the salt of the earth for God's work of reconciliation, justice, and peace on Augustine's home continent of Africa, and indeed throughout the world.

Chapter 6 Endnotes

1 I am grateful to Fr. Maurice Ashley Agbaw-Ebai, Matthew Levering, and the participants of "*Africae Munus*: Ten Years Later," sponsored by the Center for Scriptural Exegesis, Theology, and Doctrine at Mundelein Seminary, November 4–6, 2021 for their feedback on my

presentation. I also thank Garrett Peters, my graduate assistant, for his proofreading of this chapter. This essay is dedicated in fraternal charity to the Dominican Vicariate of Eastern Africa, where I served in 2003–05.

2 John S. Mbiti, *African Religions and Philosophy*, 2d revised and enlarged ed. (Oxford: Heinemman, 1989 [1999 reprint]), 223.

3 Benedict is quoting his Address on March 19, 2009 at the Special Council of the Synod for Africa, Yaoundé, Cameroon. Benedict elsewhere in this document praises the early Christian history of Africa. For example, he writes, "Africa is the cradle of the Christian contemplative life. Present from earliest times in North Africa, especially in Egypt and Ethiopia, it took root in sub-Saharan Africa during the last century" (no. 119).

4 For an overview of Augustine, I recommend Matthew Levering, *The Theology of Augustine: An Introductory Guide to His Most Important Works* (Grand Rapids, MI: Baker Academic, 2013).

5 Augustine tells us that his birthday is the Ides of November, i.e., November 13, in his early dialogue, *De Beata Vita* 1.6.

6 For context and analysis, see the address of Cardinal Peter Turkson, "A Special Assembly of the Synod of Bishops for Africa II: Le Profizie, Risorse, Ricadute," Facoltà Teologica, Firenze, March 1, 2010. For an argument that Pope Francis's encyclical *Fratelli Tutti* carries on the themes of the exhortations on Africa by John Paul II and Benedict XVI, see Patrick Ndodé-Sikossi, O.P., "L'actualité des thèmes d'Ecclesia in Africa et *d'Africae Munus* dans *Fratelli tutti*," *Revista Iberoamericana de Teología* 18, no. 34 (2022): 139–60.

7 For witness to Augustine as the favorite theologian of Joseph Ratzinger/Benedict XVI, see for example his address at Vespers on April 22, 2007 during his pastoral visit to Vigevano and Pavia at the Basilica of St. Pietro in Ciel d'Oro, Pavia. Pope Benedict speaks there of "my personal devotion and gratitude to the one who played such an important part in my life as a theologian and a Pastor, but, I would say, even more as a man and a priest." Matthew Levering emphasizes Africa's importance to Ratzinger/Benedict, which includes that Africa was "the birthplace of his most decisive mentor, Augustine of Hippo." See Matthew Levering, "Introduction," in *Joseph Ratzinger and the Future of African Theology*, eds. Maurice Ashley Agbaw-Ebai and Matthew Levering (Eugene, OR: Pickwick Publications, 2021), 1.

8 Benedict XVI, general audience on January 9, 2008 in Paul VI Audience Hall, "Saint Augustine (1)."

9 "Sermon for the Feast of Saint Augustine," translated by Matthew

J. O'Connell, in Benedict XVI/Joseph Ratzinger, *Dogma and Preaching: Applying Christian Doctrine to Daily Life*, unabridged edition, ed. Michael J. Miller (San Francisco: Ignatius Press, 2011), 362–68, at 367.

10 For an overview of Augustine's preaching, see *The Cambridge Companion to Augustine's Sermons*, eds. David V. Meconi, S.J., and Andrew Hofer, O.P., forthcoming from Cambridge University Press. New City Press's The Works of Saint Augustine is publishing English translations of the complete works of the African Doctor. Fr. Edmund Hill, O.P., Sr. Maria Boulding, O.S.B., and Fr. Boniface Ramsey translated many of Augustine's works, including much preaching. Citations are given in this essay to their translations by the volume and page number in that series.

11 Benedict XVI, Address to the Roman Curia, December 21, 2009, and cited in *Africae Munus* no. 10.

12 *Augustinus Afer: Saint Augustin, africanité et universalité. Acts du colloque internationale Alger-Annaba 1–7 avril 2001*, ed. Pierre-Yves Flux, et al. 2 vols. Paradosis 45/1–2 (Fribourg: Éditions Univeristaires Fribourg Suisse, 2003). The volume is mostly in French and English, although other languages have a presence. One reviewer notes: "The conference took place under the strictest security measures. Participants were issued with bodyguards and their visits to the sites were accompanied by the background noise of military helicopters. This, too, perhaps, is a reminder of the security situation during the last years of Augustine's life." See Josef Lössl's review in the *Journal of Theological Studies*, n.s. 56, no. 1 (2005): 231–33 at 233.

13 For accessible surveys of early African Christianity, including Augustine's place within it, see David E. Wilhite, *Ancient African Christianity: An Introduction to a Unique Context and Tradition* (New York: Routledge, 2017) and David L. Eastman, *Early North African Christianity: Turning Points in the Development of the Church* (Grand Rapids, MI: Baker Academic, 2021).

14 David E. Wilhite, "Augustine in Black and African Theology," in *The Oxford Guide to the Historical Reception of Augustine*, editor-in-chief Karla Pollmann, editor Willemien Otten, vol. 1 (Oxford: Oxford University Press, 2013), 126–134, at 131. For a more extended appreciation of the question of Augustine's Africanness and theology in recent times, see David E. Wilhite, "Augustine the African: Post-colonial, Postcolonial, and Post-Postcolonial Readings," *Journal of Postcolonial Theology and Theory* 5, no. 1 (2014): 1–34. For accessible surveys of early African Christianity, including Augustine's place within it, see David E. Wilhite, *Ancient African Christianity: An Introduction to a Unique Context and Tradition* (New York: Routledge,

2017) and David L. Eastman, *Early North African Christianity: Turning Points in the Development of the Church* (Grand Rapids, MI: Baker Academic, 2021).

15 Paulinus Ikechukwu Odozor, C.S.Sp., *Morality Truly Christian, Truly African: Foundational, Methodological, and Theological Considerations* (Notre Dame, IN: University of Notre Dame Press, 2014), 260.

16 Kolawole Chabi, O.S.A., "Augustine's Ideal of Community vis-à-vis the Communal Dimension of 'Igwebuike' African Philosophy," in *Perspectives on Igwebuike Philosophy: Essays in Honour of Professor Kanu, Ikechukwu Anthony, O.S.A.*, eds. Kanayo L. Nwadialor et al. (Bloomington, IN: Authorhouse, 2019), 1–13, at 1.

17 Chabi, "Augustine's Ideal of Community," 2.

18 *Sermon* 227 (Works of Saint Augustine III/6, Hill, 254). Adapting this Augustinian adage, Daniel Cardó insightfully writes that even in a literate culture, "preachers are the only 'books' that most people will 'read.'" See Daniel Cardó, *The Art of Preaching: A Theological and Practical Primer*, foreword by Timothy Gallagher, OMV (Washington, DC: The Catholic University of America Press, 2021), 100.

19 Brian E. Daley, SJ, "Augustine the Preacher: Practicing the Rhetoric of Love," in *The Center Is Jesus Christ Himself: Essays on Revelation, Salvation, and Evangelization in Honor of Robert P. Imbelli*, ed. Andrew Meszaros (Washington, DC: The Catholic University of America Press, 2021), 231–51, at 231.

20 Edmund Hill, OP, "St Augustine as Preacher," *Blackfriars* 416 (1954): 463–71, at 469.

21 *Exposition on Psalm* 72.34 (Works of Saint Augustine III/17, Boulding, 492). Cf. Hill, "St Augustine as Preacher," 469. This paragraph adapts material from chapter 5 of my *The Word in Our Flesh: The Power of Patristic Preaching*, forthcoming from The Catholic University of America Press.

22 *On Christian Doctrine* 4.12.27; Cicero, *The Orator* 21.69.

23 *On Christian Doctrine* 4.24.53 (Works of Saint Augustine I/11, Hill, 234).

24 Possidius of Calama, *Life of St. Augustine*, chap. 12.

25 For Augustine's teaching on the one Christ as deification, see David Vincent Meconi, S.J., *The One Christ: St. Augustine's Theology of Deification* (Washington, DC: The Catholic University of America Press, 2013).

26 For an extended study of this kind of incarnational preaching, see my *The Word in Our Flesh: The Power of Patristic Preaching*, forthcoming from The Catholic University of America Press.

27 Cardinal Peter Kodwo Appiah Turkson, Relator General of the

Synod, Report before the Discussion, II. a. Emmanuel Katongole concludes a pertinent essay on reconciliation in this way: "My goal in this exploration has been to make explicit the conviction that reconciliation is not simply a pastoral programme, among many, but the lens through which the church understands her identity and mission in the world. The post-synodal Exhortation *Africae Munus* reinforces this conviction, and thus provides a very timely set of pastoral guidelines and recommendations for the mission of the church in Africa in the twenty-first century." See Emmanuel M. Katongole, "Apostolic Exhortation, *Africae Munus*: The Church in Africa in Service to Reconciliation, Justice, and Peace," in *Mission as Ministry of Reconciliation*, eds. Robert Schreiter and Knud Jørgensen, Regnum Edinburgh Centenary Series, vol. 16 (Oxford: Regnum Books International, 2013), 66–78, at 78.

28 *Homily 2 on 1 John*.4 (Works of Saint Augustine I/14, Ramsey, 42).

29 *Sermon* 71.18 (Works of Saint Augustine III/3, Hill, 256).

30 *Sermon* 26.7 (Works of Saint Augustine III/2, Hill, 96).

31 *Sermon* 121.1 (Works of Saint Augustine III/4, Hill 234).

32 *Exposition 12 on Psalm* 118.5 (Works of Saint Augustine III/19, Boulding 398).

33 See Andrew Hofer, O.P., "Matthew 25:31–46 as an Hermeneutical Rule in Augustine's *Enarrationes in Psalmos*," *Downside Review* 126 (2008): 285–300.

34 *Sermon* 28.2 (Works of Saint Augustine III/2, Hill, 111).

35 *Sermon* 28.2 (Hill, 112).

36 *Sermon* 23B (Dolbeau 6).7 (Works of Saint Augustine III/11, Hill, 41).

37 Donald X. Burt, O.S.A., "Peace," in *Augustine through the Ages: An Encyclopedia*, ed. Allan D. Fitzgerald, O.S.A., foreword by Jaroslav Pelikan (Grand Rapids, MI: Eerdmans, 1999), 629–32.

38 For a study of the contrast of kinds of peace in *City of God*, see my "Book 19. The Ends of the Two Cities: Augustine's Appeal for Peace," in *The Cambridge Companion to Augustine's* City of God, ed. David V. Meconi, S.J. (Cambridge: Cambridge University Press, 2021), 228–50.

39 *Tractate* 77.5 on the Gospel of John (Nicene and Post-Nicene Fathers, First Series, vol. 7, Gibb and Innes, 340 [altered]).

40 For a study of true peace for hearts that have anxieties today, see my "Book VI: Augustine's Anxiety and Ours," in *Augustine's* Confessions *and Contemporary Concerns*, edited by David Vincent Meconi, S.J. (Saint Paul, MN: Saint Paul Seminary Press, forthcoming).

41 For a study of Augustine's preaching on peace in heaven, see my "Preaching on Heaven and its Peace," in *The Cambridge Companion*

to *Augustine's Sermons*, edited by David Vincent Meconi, S.J., and Andrew Hofer, O.P. (Cambridge: Cambridge University Press, forthcoming).

42 *Sermon* 53A.12 (Works of Saint Augustine III/3, Hill, 82–83).

43 (Hill, 83).

44 *City of God* 19.13.1.

45 (Hill, 83).

46 Valentine Ugochukwa Iheanacho, "The African social question: A challenge to the African church in light of the two synods on Africa," *Acta Theologica* 41, no. 2 (2021): 23–42, at 38.

47 *Exposition on Psalm* 59.2 (Works of Saint Augustine III/17, Boulding, 181).

48 *Sermon* 289.6 (Works of Saint Augustine III/8, Hill, 123).

Chapter 7
Africae Munus and the Challenge of a Political Pentecostalism

Dennis Kasule

When you see your child every day, you know that he or she is growing, but it is difficult to measure the growth daily (a bit like Mark 4:27). On the other hand, when you go away for a year or so and return, it becomes easier to recognize how tall he or she has grown during the time you were away. I visit my home parish about once or twice every year. During my visits, I look to see what has changed. Over the past number of years, I have noticed a consistent transformation in the religious landscape. This transformation is what I intend to draw attention to in this essay. It has been a joy to listen to the many theses presented during our conference. However, I am not going to put forward a theological or philosophical thesis, but to share observations and invite us to pay attention to a change that is a direct challenge to the future of Catholicism on the African continent.

In one of the shortest paragraphs in *Africae Munus*, Pope Benedict XVI makes mention of the emergence and growth of African Independent Churches on the continent. The paragraph (no. 90) reads:

> In recent decades, the Church in Africa has been asking itself a great many questions about the emergence and growth of non-Catholic communities sometimes known as African Independent Churches. Frequently an offshoot of traditional Christian Churches and ecclesial communities, they adopt elements of traditional

> African cultures. These groups have recently made an appearance in the ecumenical field. The Pastors of the Catholic Church will have to take into account this new phenomenon affecting the promotion of Christian unity in Africa, and they will consequently have to find a response suited to the context, for the sake of deeper evangelization as a way of effectively communicating Christ's truth to the people of Africa.[1]

In this paragraph, Benedict XVI acknowledges a recent transformation in the landscape of Christianity on the African continent. Newcomers are emerging and growing. Not only that, but they also do not seem to fit the patterns of mainline churches. While appearing frequently as offshoots of traditional Christian churches and ecclesial communities, they are different in this way: "they adopt elements of traditional African cultures."

While the change in the landscape of Christianity on the African continent is acknowledged, apparently not much attention can be devoted to it in the exhortation because it is depicted as a new phenomenon, sort of an unknown, a question. Nevertheless, Benedict XVI recognizes that this transformation in the landscape of Christianity on the African continent is a challenge for the Catholic Church.

Having said so, he asks the Catholic pastors to consider this new phenomenon and respond to it in ways that are suited to the contexts in which they carry out their mission in view of promoting Christian unity and a deeper evangelization.

The topic of this essay arises from paragraph 90 of *Africae Munus*. While the mentioned paragraph names the new movements as the African Independent Churches, it seems to me that African Pentecostalism can be seen as an extension of this broad category. Perhaps, it might even be its manifestation *par excellence*. In the next paragraph (paragraph no. 91), Benedict XVI describes how the emerging forms of Christianity on the African continent have garnered their growth and vibrancy. He states:

> Various syncretistic movements and sects have sprung up in Africa in recent decades. Sometimes it is hard to discern whether they are of authentically Christian inspiration or whether they are simply the fruit of sudden infatuation with a leader claiming to have exceptional gifts. Their nomenclature and vocabulary easily give rise to confusion, and they can lead people in good faith astray. These many sects take advantage of an incomplete social infrastructure, the erosion of traditional family solidarity and inadequate catechesis in order to exploit people's credulity, and they offer a religious veneer to a variety of heterodox, non-Christian beliefs. They shatter the peace of couples and families through false prophecies and visions. They even seduce political leaders. The Church's theology and pastoral care must determine the causes of this phenomenon, not only to stem the hemorrhage of the faithful from the parishes to the sects, but also in order to lay the foundations of a suitable pastoral response to the attraction that these movements and sects exert. Once again, this points to the need for a profound evangelization of the African soul.[2]

To me, this description fits well with many aspects of the African Pentecostalist movement, and there is no other movement that is causing the hemorrhaging of parish communities like this one.

In this essay, I attempt to take up Benedict XVI's invitation and challenge to the pastors of the Catholic Church regarding this transformation in the landscape of Christianity in Africa. I actively listen to his call and exhortation to Catholic leaders to determine why the emerging non-Catholic communities are causing a steady departure of the faithful from parish communities. Benedict XVI not only urges Catholic leaders to find the causes behind the exodus of the faithful but also to lay the foundations for contextually appropriate responses to arrest the situation and attend to what he calls, "the need for a profound evangelization of the African soul."[3]

Therefore, first, I explore some key reasons for the emergence and rise of Pentecostalism as a religious, social, and political force. I use Uganda as a particular case, but also show that this situation is not unique to Uganda. Secondly, I sketch in broad strokes what the Catholic response has looked like. Finally, I point out some areas to which Catholic leaders could pay attention toward stemming the growing tendency of the Catholic faithful to abandon their parish communities.

The Rise of Pentecostalism and Its Intersection with the Political Economy

Recent statistical projections indicate that the share of Christians worldwide who live in sub-Saharan Africa is expected to increase dramatically between 2015 and 2060, from approximately 26% to 42%.[4] This means that within only forty years from today, for every 10 Christians in the world, 4 will be from Sub-Saharan Africa. This projection is an indicator of the changing face of Christianity worldwide. But the change goes further. As Christianity grows in sub-Saharan Africa, it is also emerging in new forms.[5] The new expressions of Christianity involve negotiating with African cultures, sensibilities, linguistics, ethnicities, and liberative or decolonizing praxes amidst prevailing socio-economic and political exigencies.

The great strides of Christianity and the emergence of new forms of it on the African continent have tapped into a core of a typical African's existence, namely, a pervasive religiosity. In 1969, the Kenyan Anglican priest and philosopher, John Mbiti, published his insightful work *African Religions and Philosophy* in which he presented his systematic study of the attitudes of mind and belief that have evolved in the many societies of Africa. One of his remarkable insights in that work touches on the infusion of religion in all aspects of life for most Africans. Mbiti remarked that "African people are notoriously religious (and) religion permeates into all the departments of life so that it is not easy or possible to isolate it."[6] In other words, religion or religiosity is a life-shaping reality in the lives of most Africans.

But we must clarify this point further: To think of religion or spirituality as a distinct compartment in the lives of most Africans would be misleading. Rather, for typical Africans one's spirituality or religion is intertwined with one's culture, society, and environment. This remains true today despite the invasion of modernity in some aspects of African living. The success of the major missionary religions on the continent, that is, Christianity and Islam, coupled with the persistence of traditional African belief systems, as well as new forms of religious practice, is one indicator of this fact.

In an interview given in 2015, the Harvard-based professor of African religions, Jacob Olupona, remarked as follows:

> African spirituality simply acknowledges that beliefs and practices touch on and inform every facet of human life, and therefore African religion cannot be separated from the everyday or mundane. African spirituality is truly holistic. For example, sickness in the indigenous African worldview is not only an imbalance of the body but also an imbalance in one's social life, which can be linked to a breakdown in one's kinship and family relations or even to one's relationship with one's ancestors.[7]

In other words, it is characteristic that a sickness affecting the body is not seen as a merely physical occurrence for the typical African. The causes of bodily ailments are sought beyond the physical, in the trans-physical (the social, relational, etc.), and the metaphysical realms. The same can be said for the explanations about one's failure to prosper or one's prospering.

Among the many kinds of Christianity shaping the religious landscape of sub-Saharan Africa today, a particular strain is gradually showing itself as the frontrunner, that is, Pentecostalism. It is beyond the scope of this essay to go into the debate on the origins of Pentecostalism in sub-Saharan Africa. Generally, African scholars mostly attribute the origins of African

Pentecostalism to internal forces within Africa while Western scholars mostly attribute its origins to forces outside Africa.[8] In any case, what we can no longer debate is the vibrant presence of Pentecostalism in sub-Saharan Africa today. It is remarkable. It is a sweeping force.

Characteristically, unlike traditional Christian denominations which have varying degrees of structure and order, African Pentecostalism has very little in terms of structures of authority; it is very diverse and decentralized, and the various groups are, more or less, the personal possessions of their leaders. As some scholars have argued, it is conceivable to speak of "Pentecostalisms" to capture the decentralized variety of Pentecostal expression in sub-Saharan Africa.[9] Perhaps four common features that one can identify amidst this diversity are: (1) The belief that everyone and anyone can have a direct experience of God through the Holy Spirit ("Spirit baptism") and receive the Spirit's gifts, such as prophecy, healing and deliverance, speaking in tongues, and efficacious prayer; (2) The appreciation of the presence of supernatural or spiritual forces everywhere, especially the malignant as well as miracles; (3) Emphasis on Scripture; (4) leadership and rhetoric that is attentive to African sensibilities and current exigencies.

Regarding the reasons for Pentecostalism's phenomenal rise, it is possible to put them in three broad clusters: the religious, the rhetorical, and the political-economic. First, we explore the religious cluster. The vibrant presence of Pentecostalism in Africa has had a lot to do with its ability, as a movement, to tap into the religiosity and worldviews of most Africans. Pentecostal pastors are careful to address not just the spiritual but the overall human experience and the environment which, to the typical African, is perceived as filled with supernatural or spiritual significance. As such, African Pentecostalism is attractive because of its emphasis on the pneumatic, frequent acknowledgment of spiritual forces, an emphasis on spiritual warfare, healing and deliverance, vibrant and creative liturgical services, and the promise of abundant life, which focuses not only on heavenly bliss but also on prosperity here and now, thereby promising to have an answer to endemic poverty.[10]

In the second cluster, which was labeled "rhetorical," are all the reasons that have to do with leadership, communication, messaging, and relationships. Pentecostal churches[11] have excelled in the use of modern media to project their leaders and their churches, to reach out, and enhance their prayer services. By doing so, these churches have garnered massive followings on radio and television stations. In terms of institutional structures, they are small compared to mainline churches, but they reach out to a larger audience. To give an example, in Uganda, there are at least 26 Pentecostal radio stations and 16 Pentecostal television stations. The Catholic Church is only starting to attempt to open television channels. In addition to this massive mediazation, Pentecostal churches foster relaxed fellowship environments, renewal and revival camps, person-centered approaches, and lay-oriented leadership. Through all these means, they have been able to attract young Africans and to keep them. In addition, many Pentecostal leaders take on celebrity personas. They persuade, especially the poor, by telling autobiographical and biographical stories of overcoming adversity and promising them help to walk similar journeys. Moreover, Pentecostal leaders tend to operate like traditional African chiefs or monarchs with rarely questioned or challenged authority. They run their churches as independent personal kingdoms or religious enterprises. This style contrasts with the leaders of mainline churches who tend to operate institutionally, but it fits well in the traditional African socio-political-religious setting. In a way, the Pentecostal pastor has assumed the place of the traditional medicine-man.

Thirdly, in a distinct way, the success of African Pentecostalism has significantly depended on the political and socio-economic conditions prevalent in most African states. In the words of the Ibadan University-based scholar, Adeshina Afolayan, "the traction that Pentecostalism has gained in the lives of tens of millions of people in Africa alone has gone beyond the realm of religious dynamics or the movements of the Holy Spirit. Its rapid growth and spread has a lot to do with trauma and, by association, the glaring failure of the state apparatuses in Africa."[12] The hardships caused by failures of the political economy have driven men and women to both evil and God.

In this vein, Afolayan has distinguished four dynamics in the political economies of most African states that have favored the success of Pentecostalism: (1) The socio-economic circumstances of postcolonial and neocolonial suffering and trauma to which Pentecostalism has responded with a theology of worldliness and materiality; (2) the rogue African state against which Pentecostalism struggles but is also mostly complicit; (3) the fluid mediation of Pentecostal leadership determines Pentecostals' mode of reacting to political events; (4) Pentecostal leadership in mediating the tension between the care of the soul and the care for external material things or care for otherworldly and this-worldly concerns.[13]

Obviously, in its phenomenal rise, African Pentecostalism has become far distant from being apolitical. Pentecostal leaders actively work toward influencing and shaping public policies, public institutions, and public spaces or advocating for alternative public discourses. In many cases, this political presence or activism is informal but very effective. Its effectiveness can be attributed not only to the appropriation of media technologies but also to the persuasiveness of Pentecostal rhetoric on the masses of sub-Saharan Africans. Moreover, because of its highly decentralized nature, Africa's "Big Men" can easily court the support of individual Pentecostal leaders to support their political agendas or ambitions in exchange for personal favors or benefits.

The Case of Uganda

To use Uganda as an example, the presence of Pentecostalism has gone from being an urban phenomenon from the mid-1980s and into the 90s to becoming a nationwide religio-political force at the beginning of the third millennium. Driving in the countryside, one can easily hear African Pentecostal preachers blasting their megaphones, competing with the noise made by boda-bodas (motorcycle taxis).

This is all comparatively new in the history of Uganda. In the colonial period, Pentecostal churches were "positively discouraged" by the British colonialists who ruled Uganda as their Protectorate.[14] Despite this challenge, the *Balokole,* as they came to be known locally (literally meaning "the redeemed" in Luganda) have gradually emerged as an alternative to mainline churches (Anglican, Catholic, and Orthodox) that were quite unhindered by the colonialists. At first, the *Balokole* version of Christianity appeared as a Revival Movement within the Anglican Church of Uganda. This movement emphasized the inadequacy of the traditional ways of being church and promoted personal and spiritual witness. Eventually, *Balokole* came to refer to adherents of diverse forms of "born-again" or spirit-inspired upstart communities.[15]

From the 1930s into the early 1960s the *Balokole* Movement operated mostly underground. After Uganda's independence in 1962, a variety of *Balokole* churches came from the underground and new ones were established. But once again, the *Balokole* Movement returned to the underground in the 1970s during the administration of His Excellence Field Marshall president Idi Amin Dada, the Conqueror of the British Empire. Since the mid-1980s, the *Balokole* Movement has thrived under Uganda's ruling regime. But it was not until Uganda's census of 2002 that *Balokole* were distinguished from Protestants (Anglicans) for the first time. Today, however, self-proclaimed *Balokole* make up an estimated one-third of Uganda's population, and most of them are young.[16]

After all those decades of operating underground, the current regime has shrewdly patronized Pentecostalism. Uganda's first lady is known to be a devout follower of the Pentecostal Movement. She has "presided" over some state prayer functions. One of the president's daughters is a Pentecostal pastor. The *Balokole* churches see themselves as indebted to the regime for bringing them from the underground and attribute to the regime leader their public existence and freedom. Moreover, they see Uganda's first family of nearly forty years as belonging to them. The regime has taken advantage of this relationship by marshaling the support and assistance of Pentecostal leaders to influence their adherents and public discourse on political, moral, and socio-economic issues. Further, the *Balokole* Movement has been used to counterbalance the institutional mainline churches, their following, and their influence.

Coupled with being the fastest growing strain of Christianity, the *Balokole* have also become the most powerful religious presence in Uganda's politics and public discourse. This is due to *Balokole*'s strategic mediatization, political connections, lobbying, and rhetoric. To be fair, it must be acknowledged that the *Balokole* are not the first religious segment to play a role in Uganda's politics. Since the 1950s, Uganda's most influential political parties have been shaped by the Anglicans vs. Catholics difference. What is new with African Pentecostalism is that its leaders have not shied away from the political, and from trying to influence and control public discourse and policy.

As a result, over the last 30 years, there has been a gradual tightening of the relationship between politics, the Ugandan state, and the Pentecostal movement. The Ugandan leaders of Pentecostalism are committed not only to influencing the spiritual realm but also to the battle to shape the public and political sphere with the view that a Christian-Pentecostal nation will be born as a result. Given this dream, segments of African Pentecostalism have also worked against the state and the regime in Uganda. In the past 30 years, two rebel groups in Eastern and Northern Uganda have been connected to the revival movement. These are Alice Auma Lakwena's Holy Spirit Movement and Joseph Kony's Lord's Resistance Army (LRA).

Both of those groups branded themselves as religio-political liberation movements. Both arose as spirit-led movements with spiritual and political objectives in reaction to political discrimination, marginalization, victimization, state corruption, oppression, violence, repression, economic underdevelopment as well as moral and spiritual confusion from which they desired to purify society.[17] Their goal was to create alternatives to the current state and regime. For instance, the objectives of Alice Auma Lakwena's Holy Spirit Movement were to "remove Museveni's government, to remove all wrong elements from society, and to proclaim the word of the Holy Spirit."[18]

We have used Uganda as an example. However, the influence of Pentecostal leadership on politics in Africa is not limited to Uganda. In his essay, "Pentecostalism, Islam, and Religious Fundamentalism in Africa," Marinus Chijioke Iwuchukwu reports that "A popular Nigerian Pentecostal leader, Pastor T.B. Joshua is known to have publicly acknowledged that seven different African heads of state consult with him. Former Nigerian president, Goodluck Jonathan, former Ghanaian president John Atta Mills, and former president of Zambia, Frederick Chiluba, and the current Kenyan and Zambian presidents are known for vigorously courting the support and assistance of Pentecostal leaders for their political administrations."[19] The intersection of African Pentecostalism and politics is not going away anytime soon.

The Catholic Response

Ten years after Benedict XVI's invitation to pastors of the Catholic Church, one might ask: has the abandoning of parishes as a result of switching to Pentecostal churches subsided? The answer is no, at least in the case of Uganda. The challenge of African Pentecostalism to Catholic parishes continues. However, there have been Catholic responses in the form of the resurgence of various Marian movements and the growth of the Catholic Charismatic Renewal Movement.

Interestingly, these responses have not come from above, i.e., from the initiative of Catholic bishops. The Marian movements are mostly lay movements. Intuitively the Catholic faithful recognize that something needs to be done to lessen the departure of their fellow Catholics from parish communities. For its part, the Catholic Charismatic Renewal Movement (CCRM) is, as it were, meeting the African Pentecostal Movement on its turf. The two movements are sort of parallel to each other. There are fundamental differences between them concerning faith, sacraments, and ecclesial leadership. However, there are also many similarities between them including, as Karen Murphy has described, "a shared openness to the Holy Spirit, to the charisms, and to their value of an embodied, experiential, and supra-rational faith."[20] In addition, their adherents are oriented to the miraculous and the supernatural. These similarities have given powerful traction to the two movements in Africa.

It appears that one reason why these movements are growing is the search for a powerfully transformative Christianity, that is, a Christianity that is holistic, one that speaks to everything in people's lives and their environment. The growth of Marian movements and the CCRM is a response to a yearning similar to that which the African Pentecostal movement has tapped. However, there is an outstanding lacuna in the responses of the Marian and the Catholic Charismatic Renewal Movements. Both strains of Catholicism have generally been poorly shepherded, and gradually units of them have become disconnected from Catholic teaching and life. To give an example: In Western Uganda, in the 1980s and 90s, there was the Marian Movement for the Restoration of the Ten Commandments of God founded by two self-acclaimed visionaries. These self-proclaimed visionaries were excommunicated from the Catholic Church, as were the other leaders of the movement. However, the movement continued to gather a significant following with the prediction of an apocalypse, which was expected to usher in a new reality on December 31, 1999. Eventually, when the leaders' predictions of the apocalypse failed to come about, they resorted to mass-murdering their followers. The final count of the murdered was close to a thousand if not more.[21] Elsewhere, although not as physically violent, within the Charismatic Renewal Movement, theological and pastoral problems abound. The point here is that the response to the transformation going on in the landscape of Christianity on the African continent has lacked theological and pastoral leadership. Based on the above, Catholic theologians and pastoral leaders on the African continent could pay attention to the following:

I—Developing a Robust Pneumatology as a Dimension of the Ecclesiology/Spirituality of Communion Attentive to African Sensibilities

As much as the CCRM has slightly slowed the hemorrhaging of Catholics from parishes, it has faced resistance and antagonism from more traditional Catholic practitioners. Imagine the apparent difference between a solemn Latin Mass and a Charismatic Mass! On the one hand, some charismatic Catholics label "non-charismatic" Catholics as rigid, individualistic, legalistic, and limited in their appreciation of the power of the Holy Spirit. On the other hand, some non-charismatic Catholics label charismatic Catholics as *Balokole*, liberal, and liturgy abusers. The result is that today, for many, the Catholic Church and the Holy Spirit have very little to do with each other. In the light of the above, Catholic theologians and pastors on the continent would do well to develop a robust pneumatology as a dimension of the ecclesiology/spirituality of communion, specifically touching on the agency of the Holy Spirit in the daily lives of Catholics and how the Holy Spirit sets us free for ethno-praxes that open us to communion, not divisions. *Africae Munus* mentions the role of the Holy Spirit in relation to inculturation, the apostolates of reconciliation, justice, peace, evangelization, and missionary activity. However, it does not have a section dedicated to pneumatology *per se*. Was this a missed opportunity? Perhaps! In any case, it would be appropriate that the Synod of African bishops builds on a robust pneumatological foundation.

II—Taking Seriously the Healing Ministry of Jesus

A particularly vital face of Jesus for Africans is Christ the divine healer or physician. One of the strengths of the CCRM in many parts of the African continent has been to promote the relationship of Catholics to Jesus as their divine physician. This approach to Christ encompasses a strong belief in and a devotion to Jesus' authority over both spiritual and physical powers. In the case of Uganda, as Jesus' ministry of healing has tended to become a privileged aspect of the CCRM, it has tended to become neglected by the rest of the Church or to lose its priority of place in the daily pastoral care rendered to the faithful. Relatedly, the sacrament of healing, through which divine remedy is provided to the sick, is often misunderstood as a sacrament of dying. Thus, the faithful are often afraid of receiving it if they hope to live. What this misunderstanding calls for is a renewal of the catechesis about the anointing of the sick in the various vernaculars. It also points to the need for parish priests to take seriously the pastoral care of the sick whether spiritual, physical, or emotional, especially by making available the sacrament of healing in both communal and individual contexts.

III—Developing a Marian-Eucharistic Vision of African Womanhood

In *Africae Munus*, Mary, the Mother of God, is mentioned just three times and two of these are in one paragraph (the closing prayer in no. 175). However, Mary's impact and influence in Africa are exceptional. African Pentecostal preachers seem to get this. The group that they often target is women because they are often the most affected by societal and communal dysfunction. However, Pentecostal preachers realize that to sway women from their Catholic faith, they have first to undermine their Marian devotions or attachments.

There are, however, very few developed Mariological expositions by African theologians and apologists. Marian and Mariological themes remain underdeveloped and fragmented. Since Catholic women are often the movers and shakers at the grassroots level, the Church in Africa could benefit from developing Mariological themes that African women easily relate to. For instance, Mercy Oduyoye, in her contribution to African Christology, maintains that African Christian women relate closely to Jesus as the "Son of Mary." She states, "Childbearing is central to African women's self-image and the scene of Mary and Elizabeth swapping pregnancy announcements is a precious one for African women."[22] Mary also presents a model of faithful resilience for African women whose lives often so much resemble her own. In addition, developing Marian or Mariological themes with African sensibilities would curb exaggerations and excesses that provide grounds to Pentecostal preachers for discrediting both Marian devotion and Catholicism in general.

Closely connected with Marian devotion in Africa is Eucharistic devotion. This connection is not farfetched insofar as the Body and Blood of Christ take on original formation in Mary. She is the tabernacle *par excellence* in her openness and fruitfulness. Theological reflection on the place and role of women in the Church in Africa must ensue from this dimension. Some women have left the Catholic Church with the desire for their charisms to be better recognized. In many ways, this has little to do with the clamoring for the ordination of women that is heard in sections of Western cultures. It has more to do with recognizing women's contributions to the life and vitality of the Church in Africa. In most Catholic homes, women are the principal transmitters of the Catholic faith. They are the promoters of vocations. They are the ones who stand with their sons and daughters, as Mary did, in life's trials. As stated earlier in relation to pneumatology, it would be appropriate that the Synod of African bishops builds on a more robust Marian/Mariological foundation. Catechesis could benefit from these developments.

IV—A Robust Mediazation and Contextualized Biblical Rhetoric

The Church has been instrumental in developing the print media channels in Africa. Many of the first newspapers on the continent were church founded. *Africae Munus* (nos. 142–146) touches on the need to evangelize the media. However, the Church has lagged in relation to telecommunication media including radio, television, and social media. In the case of Uganda, for instance, as mentioned earlier, there are only two upstart small Catholic television channels covering only the Kampala area. Compare this with thirteen well-established Pentecostal television channels that cover the entire country. By extension, Catholic rhetoric and messaging at times answer questions that Africans are not asking. Catholic leaders have to touch base profoundly with the worldviews, concerns, and environment of Africans. It must be recognized that often Western missionaries had dismissive, derogatory, or misconstrued interactions with the symbolic elements of African cultures and worldviews. But dismissing a worldview does not make it go away. Those worldviews are the waters in which typical Africans swim. Inculturation has helped to bring the liturgy closer to home for some Africans; but in many ways, Catholic rhetoric has not been fully translated into African languages.

The reason for this gap may be because the theological education of Catholic leaders is conducted in foreign languages. However, the problem here is not only translation. It also has to do with people's longing for the word of God, which is not typically satisfied because many communities go for months without immersing themselves in the word of God. Pentecostal leaders have found ways to bring the word of God to unchurched yet thirsty people on radios, televisions, and megaphones, to present it powerfully and as powerful.

Also, it must be recognized that African cultures are typically *logia-cultures*. Words are taken to be powerful, to create realities or transform them. Pentecostal preachers are attuned to these African sensibilities about words. In several sections (nos. 16, 39–41, and 150–151), *Africae Munus* calls for the promotion of the biblical apostolate at various levels, but perhaps most importantly at the grassroots level of small Christian communities. The challenge is that the appropriate vehicles are lacking.

V—Retooling Ministries to Young Catholics, Avoiding Both the "Prosperity" and "Gnostic" Gospels

The segment most impacted by the failure of post-colonial African states are the young people who make up most populations of these states. Many finish university degrees but are not able to find employment; they can't afford to build livelihoods; they end up crippled by poverty or their lives are upended by violence. The hemorrhaging of Catholics from parishes mostly comprises young people. The leaders of Pentecostal churches present themselves not only as spiritual or religious leaders but also as "*Moses-figures,*" politico-economic visionaries who promise to lead young people from abject poverty in failed states to a better world. Catholic leadership must open the Church wider to young people, embrace the mission to attend to young people, and comfort them in their afflictions. The messaging to young people must go beyond sexual ethics to address the socio-economic and emotional afflictions that young people face. It must include expressions of compassion, comfort, and a commitment to creating opportunities for young people to get out of poverty and inequality.

In *Africae Munus,* Benedict XVI acknowledges the fact that most Africans are young people, and he dedicates a section to their instruction (nos. 60–64). He is right. Some statistics indicate that 60% of Africa's population is younger than 25 years old. However, there is little in Benedict XVI's instruction that goes beyond exhortative invitations. The Church in Africa must look at how to generate economic opportunities for young people. Many youths gravitate into Pentecostal churches because in those spheres economics is not relegated to a non-essential amidst economic and psychological destitution. Certainly, balance is key. The prosperity gospel is dangerous. However, equally dangerous is a gnostic-leaning reading of the gospel.

VI—Resourcing Small Christian Communities

Small Christian Communities (SCCs) are the mainstay of parish communities in most of Africa. In most areas, the structuring of these SCCs was functionally suited to rural frameworks in which families in particular locations tended to know each other well and to organize themselves for Church purposes along already existing neighborly as well as intra-family relationships. With ongoing urbanization in many areas, there has been increased mobility and instability in family-to-family relationships. Consequently, there are all kinds of new barriers to integration into SCCs today that were rare in the past. These include, among others, many people becoming more self-reliant, which has diminished the spirit of participatory or communal living, increased reliance on technology instead of other human beings for relationships and other human needs, and the breakdown of family ties. One implication of this change in the landscape of Catholic communities is that the formation, fostering, and sustenance of SCCs require more intentionality than before on the part of Catholic leaders, both clergy and laity. When a family or an individual moves into an area, Catholic leaders cannot assume that the newcomers will simply fit into the existing SCC structures without invitation. A key strength of the SCC structure is allowing for a more participatory model of Christian living, which also gives the lay faithful, both men and women, spaces to exercise leadership in the Church. Fostering SCCs would also mitigate the tendency of parishes to become impersonal due to their often-large sizes.

VII—Advocating the Politics of Jesus

Lastly, in a paper given at the 2019 Africa-Ratzinger Conference, I attempted to use the example of Uganda to make the case that the demands of the gospel place the Church in Africa, (the hierarchy and the laity) in vital roles in addressing the colonial and neocolonial violent socio-political history of much of the continent. I argued that the new evangelization, which according to *Africae Munus* is the task of the Church in Africa, must not overlook the parable of the Good Samaritan (Luke 10:25–37). Jesus did not praise the self-referential dispositions of the "Priest'" and the "Levite" in that story. The love to which he calls his followers has something to do with attending to socio-political and economic realities. I showed that the new evangelization cannot take a one-size-fits-all approach. Rather, it must address the needs of men and women in a holistic way mindful of their spiritual transcendence and their historical situatedness. Thus, whereas the task of the new evangelization in Europe and North America may be to address the secularizing cultural crisis and ongoing paganization in those parts of God's creation, the new evangelization in Africa must not overlook the socio-political history of modern Africa and its underlying causes, both internal and external, in view of immersing Africans in the Trinitarian life.

Conclusion

We have looked at the challenge of political Pentecostalism to the Catholic Church in Africa, painted a picture of how Catholics have responded to the challenge and pointed out some areas to which theologians and pastoral leaders could pay attention. At the heart of it all, the invitation has been for the leaders of the Church in Africa and her theologians to take a more self-critical stance. A superficial assessment of issues leads to quick solutions but does not deeply heal them. As we look back at *Africae Munus*, 10 years later, we can ask this question. Did *Africae Munus* embrace the real concerns and issues of Africa? The answer is, perhaps, yes, and no. This essay indicates that Catholicism on the continent is facing a new significant challenge that requires putting our house in order or adjusting some of our dispositions. Perhaps this is something that the Synod of Bishops of Africa could investigate in the search for the renewal of our life as sons and daughters of our heavenly Father in Christ and the Spirit.

Chapter 7 Endnotes

1 Benedict XVI, *Africae Munus* (November 19, 2011), no. 90.
2 Benedict XVI, *Africae Munus* (November 19, 2011), no. 91.
3 Ibid.
4 Pew Research Center, "The Changing Global Religious Landscape," April 15, 2017, 12.http://www.pewforum.org/2017/04/05/the-changing-global-religious-landscape/.
5 Lamin Sanneh & Joel Carpenter, *The Changing Face of Christianity:*

Africa, the West, and the World, London: Oxford University Press, 2005.

6 John Mbiti, *African Religions and Philosophy*, London: Heinemann, 1969, 1.

7 Jacob Olupona and Anthony Chiorazzi, "The Spirituality of Africa," *Harvard Gazette* (October 6, 2015). Available at https://news.harvard.edu/gazette/story/2015/10/the-spirituality-of-africa/

8 Cf. Fred Jenga, "Selling God in Uganda": *A Critical Cultural Study of Persuasion in Mediatized Neo-Pentecostalism*, Dissertation: University of Texas at Austin, 2020, 11–14.

9 Ogbu Kalu, *African Pentecostalism: An Introduction*, London: Oxford University Press, 2008.

10 Olufunke Adeboye, The Growth of the Pentecostal Movement in Africa," *Pentecostalism and Politics in Africa*, edited by Adeshina Afolayan, Olajumoke Yacob-Haliso, and Toyin Falola, Cham, Switzerland: Springer, 2018, 27–30.

11 Catholic theology would not officially apply the term churches to these Christian communities. Instead, they would be referred to as ecclesial communities. Cf. Vatican II, *Unitatis Redintegratio* (1964), nos. 13–24; Congregation for the Doctrine of the Faith, *Dominus Iesus* (2000), nos. 16–17. However, in this paper, for practical purposes, the term "churches" is used. More appropriately they could be called "personal ecclesial communities."

12 Adeshina Afolayan, "Pentecostalism, Political Philosophy, and the Political in Africa" *Pentecostalism and Politics in Africa*, edited by Adeshina Afolayan, Olajumoke Yacob-Haliso, and Toyin Falola, Cham, Switzerland: Springer, 2018, 224.

13 Adeshina Afolayan, "Pentecostalism, Political Philosophy, and the Political in Africa" in Pentecostalism and Politics in Africa, edited by Adeshina Afolayan, Olajumoke Yacob-Haliso, and Toyin Falola, Cham, Switzerland: Springer, 2018, 224.

14 Paul Gifford, *Christianity on the African continent: Its Public Role*, London: Hurst & Company, 1998, 154–168.

15 Fred Jenga, "Selling God in Uganda," 15.

16 Barbara Bompani, "For God and For My Country: Pentecostal-charismatic Churches and the Framing of a New Political Discourse in Uganda," *Public Religion and the Politics of Homosexuality in Africa., 1, Religion in Modern Africa*, E Chitando & A van Klinken (eds), Surrey, UK: Ashgate Publishing, 2016, 1.

17 Olajumoke Yacob-Haliso and Rachael O. Iyanda, "Pentecostals, Conflict, and Peace in Uganda," in Pentecostalism and Politics in

Africa, edited by Adeshina Afolayan, Olajumoke Yacob-Haliso, and Toyin Falola, Cham, Switzerland: Springer, 2018, 311–312.

18 Behrend, *Alice Lakwena and the Holy Spirits*, 3 cited by Olajumoke Yacob-Haliso and Rachael O. Iyanda, "Pentecostals, Conflict, and Peace in Uganda," in Pentecostalism and Politics in Africa, edited by Adeshina Afolayan, Olajumoke Yacob-Haliso, and Toyin Falola, Cham, Switzerland: Springer, 2018, 312.

19 Marinus C. Iwuchukwu, "Pentecostalism, Islam, and Religious Fundamentalism in Africa," *Pentecostalism and Politics in Africa*, 51. It must be noted that the leader referred to in this quote as the current president of Zambia is Edgar Lungu. He passed away in August 2021. He is no longer the current president of Zambia.

20 Karen R.J. Murphy, "Chapter 1 Introduction," *Pentecostals and Roman Catholics on Becoming a Christian*. Leiden, The Netherlands: Brill, 2018, 2.

21 For an introduction to this group confer Emmanuel K. Twesigye, *Religion, Politics and Cults in East Africa: God's Warriors and Mary's Saints*, Oxford, UK: Peter Lang, 2010.

22 Mercy Amba Oduyoye, *Introducing African Women's Theology*, Sheffield: Sheffield Academic Press, 2001, 51.

Chapter 8
The Church as the Family of God: Benedict XVI's Africae Munus *and Joseph Ratzinger's* The Meaning of Christian Brotherhood

Matthew Levering

I. Introduction

Defending the Catholic Church in 1850 against the argument that the political and economic backwardness of southern European Catholics nations tells against the Catholic Church's claim to have a divine origin, St. John Henry Newman observed that the Catholic Church does not exist to do the work of civil governments, but rather "has a work of its own, and this work is, first, *different* from that of the world; next, *difficult of attainment*, compared with that of the world; and lastly, *secret* from the world in its details and consequences."[1] This purpose of the Church is to make saints. Thus, says Newman, Catholic countries will not necessarily possess good governance or economic prudence, beneficial though a flourishing Catholicism must be to civil government's pursuit of the common good.

At the same time, Catholics in Newman's day and our own have always sought human development and have attempted to improve the earthly conditions of life.[2] Joseph Ogbonnaya has illustrated this point by reference to the African Church: "From the days of the missionaries to the present, the Church in Africa has focused its development strategy in Africa in two areas: education and health care," with over 35,000 schools and hundreds of hospitals, orphanages, and homes for the elderly and handicapped.[3] Ogbonnaya urges, however, that the Church in Africa needs to do more. He remarks for instance that clergy often live much better than the people whom they serve; the laity need to be catechized more with respect to their social responsibilities; HIV/AIDS needs to be more openly addressed; and economic and ecological degradation needs real attention.[4]

Theologies that focus upon liberation from economic and political injustice often suggest that the measure of the Catholic Church's success consists in how successfully it uplifts societies. An evident problem with such theologies is that in many countries whose population is heavily Catholic, no uplift in economic and social conditions results from efforts to radically reshape political and economic institutions. Indeed, as the history of liberation theology's implementation shows, poverty and hardship may become even worse. Even the Papal States were hardly models of good governance!

In light of this problem, this essay will propose in what follows that understanding the Church as God's family—as *Africae Munus* does—serves to highlight the Church's unique mission of deification while equally affirming, in a proper way, the role of Catholics in shaping a better social order and in caring for the poor and oppressed. In order to make this argument, I will compare the understanding of the Church as God's family in Pope Benedict XVI's *Africae Munus* with Joseph Ratzinger's ecclesiology in his early work *The Meaning of Christian Brotherhood*.

Before proceeding, let me note that the *Catechism of the Catholic Church* does not mention the image of "God's family" among the various scriptural images of the Church, such as the body of Christ, a sheepfold, a flock, a cultivated field, a vineyard, a building or house, a temple, the New Jerusalem, a mother, and the bride of God. However, the *Catechism* does say that the Church is "the house of God in which his *family* dwells" and also that the Church is "the household of God" (1 Tim 3:15).[5] Moreover, the *Catechism* adds that God, in building up his Church over the generations, ensures that the ecclesial "family of God" is gradually formed and takes shape during the stages of human history."[6] Like the *Catechism*, Vatican II's Dogmatic Constitution on the Church, *Lumen Gentium*, focuses on the Church as the people of God, the Body of Christ, and the Temple of the Holy Spirit. Even so, *Lumen Gentium* does urge: "Since the human race today is tending more and more toward civil, economic and social unity, it is all the more necessary that priests should unite their efforts and combine their resources under the leadership of the bishops and the Supreme Pontiff... so that all mankind may be led into the unity of the family of God."[7]

Given the notable importance of familial and tribal bonds in African cultures, African bishops and theologians have long emphasized the Church's status as God's family. In fact, as Alex Ojacor remarks, African understandings of family profoundly illumine the biblical testimony to the Church as God's family. Ojacor observes regarding the nature of the family, "The African experience of family is much wider than the word suggests in Europe and America.... [A] family in Africa includes children, parents, grandparents, uncles, aunts, brothers, and sisters.... [T]he family also includes departed relatives and unborn members still in the loins of the living."[8] Laurenti Magesa similarly emphasizes the breadth of the word "family"—it is not simply a nuclear family headed by a father. Referencing the work of John Mary Waliggo, Magesa explains that "the authentic family... consists of father, mother, brothers and sisters, aunts and uncles, and so on, and so should the authentic Church-family. It is not constituted only of the bishop but is made up of all the faithful in the diocese."[9]

Not surprisingly, African bishops have recognized that the African understanding of family illuminates the significance of the biblical testimony to the Church as God's family. Teresa Okure points out, "The First African Synod adopted the NT and Vatican II's all-inclusive definition of church as God's people by choosing the family as the model for what it means to be church in Africa."[10] Yet, Okure identifies not only positive but also negative aspects of this image. On the negative side, she observes that the family in Africa is heavily patriarchal. Positively—and, as she says, theologically fruitful in the ways intended by the Synod—"family in Africa embraces all members on equal terms regardless of personal, social, religious, and other affiliations since one ancestral blood flows in all members and bonds them inseparably."[11]

Okure observes that a number of eminent African theologians have taken up the theme of the Church as family, including Agbonkhianmeghe Orobator in his 2000 book *The Church as Family of God: African Ecclesiology in Its Social Context*.[12] Likewise, in the perspective of Bénézet Bujo, "A genuinely African ecclesiology seems to rely on a correct understanding of community and family."[13] Bujo conceives of Jesus as transcending, but as analogously understandable within, the traditional African view of the tribal father or "primordial ancestor who is the sustaining force for later ancestors, who form a chain of unity and through whom the contemporary generation is able to trace its origins back to the first ancestor."[14] From this perspective, which strikes me as having much ecclesiological value in a time when the communion of saints is often no longer understood, Jesus the Last Adam (1 Cor 15:45) is accomplishing "the eschatological 'gathering of Israel' [the family of God]... as the eschatological tribal father."[15]

Similarly, Paulinus Odozor maintains that the African family's unity in ancestral blood is in certain ways analogous to the Church as "a family made so by one faith, one baptism, one Lord, and sharing a bond on the basis of the blood of Christ into whom we are all baptized."[16] Odozor emphasizes the blood of Christ that unites believers, since Christ draws together his followers by his "blood of the covenant, which is poured out for many" (Mark 14:24). As Paul puts it, "The cup of blessing which we bless, is it not a participation in the blood of Christ?" (1 Cor 10:16). All who are in Christ are so by "redemption through his blood" (Eph 1:7; Col. 1:14), and Christ has reconciled to God "all things, whether on earth or in heaven, making peace by the blood of his cross"

(Col 1:20). Of course, as Odozor recognizes, Christians do not have Christ's literal blood or genetic markers coursing through our veins, and so we are not one family with him in that sense of "blood relations."

Looking back on his own participation in the Synod, Odozor remarks, "The Second African Synod [from which *Africae Munus* came] was... very much an ecclesiological synod," insofar as it "spent a lot of time discussing the nature, mission, and spirituality of ecclesial communion in Africa."[17] *Africae Munus* devotes much attention to the distinct offices and tasks within the Church, including bishops, priests, deacons, religious, and laity. It also explores how the Church, can contribute to peace, justice, and reconciliation in Africa, given the endemic political and economic crises that have afflicted the continent. Tragically, many of these crises, as in the Rwandan genocide, have divided African Catholics along familial or tribal lines. Since this is so, the image of the Church as God's "family" might have unfortunate overtones. Either the image of the "family of God" might seem to have exclusionary and thus prone to encouraging violence and pride, or it might seem frankly unrealistic in light of ongoing tribal conflicts in Africa. As Stan Chu Ilo has commented, "In a continent wounded by ethnocentrism, seen, for example, in the post-Rwandan genocide, African ecclesiology must show the African faithful the reason to believe that the waters of baptism are stronger than the blood of ethnicity."[18]

When the Church is true to itself, the Church as God's family is marked not by the divisive arrogance of status or by powerful familial connections, but by the self-giving love of Christ and by the witness of martyrdom. Emmanuel Katongole has reflected upon this distinctively Christian family in describing the martyred Sisters of the Resurrection in Busamana, Rwanda. He remarks astutely, "In a world marked by the deep divisions of racial, national, and ethnic loyalties, martyrs point to a communion that cuts across these boundaries."[19]

Katongole is more optimistic than I am, however, about the prospects for "a thorough theological reinvention of politics."[20]

I agree with Katongole that the world's current politics is in very bad shape, and that the truths of Catholic social teaching need to be put into practice. But as a matter of socio-political fact, neither the truths of Catholic Social Teaching nor the sacraments as such seem to be able to transform majority-Catholic countries into exemplars of political and economic wellbeing for the world to admire, whereas some majority-Protestant and secular nations are governed skillfully. In this regard, bishops and theologians would do well to learn humbly from scholars who study poverty and who possess insights into the political, legal, and economic structures that decrease poverty levels and enhance social well-being.[21]

More than Katangole, therefore, I would emphasize that the Church as God's family is a "new politics" not as a competitor to or replacement for the world's political structures, but as something entirely different—challenging the totalizing claims of both politics and economics by transcending them through a resolute God-centeredness and Christ-centeredness.[22] The image of the Church as God's family integrates the theocentric, Trinitarian, Christological, eschatological, and ethical dimensions of the Church. It does so without minimizing the ethical dimensions: God's children are called to "walk as children of light" (Eph 5:8) and to draw the whole world into "the household of God" (1 Tim 3:15). Emeka Xris Obiezu has aptly described the Church as "a socially transformative family that seeks to make the Christian moral ideal of love of neighbor part of the common good."[23]

Reflecting the depths of evildoing and suffering found in recent African history, Katongole asks, "What should Christian missions look like after the Rwandan genocide? In the aftermath of colonialism, how should Christians engage the social systems that we are part of?"[24] A significant part of the answer, I suggest, can be found in the image of the Church as the family of God. Christians should the non-exclusionary truth that we are adopted sons and daughters in the incarnate Son, called to dwell with the Father and Son here and now in justice and charity through the Spirit, and called to enter into the everlasting glory of the Lord Jesus through configuration to his self-sacrificial love. Such a perspective will foster Christians who, in Katangole's words, dare "to take the gospel seriously" and who by the grace of the Holy Spirit are able to "resist the temptation to transfer [their] citizenship from God's kingdom to this world."[25] As we will see, just such a perspective is supported by Benedict's *Africae Munus* and Ratzinger's *The Meaning of Christian Brotherhood*, read in light of Scripture's testimony to believers' adoptive sonship.

II. Scriptural Background: The Family of God

In *Adopted into God's Family: Exploring a Pauline Metaphor*, Trevor Burke explores Paul's understanding of our "adoption as sons" in the incarnate Son Jesus Christ (Rom 8:23).[26] Burke also notes that Paul is not the only New Testament author to proclaim that believers belong to God's family: John does too, as for instance in 1 John 3:1–2, "See what love the Father has given us, that we should be called children of God; and so we are." In Christ and through the Spirit, God has made us not only into his friends but into his beloved family, with whom God shares all that he is and has. Whereas John describes this new familial relationship largely in terms of new birth (see also John 1:12–13 and John 3), Paul describes it in terms of adoption.

As Burke says, the metaphor of adoption indicates that Christ transfers us from one family to another: We begin in a family caught up in sin and death, the family of the fallen Adam, and we are transferred into the family of Christ the New Adam. The notion of coming to be part of God's family in Christ is metaphorical in the sense that God the Holy Trinity does not really have a "family": the Father's generation of the Son cannot be understood to be a divine instance of human fatherhood, since such an understanding would subordinate the Son to the Father. The Son is not the Father's child. Yet, the bond of intimacy shared by Father and Son—the communication of divine life—is indeed shared in by believers through the power of the Holy Spirit. God's family is constituted by profoundly intimate relational bonds.

Burke points out that the Pauline notion of adoption into God's family has ethical ramifications: Believers are expected to behave in a manner appropriate for children of God. This manner is cruciform, self-surrendering love, as we are configured by the Spirit to the love of Christ. As Brant Pitre, Michael Barber, and John Kincaid say in their *Paul, a New Covenant Jew,* for Paul "the righteous act of Christ enables those who are in him to *become* righteous.... Those in Christ are so truly united to him that they share in the Lord Jesus's own divine sonship, becoming adopted children of God in him, living in union with him and in conformity to his character."[27]

Adoption into God's family comes from God's will in Christ and his Spirit, rather than from mere human resources. According to Paul, "in Christ Jesus you are all sons of God, through faith. For as many of you as were baptized into Christ have put on Christ" (Gal 3:26–27). God has chosen us to be his own children—"and if children, then heirs, heirs of God and fellow heirs with Christ" (Rom 8:17). In receiving the Holy Spirit, we receive the "spirit of sonship" and we are enabled to call out with Christ, "Abba! Father!" (Rom 8:15).[28] In Christ the Son, we will receive the inheritance that Christ already fully enjoys, namely the riches of an intimate and everlasting communion with God the Father. Paul proclaims that Christ came "so that we might receive adoption as sons. And because you are sons, God has sent the Spirit of his Son into our hearts, crying, 'Abba! Father!'" (Gal 4:6). In Christ God has made us into his family and heirs, with the Church as "our mother" (Gal 4:26).[29]

In the family of God, Christ is the "first-born," but not for himself alone: he is the "first-born among many brethren" (Rom 8:29). It is Christ who, by his Cross and Resurrection and by pouring out his Spirit, brings about the family of God. This has been the plan of God from the outset of creation. God has eternally elected believers "to be his sons through Jesus Christ" (Eph 1:5). God even now gives us "the riches of his glorious inheritance"

(Eph 1:18). Thus, Paul makes clear that "the goal of the Christ-event is familial."[30]

It is noteworthy that the Scriptures of Israel already describe the people of Israel as God's son or sons / children. For instance, in Isaiah 1:2, God bemoans the fact that "sons I have reared and brought up, but they have rebelled against me." Hosea 11:1, cited in Matthew 2:15, portrays God as saying, "When Israel was a child, I loved him, and out of Egypt I called my son." In Exodus 4:22, God instructs Moses to say to Pharaoh, "Thus says the Lord, Israel is my first-born son." Deuteronomy 32:18 rebukes rebellious Israel by appealing to Israel's status as God's son: "You [Israel] were unmindful of the Rock that begot you, and you forgot the God who gave you birth." In Jeremiah 3:19, has God mournfully proclaims to his people, "I thought you would call me, My Father, and would not turn from following me." In this same passage God begs his people, "Return, O faithless sons, I will heal your faithlessness" (Jer 3:22). Further instances along these lines could be cited, demonstrating over and over again that "God's covenant people" are "the family of God"—a point that while already true in the Old Testament, is far truer in the new covenant through the death and Resurrection of the incarnate Son.[31]

In the Pauline understanding of adoptive sonship, as Burke says, believers enjoy "a belonging where God as 'Father' occupies centre stage in his 'family.'"[32] Believers do so not merely individually but corporately, as the Body of Christ. The Church flows from God's eternal electing of a people in Christ. Another relevant point is that the intimate term "*abba*" appears to have been distinctively used by Jesus vis-à-vis God the Father and extended by Paul to the way in which Jesus' followers are to address the divine Father.[33] This use of the term "*abba*" goes beyond the earlier references to God as a Father to his people, whether in the Old Testament or in Second Temple literature. Jesus addresses God as Father in relation to himself and not simply in relation to all Israel.[34]

Furthermore, Jesus insists that henceforth, adherence to one's blood-family or ancestral family must bow before his own claims.

He states in the Gospel of Matthew, "I have come to set a man against his father, and a daughter against her mother, and a daughter-in-law against her mother-in-law; and a man's foes will be those of his own household. He who loves father or mother more than me is not worthy of me; and he who loves son or daughter more than me is not worthy of me" (Matthew 10:35–37). Such statements have been taken by recent scholars to mean that Jesus rejected marriage and family, due to his apocalyptic worldview.[35] Candida Moss and Joel Baden recognize that things are not quite so simple, but they remark that "[f]or Mark, the author of our earliest Gospel, life begins at baptism."[36] On this view, biological familial life is no longer of significance, at least in the sense that the family "is constructed at the foot of the cross."[37] Marianne Blickenstaff puts the matter even more sharply, arguing that the Gospel of Matthew depicts Jesus as "the *only* bridegroom, and all references to weddings are marked by violence."[38] According to Blickenstaff, the choice for the early Christians is "between biological and fictive family ties, between earthly masters and the heavenly kingdom."[39]

These sharp dichotomies misunderstand Christ's teaching. In proclaiming the imminent arrival of the kingdom of God (which he himself *is* in person), Christ opens up the path of virginity witnessing to the new life of the kingdom. But Christ does not reject marriage or family, so long as they are subordinate to the new family—the eschatological Israel, the Church—that he is bringing about. He knows that fidelity to the Gospel will strain familial ties in many instances, and such familial ties cannot be set above the Gospel. In this sense, those who do the will of God are indeed the truest family (Mt 12:49-50)—since they are adoptive sons and daughters in the Son, sharing through the Spirit in the divine life. To be united to Christ is indeed far greater than any biological familial or ethnic bond, but Christ condemns those who ignore God's commandments about the biological family, "'Honor your father and your mother,' and, 'He who speaks evil of father or mother, let him surely die'" (Matthew 15:4; cf. Exod 20:12 and 21:17).

In the Gospel of John, Christ on the Cross establishes the Church as the family of God. We read, "Jesus saw his mother, and the disciple whom he loved standing near, [and] he said to his mother, 'Woman, behold, your son!' Then he said to the disciple, 'Behold, your mother!'" (Jn 19:26-27). This exchange seals the Church as God's family in Christ. In John 14, too, Jesus promises that believers will receive the indwelling of the Father and the Son and that believers will receive the Holy Spirit. All this is framed by the evangelist's proclamation in John 1 that those who believe in Jesus are members of God's family: "To all who received him, who believed in his name, he gave power to become children of God; who were born, not of blood nor of the will of the flesh nor of the will of man, but of God" (Jn 1:12-13). In light of the whole Gospel of John, Sherri Brown observes that when Jesus on the Cross teaches that his own mother is now the mother of the beloved disciple (representative of all believers), the point is to establish the covenantal community as "the family of the new community of God."[40] Similarly, Francis Moloney remarks, "As a result of the lifting up of Jesus on the cross the Beloved Disciple and the Mother become one.... Because of the cross and from the moment of the cross a new family of Jesus has been created."[41]

III. *Africae Munus* on the Church as the Family of God

With regard to the Church as a family, *Africae Munus* first testifies to our connection to our "forebears in faith." The Church today is united to the forebears portrayed in the Old Testament. In drawing out this connection, *Africae Munus* recognizes that given the enormous challenges faced by the nations of Africa, "the Church, like Israel, could easily fall prey to discouragement" (*AM* §5). Thus the trials faced by forebears such as Moses (Heb 11:27) show the way forward. The family of Israel—the twelve tribes led by Moses on the exodus—provides a model for how to get through a seemingly overwhelming onslaught of political, economic, and spiritual disasters. The people must not give up hope of entering the Promised Land.

Africae Munus recalls that *Ecclesia in Africa* "made its own the idea of 'the Church as God's Family,' which the Synod Fathers 'acknowledged... as an expression of the Church's nature particularly appropriate for Africa'" (*AM* §7; cf. §15). Pope Benedict XVI explains that "to see the Church as a family and a fraternity is to recover one aspect of her heritage" (*AM* §8). The Church is comprised of God's adopted sons and daughters in the first-born Son. The reception of the Eucharistic body and blood of Christ makes believers to be "truly one," so that believers become "blood relations and thus true brothers and sisters," possessed of a fraternal bond in the Church that "is stronger than that of human families, than that of our tribes" (*AM* §152). As members of the family of Christ, Christians are called to share in his self-sacrificial love. In the midst of "fratricidal conflicts" and poverty, the Church in Africa must bear witness to the "fraternal solidarity" that God intends for all his children (*AM* §§8–9; cf. §18), by calling upon "the power of the Spirit to transform the hearts of victims and their persecutors and thus to re-establish fraternity" (*AM* §20).

Africae Munus makes a connection between Africa and the parable of the prodigal son: Not only must the younger son be reconciled to his father (representing the divine Father), but also the younger son must be reconciled to his brother. This is the situation that characterizes some nations in the African Catholic Church, where real reconciliation between brothers who have sinned against each other is needed, so that "serene coexistence" can be restored (*AM* §21). Familial solidarity with Christ will ensure that a justice grounded in love will truly characterize the Church in Africa (*AM* §26). The human family in Africa cries out for assistance in the midst of economic and political suffering. In response, the family that is the Church must offer "fraternal service" (*AM* §29) in accordance with the beatitudes, rising above selfish self-seeking.[42] Christ's Paschal mystery functions as "the principle and bond of a new fraternity" (*AM* §41). All this depends upon encountering Jesus through the proclamation and witness of the Church (*AM* §149), an encounter that, when it generates faith, "heals, sets free and reconciles" (*AM* §149).

Africae Munus points out that in Africa, the elderly are fully integrated into the family and indeed stand at the head of the family. Among Africans in rural areas, "stability and social order are still frequently entrusted to a council of elders or traditional chiefs" (*AM* §49), and their primary task is justice and reconciliation. This example should instruct the bishops in serving the Church as the family of God.

In light of the Church as God's family, *Africae Munus* attends to the roles of men, women, and children. It urges men to ground themselves in prayer and to manifest "God's own fatherhood (cf. Eph 3:15)," not by power but by "guarantee[ing] the personal development of all members of the family," especially through justice and reconciliation (*AM* §53). The equal dignity of women must be promoted, including by protesting ancestral or cultural practices that are contrary to the equality of women.[43] *Africae Munus* calls for initiatives that support women and that recognize women's role in the Church and the world.[44] Inspired by the figure of Mary of Bethany, all believers, men and women, should read "the Bible daily," so as to increase in "the knowledge of Jesus Christ" and to enable the word of God to build "up the community of Christ's disciples" (*AM* §151).

Regarding the status of children, *Africae Munus* first proclaims that "the Church is Mother and could never abandon a single one of them" (*AM* §67). This image of Mother Church fills out the portrait of the Church as God's family. Believers should have a childlike "spirit of trusting abandonment," since it is such believers who "find in God a Father and become, through Jesus, children of God"—"adopted children by grace" (*AM* §67). Catholics can learn from the traditional African religious belief that life here and now includes the ancestors, as well as those yet to be born, and indeed all creation. In the African perspective, the world is "a space of communion where past generations invisibly flank present generations, themselves the mothers of future generations" (*AM* §69).

Not surprisingly, other ecclesiological motifs, in addition to the theme of the Church as God's family, are present in *Africae Munus*. For instance, the document describes the Church as guided by the Holy Spirit and as acting as a single body, whose members exhibit a diversity of gifts (AM §97). The Church is Christ's "Body," united by his gift of the Holy Spirit (AM §132). The Church is a sacrament of communion with God and is a sacrament of God's will that the human race be one (AM §133). *Africae Munus* also describes the office and task of bishops, and the importance of their communion with the presbyterate and with the pope. The theme of the Church as communion receives a paragraph. *Africae Munus* concludes that believers who truly live the path of charity in the Holy Spirit will find themselves acting as "protagonists of a renewed African society" (AM §109; cf. §§171-72).[45]

IV. Joseph Ratzinger's Ecclesiology in *The Meaning of Christian Brotherhood*

In light of the perspective of *Africae Munus*, let me now turn to Ratzinger's 1960 book *The Meaning of Christian Brotherhood*, which Ratzinger's biographer Peter Seewald describes as the place where the young Ratzinger "spoke for the first time to a wide readership."[46] In *The Meaning of Christian Brotherhood*, Ratzinger defines the Christian community—the Church—by citing Matthew 23:8, "you have one teacher, and you are all brethren."[47] Christians are brothers due to the Holy Spirit who unites the Church. The graced ontological status of Christians as brothers (and sisters) in Christ carries with it a moral imperative, which Ratzinger terms the "ethos of brotherliness."[48]

Ratzinger observes that Plato describes fellow citizens as brothers, and Xenophon describes friends as brothers. Yet, the problem is that by defining a particular group as a brotherhood, one excludes those who do not belong to this group from the circle of brotherhood. Within the brotherhood or "extended family," the members have an ethical responsibility to treat each other as brothers; but it may seem that toward people who are outside the brotherhood, there is no such ethical duty. Along such lines, Israel understood itself as God's family by contrast to the Gentile nations who were not God's family in the intimate sense rooted in divine election and covenant. Their common father was Jacob-Israel (or Abraham); but their familial unity stemmed most fundamentally from the fact that the people Israel was the chosen "son" of the divine "father" YHWH. Although they were a family by ancestral blood, their shared relationship to YHWH primarily constituted them as a family. Ratzinger observes, "God had a special paternity toward Israel: whereas he was the Father of all the peoples of the world through creation, he was beyond that the Father of Israel through election."[49]

In Ratzinger's view, however, this relationship always had a certain contingency to it.[50] If Israel failed to live as true children of God and as true brothers of each other, God could renounce the election of Israel just as freely as God had once chosen Israel. The prophets dangled this threat over the people of Israel, while at the same time foretelling the ultimate salvation of the people. Ratzinger adds that in later Judaism, the idea would arise that God had offered the Torah to all peoples but only Israel had accepted it. Ratzinger suggests that this viewpoint closes off the circle of brotherhood, whereas in the prophets the circle of brotherhood had remained open due to the fact that Israel's status continued to be dependent upon God's free choice.

While Israel is uniquely chosen, Israel's story plays out in relation to the nations. The first chapters of Genesis make clear that God is the Creator of all humans. All humans in this sense are one family, sharing "a single humanity because of their single human source and the single creative act of God."[51] The unity of all humans is underlined by Genesis through the story of Noah and the Flood, which entails that all humans descend not only from Adam but also from Noah. Indeed, Israel is not the only people to receive a covenant, since all the nations (including Israel) live under the terms of the Noachide covenant. Humanity has a common divine Father and a common human father (Adam and Noah), and so the unity of humanity as the family of God is clear. Yet, also clear is "the elective exclusiveness of God toward Israel and the exclusive descent from the fathers of the covenant, Abraham, Isaac, and Jacob."[52]

Ratzinger highlights this duality: God's family is exclusively Israel, and yet God's family also includes the entire human race in some way. The duality enables the moral imperative of brotherliness to apply not only to fellow Israelites, but to all humanity. Repeatedly, God commands Israel to care for strangers and sojourners. In fact, strangers—those who do not belong to God's family Israel—are shown to be related to Israel by means of pairs of brothers. The most important such pair of brothers is Jacob and Esau, since the nations round about Israel descend from Ishmael and Esau. The nations are related to Israel, originally speaking, in the relation of a blood brother. Ratzinger comments, "we can… see here that even the partners of Israel who were expelled from the election [e.g., Esau] could yet be understood in a wider sense as 'brothers,' that even he who was rejected remained a 'brother.'"[53]

The central issue that Ratzinger is addressing, as will be clear by now, is how God's chosen family—Israel and ultimately all who by grace are adopted sons and daughters in the Son—does not instantiate yet another instance of exclusion and division in the human race.[54] In his reflections, Ratzinger observes that the claim to be God's family is not limited to Jews (or Christians), but instead has numerous parallels in the ancient world. He states, "In the Syrian Baal cults, the tribes and groups who were united through blood and the unity of the protective deity had long regarded themselves as sons of this god and as brothers of one another."[55] He finds a similar sense of brotherhood among the members of Syrian Jupiter cults, the members of the cult of the Great Mother, and the members of various Jewish syncretistic communities. The members of the Mithras community, the Essenes, and the Qumran sect (perhaps Essenes) thought of their fellow community members as their brothers.

Similarly, the Stoics conceived of humans as God's family, although the Stoics did not limit this status to members of a particular nation or religious group. Ratzinger observes that Roman "[p]olitical unification had its philosophical parallel in Stoic cosmopolitanism which discovered the unity of the world and of men. Epictetus saw all men as brothers, for all came from God. The ideas of the Stoa, of Seneca, Musonius, and Marcus Aurelius, followed the same direction."[56] According to Ratzinger, perhaps the fullest expression of this Stoic perspective on the universal brotherhood of humans as children of the one Father God is found in the Hermes mystery cult. No one was excluded, since the uninitiated were still brothers, still children of the one Father God, even if to be pitied due to their ignorance. The initiated prayed to be given the strength to illumine the uninitiated with the truth about the brotherhood of all the Father's children.[57]

Ratzinger attends briefly to the versions of "brotherhood" prevalent during the period of the Enlightenment. By comparison with the ancient viewpoints, God has moved into the background. Enlightenment thinkers derived the brotherhood of humanity simply from the fact that we all share the same human nature. They argued that all humans would be equal were it not for accidental circumstances of history. Against monarchical and feudal systems, they called for recognition of the natural equality of all humans and for a new social order based upon this equality. Christian brotherhood was rejected as insufficient, since it promoted a distinctive ethos for Christians and separated Christians from non-Christians. Ratzinger explains that "in the name of brotherhood all barriers were removed and a unified ethos was proclaimed as binding on all men in equal measure."[58]

The problem with the Enlightenment ideal is that if everyone is a "brother," then the intensity or intimacy of the word "brother" no longer holds. In fact, if everyone is equally a "brother," then no one really is a brother. Unsurprisingly, the Enlightenment ideal was never widely practiced. Those who proclaimed it most prominently were often themselves Freemasons—an esoteric brotherhood—and the Enlightenment ideal easily gave way among the intelligentsia to Marxism, with its sharp division of

greatly on its ability to provide Christians with concrete resources with which to face Africa's social history."[69] For *Africae Munus*, the fundamental "concrete resources" the Church possesses are Christ, his teachings, and his sacraments. Through the Holy Spirit, these resources have the power to configure God's family to the image of Christ—and in this way to reshape the world, by reorienting the world toward the Trinitarian life of self-surrendering love.[70] For those who possess faith, these resources bear fruit in love. As Bekeh Ukelina Utietiang says, the members of God's family will "differentiate themselves from others by the way they love not just each other, but those who do not love them as well," including by "reach[ing] out in love to traditional religionists and Muslims."[71]

Read in light of *The Meaning of Christian Brotherhood, Africae Munus* reminds us that if the Church is to have a future in Africa or anywhere else in this power- and wealth-hungry world, it will be the future of the family of God, living through the Spirit as children of God and as the brothers and sisters of Christ crucified, desirous of the full inheritance of the Father, and therefore standing as a sign of contradiction to every this-worldly politics even while living fully in the world in service to the life of the world.[72] May the retrieval of the Church as God's family—the Church as Christian brotherhood in Ratzinger's sense—begin in Africa and spread to Rome and the whole world.

Chapter 8 Endnotes

1 John Henry Newman, *Certain Difficulties Felt by Anglicans in Catholic Teaching*, vol. 1 (London: Longmans, Green, 1897), 241.

2 Here I place the emphasis somewhat differently from Stan Chu Ilo, who praises "a diversity that respects the new narratives of faith emerging in places such as Brazil, Mexico, Kenya, Nigeria, and India, as well as the renewal of faith happening in Nairobi, Taize, Lyon, Cebu, Rimini, and many unheralded but flourishing parishes throughout the world. The future of the church will be constructed through a learning church that is at home in the world, with women,

LGBTQ, the poor, and those on the margins" (Ilo, *A Poor and Merciful Church: The Illuminative Ecclesiology of Pope Francis* [Maryknoll, NY: Orbis, 2018], 287). I hold that a Church learning from Jesus Christ will always live in a dialectical relationship with the world, in accord with Romans 12:2, "Do not be conformed to this world but be transformed by the renewal of your mind." Ilo seems to focus the Church largely upon social programs, with the resultant risk of instrumentalizing and immanentizing the Gospel, and with the danger of giving the Church over to the false promises of contemporary progressive visions.

3 Joseph Ogbonnaya, "The Church in Africa: Salt of the Earth?," in *The Church as Salt and Light: Path to an African Ecclesiology of Abundant Life*, ed. Stan Chu Ilo, Joseph Ogbonnaya, and Alex Ojacor (Eugene, OR: Pickwick, 2011), 65–87, at 74.

4 Alex Ojacor points out, "Up to 25 percent of the African population is infected with HIV / AIDS" (Ojacor, "The Church in Africa and the Search for Abundant Life: Signposts for Renewal and Transformation of God's People in Africa," in *The Church as Salt and Light*, 88–98, at 88.

5 *Catechism of the Catholic Church*, 2nd ed. (Vatican City: Libreria Editrice Vaticana, 1997), §756.

6 Ibid., §759.

7 *Lumen Gentium*, §28, in *Vatican Council II*, vol. 1: *The Conciliar and Postconciliar Documents*, rev. ed., ed. Austin Flannery, O.P. (Northport, NY: Costello, 1996), 350–426, at 386–87.

8 Ojacor, "The Church in Africa and the Search for Abundant Life," 92. At the same time, Ojacor grants that today "the African family is in mortal danger. The migrant labor system, social and geographical mobility, unemployment, housing shortages, rural-urban migrations, internal displacement due to civil wars (placing people in squalid 'displaced person' camps), refugees, the corrosive influence of the Western neo-pagan culture, and [other] factors are destroying the traditional family and its many positive values" (ibid., 92–93).

9 Laurenti Magesa, "The Future of the African Synod," in *The African Synod: Documents, Reflections, Perspectives*, ed. Maura Browne, S.N.D. and the Africa Faith and Justice Network (Maryknoll, NY: Orbis, 1996), 163–71, at 168. Magesa goes on to make the troubling claim, however, that the de facto Church is separated from the "official Church." I am unsure what this implies; does he mean separated not only from the bishops but also from the solemn dogmatic and moral teachings of the Church? He argues that "there are in reality

two parallel Churches [in Africa], the juridical Church and the Church of the Spirit" (ibid., 169). This claim implies a mistaken notion of the relationship between Spirit and institution. For Waliggo's perspective, see John Mary Waliggo, "'The Synod of Hope' at a Time of Crisis in Africa," in *The African Synod*, 199–210. Although critical of the Synod's lack of input (in the preparation period) from the laity, Waliggo has many positive things to say about the Synod itself. He appreciates the theme of the Church as a family, while warning against the patriarchal and overly hierarchical elements of the traditional African family.

10 Teresa Okure, "Becoming the Church of the New Testament," in *The Church We Want: African Catholics Look to Vatican III*, ed. Agbonkhianmeghe E. Orobator, S.J. (Maryknoll, NY: Orbis, 2016), 93–105, at 95. See also Pope John Paul II, Apostolic Exhortation *Ecclesia in Africa*, §63, available at www.vatican.va.

11 Okure, "Becoming the Church of the New Testament," 95. However, Okure concludes, "African theologians need to make the call to be Eucharistic church, anchored in the new commandment of love, the soul of their theologizing in service to the church we want to be. We need to help the church hierarchy evolve new practical measures for internalizing this. This requires courageous revision of age-old church structures and the evolution of a new testament ecclesiology and Christology that serve as antidotes to those anti-gospel value systems that infiltrated the church from the empire" (ibid., 104). I concur with the call to be a Eucharistic Church, but it seems like an unpropitious moment to undertake the revision Okure proposes, because Catholic theologians increasingly see the Church as changeable (doctrinally and practically) in any way, by contrast to the dogmatic teaching of *Lumen Gentium* regarding the offices of the Church. For Okure's critique of hierarchy as rank, see Okure, "Church-Family of God: The Place of God's Reconciliation, Justice, and Peace," in *Reconciliation, Justice, and Peace: The Second African Synod*, ed. Agbonkhianmeghe E. Orobator, S.J. (Maryknoll, NY: Orbis, 2011), 13–24, at 21. She appears to favor moving away from hierarchy and the priest/laity distinction, along with including women in the "ministerial priesthood," now to be understood in functional rather than hierarchy-rank terms; and she assumes that the constitution of the Catholic priesthood (the sacrament of orders in its various dimensions) has been fundamentally shaped by "outdated empire values 're-baptized' as gospel"—a claim that logically implies that Protestants were right

to deny the sacramental status of holy orders (and to reject the Council of Trent). The dogmatic implications of her perspective are firmly Protestant; and in her view, Catholic ecclesiology needs to be re-thought from the ground up, in light of Jesus as proclaimed in Scripture.

12 See Agbonkhianmeghe Orobator, S.J., *The Church as Family of God: African Ecclesiology in Its Social Context* (Nairobi: Paulines, 2000). See also Nicholas Fogliacco, "The Family: An African Metaphor for Trinity and Church," in *Inculturating the Church in Africa: Theological and Practical Perspectives*, ed. Cecil McGarry and Patrick Ryan (Nairobi: Paulines, 2001), 120–58; Charles Nyamiti, *Studies in African Christian Theology*, vol. 4: *Christ's Ancestral Mediation Through the Church Understood as God's Family: An Essay on African Ecclesiology* (Nairobi: CUEA, 2010); Joseph G. Healey, *Building the Church as Family of God: Evaluation of Small Christian Communities in Eastern Africa* (Nairobi: AMECEA Gaba Publications, 2012).

13 Bénézet Bujo, "On the Road toward an African Ecclesiology: Reflections on the Synod," trans. T. Allan Smith, in *The African Synod*, 139–51, at 140. In the latter part of his essay, Bujo argues for an "African palavar model" of the Church, and he criticizes the "West-European model" of the Catholic Church as "a culturally conditioned concept of Church that arose in the West" (ibid., 149). I think here he has adopted a simplistic view of the roots and dogmatic development of Catholic ecclesiology.

14 Ibid., 140.

15 Ibid., 141. Bujo continues, "In many Black African ethnic groups the presence of the ancestors is visually represented by means of a special tree, the ancestor tree. The tree in question is an ever-verdant tree, such as the ficus, which symbolizes the life that never dies. Among the Bahema of eastern Zaire the ficus is planted on the grave of a family father. The father lying in the grave is not dead at all but shoots forth to new life as a ficus tree so that he now becomes shelter and vivifying 'spirit.' The branches and leaves of this tree symbolize the numerous descendants of the deceased. They owe to him their verdure. Separated from him they cannot survive.... It is not out of place to transfer this fundamental reality to Jesus Christ. Primarily by means of his cross the murdered Jesus becomes a green tree that dies no more. He owes this new life to God the Father, who raised him up in such a way that he definitively overcame death. The Father, however, operates together with the Holy Spirit, who is the inner vitality represented by the white resin of the ficus. The ficus

tree or the cross as the tree of life thereby has a trinitarian dimension. Only if the branches and leaves of the ficus obtain its life-giving energy do they stay green. Similarly, as his members, Christ's disciples are guaranteed the life that never dies when they are rooted in the life of the Trinity through the very same Christ risen to life.... The faithful whose life is played out under the tree, which symbolizes the Risen One and the Church simultaneously, receive their vitality and sense of belonging in the Spirit through whom the Father raised the Son" (ibid., 141–42). From the perspective of African Traditional Religions—sharply critical of Christianity—the Ugandan writer Jennifer Nansubuga Makumbi depicts the tribal father and the ancestor tree in her recent popular novel *Kintu* (Oakland, CA: Transit Books, 2017).

16 Paulinus Ikechukwu Odozor, C.S.Sp., *Morality Truly Christian, Truly African: Foundational, Methodological, and Theological Considerations* (Notre Dame: University of Notre Dame Press, 2014), 275.

17 Odozor, *Morality Truly Christian, Truly African*, 280.

18 Stan Chu Ilo, "African Ecclesiologies," in *The Oxford Handbook of Ecclesiology*, ed. Paul Avis (Oxford: Oxford University Press, 2018), 615–38, at 635. See also Jana Marguerite Bennett, *Water Is Thicker Than Blood: An Augustinian Theology of Marriage and Singleness* (Oxford: Oxford University Press, 2008).

19 Emmanuel Katongole, *Born from Lament: The Theology and Politics of Hope in Africa* (Grand Rapids, MI: Eerdmans, 2017), 256. Martyrs also direct theological attention to concrete situations and practices, with regard to which Katongole remarks, "For the African Church to live into this kind of self-emptying *kenosis* that Paul talks about, it as to sacrifice the elegance and magisterial authority that comes with distance. It has to come down within the confused mess of everydayness and risk becoming less and less churchly, so as to nurture and gestate, to use Éla's expression, 'a different world right here,' which is what the new future in Africa must be about" (Katongole, *The Sacrifice of Africa: A Political Theology for Africa* [Grand Rapids, MI: Eerdmans, 2011], 144). I agree with this emphasis on the local parish, but keeping in mind that the focus must be on Christ and sharing in the Trinitarian life—building up a Eucharistic life—and the "different world" that emerges may be marked more by suffering than by success, due to the resistance of the world. I note my discomfort with Katongole's repeated description of "a church committed to a new future in Africa" (ibid., 146). The Church is committed to Jesus Christ crucified and to his Kingdom which, however

much we might want it to be so, is not of this world—unlike things like "The Lord's Resistance Army" and the Prosperity Gospel. Katongole assuages my concerns when he highlights Angelina Atyam's Christ-centered ministry of mercy in the context of the atrocities of Northern Uganda, and when he proclaims that "[t]he new future is a gift grounded in God's forgiveness and reconciliation" in Jesus Christ" (ibid., 162). Thus the "new future" may simply be the presence and power of Christ's mercy, embodied in believers such as Angelina Atyam, in the midst of a horrific situation characterized by human sinfulness and interior resistance to the Gospel. Katongole shows the depth of his theology when he concludes, "what drives Angelina and the CPA is an ecclesiological vision of a community whose calling is to 'be in the world and yet not of this world' (John 17:15–16) and to be the recipient of God's precious gift of a new creation that Paul talks about in 2 Corinthians 5:17–18: 'So, for anyone who is in Christ, there is a new creation. The old order is gone, the new is here. All this is from God, who has reconciled us to himself through Christ and has given us the ministry of reconciliation'" (ibid., 164–65). The "new creation," I add, is the family of God, adoptive sons and daughters in the incarnate Son, inheritors with Christ of the riches of Trinitarian life.

20 Katongole, *Born from Lament,* 262. I would be very surprised if Catholic theologians had the answers to addressing the problems of political economy in Africa, although I am certain that Catholic theologians (especially African Catholic theologians) have many important contributions to make even in this regard. Emeka Xris Obiezu, O.S.A. makes the point that Africans "look beyond economics. They consider issues of division—ethnic and religious—as worse factors militating against sustainable development of the African people. These factors endanger if not peace, at least the pursuit of the common good of society. While Africans do not denigrate economics-based solutions to Africa-specific cases, they insist that any attempt toward a true development of Africa must include the issues of division" (Obiezu, "The Church in Africa and the Search for Integral and Sustainable Development of Africa: Toward a Socio-Economic and Politically Responsive Church," in *The Church as Salt and Light,* 34–64, at 35–36). In making this valuable point, Obiezu directs attention to Stan Chu Ilo, *The Face of Africa: Looking Beyond the Shadows* (Ibadan, Nigeria: Spectrum, 2008).

21 See Paul Collier, *The Bottom Billion: Why the Poorest Countries Are Failing and What Can Be Done About It* (Oxford: Oxford University Press, 2007); and Angus Deaton, *The Great Escape: Health, Wealth, and the*

Origins of Inequality (Princeton, NJ: Princeton University Press, 2013). See also Daron Acemoglu and James A. Robinson, *Why Nations Fail: The Origins of Power, Prosperity, and Poverty* (New York: Penguin Random House, 2012). I note that for Katongole—and he may be right—such scholars are not likely to have much to offer the Church in Africa, since what is needed instead is for Christians to determine what kind of politics and economics the Gospel requires and to follow that path in living out the Christian story faithfully. Katongole is indebted here to Jean-Marc Éla and Stanley Hauerwas, among others. For Katongole as for Hauerwas, "politics is not simply about the struggle for power and the management of society, but also about the everyday and ordinary practices of life—potluck dinners, babies, sex, and caring for the sick, aged, or handicapped. The Kingdom of God, Hauerwas notes, is primarily present in such ordinary practices, which constitute the politics of the church" (*The Sacrifice of Africa*, 120). Katongole also thinks that so long as Western scholars presume the existence of the nation-state, they will not be of much help to the situation on the ground in Africa.

22 Katongole emphasizes that "Jesus resists the spiritualization of his ministry. His ministry is not simply about a spiritual message to be listened to and later applied. The Good News that Jesus proclaims is a material vision, which involves a reordering of such material realities as geography, time, food, bodies, and communities" (*The Sacrifice of Africa*, 167). This is true, but it may still be misleading. To call the Gospel "a material vision" is true in one sense but not in another, since the Gospel has the Trinity at its very center. The term "spiritualization" may also be appropriate in certain contexts, insofar as Jesus insists that his "kingship is not of this world" (John 18:36). I concur strongly with Katongole when he observes, "the twelve baskets represent the twelve tribes of Israel, foreshadowing the new Israel, God's new family that is beyond boundaries of race, nation, tribe, and geography" (ibid., 168–69). Katongole goes on to tell the extraordinary story of Maggy Barankitse, who has truly lived out the Church as the family of God, partly by seeking in the context of Burundi to raise "children beyond the story of ethnicity" and "into the new story of God's love" (ibid., 175–76).

23 Obiezu, "The Church in Africa and the Search for Integral and Sustainable Development of Africa," 62. Obiezu is aware of the problems with traditional family life in Africa, including discrimination against women.

24 Emmanuel Katongole with Jonathan Wilson-Hartgrove, *Mirror to the Church: Resurrecting Faith after Genocide in Rwanda* (Grand Rapids,

MI: Zondervan, 2009), 93. Katongole maintains a necessary, but in my view overly undifferentiated, critique of "the systems of this world"; and he holds that the kingdom of God aims to replace such systems by introducing "a new political order in the world" (ibid., 146). In *The Sacrifice of Africa,* Katongole argues that the politics of the nation-state is intrinsically linked with war, corruption, and chaos. Given the universality of fallen human nature, I think Katongole exaggerates when he contends "the key actors of Africa's post-independence history—Idi Amin, Bokassa, Mobutu, and Mugabe—were but colonial 'types,' that is, mimetic reproductions of colonial actors like Kurtz, Leopold, and Ian Smith" (*The Sacrifice of Africa,* 12). At the same time, Katongole insightfully critiques the story of "civilization" and "progress," and he shows how Christians (under both colonial and post-colonial regimes) have been complicit in this false story. Katongole appreciates that the Church distinctively bears Christ's "theological grammar of hope," participating in "the mystery of God's own suffering, death, and resurrection" (*Born from Lament,* 264).

25 Katongole, *Mirror to the Church,* 123, 137. Katongole argues, "if we know that worship of the true and living God is what we are made for, we will also remember who we are: a community of resident aliens in a world that is both broken and redeemed. Because we know a new creation in Christ, we will live as ambassadors, welcoming strangers as though we belong here while also praying for the heavenly city, our true home, to descend to where we are" (ibid., 138–39).

26 Trevor J. Burke, *Adopted into God's Family: Exploring a Pauline Metaphor* (Downers Grove, IL: InterVarsity, 2006). See also Burke, *Family Matters: A Socio-historical Study of Kinship Metaphors in 1 Thessalonians* (London: T&T Clark, 2003); Jeanne Stevenson-Moessner, *The Spirit of Adoption: At Home in God's Family* (Louisville, KY: Westminster John Knox, 2003); James M. Scott, *Adoption as Sons of God: An Investigation into the Background of HUIOTHESIA* (Tübingen: Mohr, 1992), whose emphasis upon 2 Samuel 7:11–16 rightly comes in for significant criticism from Burke; and Brendan Byrne, S.J., *'Sons of God'—'Seed of Abraham': A Study of the Idea of the Sonship of God of All Christians in Paul against the Jewish Background* (Rome: Biblical Institute, 1979). See also, for discussion of the early Church's understanding of itself as a new family, Joseph H. Hellerman, *The Ancient Church as Family* (Minneapolis, MN: Fortress Press, 2001); P. F. Esler, "Family Imagery and Christian Identity in Gal. 5:13–6:10," in *Constructing Early Christian Families: Family as Social Reality and Metaphor,*

ed. H. Moxnes (London: Routledge, 1997), 121–49; and Karl Olav Sandnes, *A New Family: Conversion and Ecclesiology in the Early Church with Cross-Cultural Comparisons* (Bern: Lang, 1994).

27 Brant Pitre, Michael P. Barber, and John A. Kincaid, *Paul, a New Covenant Jew: Rethinking Pauline Theology* (Grand Rapids, MI: Eerdmans, 2019), 195, 209.

28 Joseph H. Hellerman adds the claim that Paul sought to overcome divisions in this way: "the Corinthian and Roman churches can be viewed as archetypical examples of the two ways in which human beings have been divided throughout history. Ethnicity divides us at the horizontal level, so that we gravitate toward those of similar racial and cultural backgrounds, and we fear those who are different. Socio-economic inequalities generate a vertical hierarchy of human persons, so that we look down with disdain, or up with desire, at those who stand on different rungs of the social ladder. The church family model is Paul's divinely inspired solution to these seemingly intractable human issues of race and rank. Ethnicity no longer matters: 'There is no Jew or Greek'; social status is now irrelevant: 'slave or free'; even gender is a nonissue: 'male or female' (Gal 3:28). This is true because we are now members of a family whose social solidarity must transcend all the differences that divide us" (Hellerman, *When the Church Was a Family: Recapturing Jesus' Vision for Authentic Community* [Nashville, TN: B&H Academic, 2009], 96).

29 As a frustrated Paul says earlier in his letter to the Galatians, "O foolish Galatians! Who has bewitched you, before whose eyes Jesus Christ was publicly portrayed as crucified?" (Gal 3:1). Having condemned many of the Galatian Christians for their actions, Paul is quick to urge mercy and humility: "Brethren, if a man is overtaken in trespass, you who are spiritual should restore him in a spirit of gentleness. Look to yourself, lest you too be tempted. Bear one another's burdens, and so fulfil the law of Christ. For if any one thinks he is something, when he is nothing, he deceives himself" (Gal 6:1–3). In his book on the Church as family, Hellerman points out (from a Protestant perspective on "salvation," but otherwise along lines that Catholics fully affirm) that "we continue to wrestle with sin and selfish behavior in our lives long after salvation. This is precisely what makes it so very difficult to live as family, to stay together, to embrace the pain, and to grow up in community with one another… . One of the dangers in all this talk about community is the temptation to idealize the concept of the church as a family and to fail to embrace the reality that doing family right is tough stuff—at church

and at home. It was difficult for Paul, and it is difficult for us" (*When the Church Was a Family*, 151). On the ways the Church is and is not holy, see my *Engaging the Doctrine of the Holy Spirit: Love and Gift in the Trinity and the Church* (Grand Rapids, MI: Baker Academic, 2016), chapter 7.

30 Pitre, Barber, and Kincaid, *Paul, a New Covenant Jew*, 199.

31 Ibid., 207. I have turned Pitre, Barber, and Kincaid's sentence about Pauline theology ("those who are justified belong to God's covenant people—that is, the family of God") to my own purposes.

32 Burke, *Adopted into God's Family*, 73.

33 See ibid., 93–95, addressing concerns raised by James Barr and others.

34 See ibid., 95n55, citing Ben Witherington III and Laura M. Ice, *The Shadow of the Almighty: Father, Son, and Holy Spirit in Biblical Perspective* (Grand Rapids, MI: Eerdmans, 2002), 60.

35 See for instance April D. DeConick, *Holy Misogyny: Why the Sex and Gender Conflicts in the Early Church Still Matter* (London: Continuum, 2011), 49: "Since Jesus thought that the age of the world was very advanced, and the end so near that God's kingdom was already inbreaking, stories about him suggest that he questioned whether or not it was necessary to continue to procreate in the short interim before the new world fully appeared and sexual behavior was abandoned altogether." On the other hand, DeConick earlier deems Jesus to be "a strong advocate for marriage, and staying married" on the grounds that he rejected divorce entirely (ibid., 45; DeConick adds, "This teaching does not appear to have been modified to allow for a man to divorce his wife for infidelity until sometime after Paul wrote his first letter to the Corinthians" [ibid.]). For further arguments that Jesus rejected marriage, see Calum Carmichael, *Sex and Religion in the Bible* (New Haven, CT: Yale University Press, 2010); David Wheeler-Reed, *Regulating Sex in the Roman Empire: Ideology, the Bible, and the Early Christians* (New Haven, CT: Yale University Press, 2017). Wheeler-Reed maintains that Jesus and his early followers "put all their eggs (literally, we may think, if we are thinking ovaries) in one basket: the kingdom of God" (*Regulating Sex in the Roman Empire*, 83).

36 Candida R. Moss and Joel S. Baden, *Reconceiving Infertility: Biblical Perspectives on Procreation and Childlessness* (Princeton, NJ: Princeton University Press, 2015), 169.

37 Ibid., 170. Moss and Baden argue that the New Testament deliberately problematicizes the notion that "fertility is a blessing and a

good," and they suggest that today we too should consider embracing infertility (whether biological or freely chosen) as a blessing and a good (ibid., 236). In my view, they have missed the point of the New Testament's stories about infertility and about freely chosen virginity.

38 Marianne Blickenstaff, *"While the Bridegroom Is with Them": Marriage, Family, Gender, and Violence in the Gospel of Matthew* (London: T&T Clark, 2005), 9.

39 Ibid.

40 Sherri Brown, *Gift upon Gift: Covenant through Word in the Gospel of John* (Eugene, OR: Pickwick, 2010), 196.

41 Francis J. Moloney, S.D.B., *The Gospel of John* (Collegeville, MN: Liturgical Press, 1998), 503–504.

42 John Olorunfemi Onaiyekan, commenting on the First African Synod (from which came *Ecclesia in Africa*), states: "The Synod emphasized the political arena, showing its conviction that most of the problems facing our continent result from inept or corrupt governments. Effective government is essential to tackle poverty and disease, civil wars and social unrest, rampant corruption, and blatant abuse of human rights. This is a direct challenge to the laity, whose role it is to make the Gospel values present in these areas. The Synod recognized that many children of the Church in positions of authority have not lived according to the principles of their faith. This is a call for a serious rededication of the African lay Christian to the service of God and of neighbor, guided by a careful reading of the social teachings of the Church" (Onaiyekan, "The Church in Africa Today: Reflections on the African Synod," in *The African Synod*, 211–19, at 217).

43 For further background, with attention to contemporary developments, see Bosco Ebere Amakwe, H.F.S.N., "Globalization and the African Woman: A Socio-Cultural Analysis of the Effect of Information and Communication Technology (ICT) on Women," in *The Church as Salt and Light*, 99–129.

44 Stan Chu Ilo remarks in a critical vein, "Effective evangelization in Africa calls for greater involvement of African women in African churches, where women are treated as second-class citizens, holding any position at the mercy of a male-dominated hierarchy and leadership across the board. Such treatment of women in the Catholic churches in Africa parallels the patriarchal cultural frameworks that furnish and legitimize the ongoing marginalization of women through various uncritical cultural assumptions" (Ilo, "Conclusion,"

in *The Church as Salt and Light*, 149–56, at 152). I note that a key question is how to integrate women without dissenting from Catholic teaching on the male-only ordained priesthood and its sacramental ministries and authority within the Church. The key is to resist limiting the exercise of Christian love to positions of power and to sacramental ministry. For a fruitful reflection (prior to the First African Synod)—but one that nevertheless falls into the mistake of advocating that women perform ministries for which priestly ordination is required, such as the administering the sacrament of reconciliation—see Bernadette Mbuy-Beya, "Women in the Churches in Africa: Possibilities for Presence and Promises," in *The African Synod*, 175–87.

45 See Bekeh Ukelina Utietiang, "New Evangelization in Africa: Learning from the Culture of Love in the Early Church," in *The Church as Salt and Light*, 130–48, at 132.

46 Peter Seewald, *Benedict XVI: A Life*, vol. 1: *Youth in Nazi Germany to the Second Vatican Council, 1927–1965*, trans. Dinah Livingstone (London: Bloomsbury, 2020), 322. Aidan Nichols, O.P. observes, "Christian brotherhood was a theme he had already touched on in Augustine, and Augustine's African predecessor, Optatus. It was also, perhaps, an obvious ecclesiological subject in a self-consciously democratic European world, and especially so on the eve of a great Church council which would underline the fundamental equality of all the baptised" (Nichols, *The Thought of Pope Benedict XVI: An Introduction to the Theology of Joseph Ratzinger*, 2nd ed. [London: Continuum, 2007], 45; see also Emery de Gaál, *The Theology of Pope Benedict XVI: The Christocentric Shift* [New York: Palgrave Macmillan, 2010], 169). It is intriguing—and a missed opportunity—that Vatican II did not really take up this theme. In his *Joseph Ratzinger: Life in the Church and Living Theology. Fundamentals of Ecclesiology with Reference to* Lumen Gentium, trans. Michael J. Miller (San Francisco: Ignatius Press, 2007), Maximilian Heinrich Heim does not discuss *The Meaning of Christian Brotherhood*. In his summary of *The Meaning of Christian Brotherhood*, de Gaál rightly connects "brotherhood" to "communion" (with Christ and each other), and so it is not surprising that Ratzinger's later ecclesiology emphasizes communion. I should note that Aidan Nichols's excellent survey of Ratzinger's book is more detailed in certain ways than the one I offer here. See also Fergus Kerr, O.P., "Church: Brotherhood and Eschatology," *New Blackfriars* 51, no. 598 (March 1970): 144–54.

47 Joseph Ratzinger, *The Meaning of Christian Brotherhood* (San Francisco: Ignatius Press, 1993), 3.

48 Ibid. It is likely that the non-gender-neutral language makes Ratzinger's insights more difficult to appropriate today. In this essay, following *Africae Munus* (and *Ecclesia in Africa*), I employ "family" rather than "brotherhood."

49 Ibid., 8. See also—in light of Christ—Joseph Ratzinger / Pope Benedict XVI, *Jesus of Nazareth*, vol. 1: *From the Baptism in the Jordan to the Transfiguration*, trans. Adrian J. Walker (New York: Doubleday, 2007), 137–39.

50 For Ratzinger's Israelology, see also his *Many Religions—One Covenant: Israel, the Church, and the World*, trans. Graham Harrison (San Francisco: Ignatius Press, 1999); Ratzinger, "The Heritage of Abraham," in his *Pilgrim Fellowship of Faith: The Church as Communion*, trans. Henry Taylor (San Francisco: Ignatius Press, 2005), 270–73; and Pope Emeritus Benedict XVI, "Grace and Vocation without Remorse: Comments on the Treatise *De Iudaeis*," trans. Nicholas J. Healy, Jr., *Communio* 45 (2018): 163–84.

51 Ratzinger, *The Meaning of Christian Brotherhood*, 9. See also Joseph Ratzinger, *'In the Beginning…': A Catholic Understanding of the Story of Creation and the Fall*, trans. Boniface Ramsey, O.P. (Grand Rapids, MI: Eerdmans, 1995).

52 Ibid., 10.

53 Ibid., 11.

54 See the concerns of Regina Schwartz, *The Curse of Cain: The Violent Legacy of Monotheism* (Chicago: University of Chicago Press, 1997), to which I respond in my *The Betrayal of Charity: The Sins that Sabotage Divine Love* (Waco, TX: Baylor University Press, 2011).

55 Ratzinger, *The Meaning of Christian Brotherhood*, 12.

56 Ibid., 14.

57 See Hermann von Soden, "Adelphos," in *Theologisches Wörterbuch zum neuen Testament*, ed. Gerhard Kittel, vol. I (Stuttgart: Kohlhammer, 1964), 144–46; and Karl Hermann Schelkle, "Bruder," in *Reallexikon für Antike und Christentum*, vol. III, ed. T. Klauser (Stuttgart: Hiersemann, 1954), 631–40; Gottlieb Söhngen, "Vom Wesen des Christentums," in *Die Einheit in der Theologie* (Munich: Zink, 1952), 288–304. On Söhngen's interests more broadly, see Tracey Rowland, *Beyond Kant and Nietzsche: The Munich Defense of Christian Humanism* (London: Bloomsbury, 2021), chapter 4.

58 Ratzinger, *The Meaning of Christian Brotherhood*, 15.

59 Ibid., 25.

60 For background, see Daniel Daley, *God's Will and Testament: Inheritance in the Gospel of Matthew and Jewish Tradition* (Waco, TX: Baylor University Press, 2021). Daley emphasizes that the inheritance is the

kingdom of God in its various dimensions, and I note that the kingdom is fundamentally a sharing in the everlasting life of Christ and of God the Father.

61 Ratzinger, *The Meaning of Christian Brotherhood*, 27.

62 Ibid., 29.

63 Ibid., 29.

64 Ibid., 55. See also Ratzinger/Benedict XVI, *Jesus of Nazareth*, vol. 1, 138: "Jesus is 'the Son' in the strict sense—he is of one substance with the Father. He wants to draw all of us into his humanity and so into his Sonship, into his total belonging to God. This gives the concept of being God's children a dynamic quality: We are not ready-made children of God from the start, but we are meant to become so increasingly by growing more and more deeply in communion with Jesus. Our sonship turns out to be identical with following Christ. To name God as Father thus becomes a summons to us to live as a 'child,' as a son or daughter."

65 Ratzinger, *The Meaning of Christian Brotherhood*, 73. For further discussion see Pope Benedict XVI, *Heart of the Christian Life: Thoughts on the Holy Mass* (San Francisco: Ignatius Press, 2010), 59, 61: "Through the Eucharist, the Lord not only gives himself to his own but also gives them the reality of a new communion among themselves which is extended in time, 'until he comes' (cf. 1 Cor 11:26). Through the Eucharist, the disciples become his living dwelling place which, as history unfolds, grows like the new and living temple of God in this world.... The Church, established in the institution of the Eucharist, in her inmost self is a Eucharistic community, hence, communion in the Body of the Lord."

66 Ratzinger, *The Meaning of Christian Brotherhood*, 79

67 Ibid., 84. For discussion, see Aaron Pidel, S.J., "The Church of the 'Few' for the 'Many': Ratzinger's Missiology of Vicarious Representation," in *Joseph Ratzinger and the Healing of the Reformation-Era Divisions*, 297–318; Christopher Ruddy, "'Smaller but Purer?': Joseph Ratzinger on the 'Little Flock' and Vicarious Representation," *Nova et Vetera* 13 (2015): 713–41; Ruddy, "'For the Many': The Vicarious-Representative Heart of Joseph Ratzinger's Theology," *Theological Studies* 75 (2014): 564–84; Anna Elisabeth Meiers, *Eschatos Adam: Zentrale Aspekte der Christologie bei Joseph Ratzinger/Benedikt XVI* (Regensburg: Friedrich Pustet, 2019), 210–20. Pidel sums up, "Ratzinger, by retrieving the salvation-historical pattern of vicarious representation, extricates himself—at least to some extent—from the horns of the dilemma posed by minority Christianity. Because the 'invisible order of grace' overflows the visible Church, the 'many' may still

be saved. This neutralizes one horn. But because the extension of the invisible order of grace everywhere depends upon its definite *repraesentatio* somewhere, none is ultimately saved without the 'little flock.' This neutralizes the dilemma's other horn. The key to negotiating the dilemma lies for Ratzinger in recasting the Church's universalism as a representational dynamic. The Church's life, even if not lived by all to the same degree, is nevertheless lived for all" ("The Church of the 'Few' for the 'Many,'" 316–17). Pidel draws a connection between Ratzinger's theology of representation and Erich Przywara, S.J.'s theology of *sacrum commercium*, in addition to the evident impact of Karl Barth's theology of election. Other theologians, such as Henri de Lubac, S.J., Yves Congar, O.P., and Hans Urs von Balthasar follow a similar path, as Pidel shows (see ibid., 301n13). In addition to *The Meaning of Christian Brotherhood*, Pidel cites such works as Ratzinger, "Stellvertretung," in Ratzinger, *Das Neue Volk Gottes: Entwürfe zur Ekklesiologie* (Düsseldorf: Patmos, 1969), 566–75; and Ratzinger, "Die neuen Heiden und die Kirche," in *Das Neue Volk Gottes*, 325–38.

68 Philip A. Rolnick, *The Long Battle for the Human Soul* (Waco, TX: Baylor University Press, 2021), 122.

69 Katongole, *The Sacrifice of Africa*, 20. Utietiang urges similarly, "The Church must rise and take active roles in society to change the lives of the people. Jesus Christ did not sit on the sidelines when his people were sick, dying, or imprisoned. At each point, he stepped in to set them free. In this way, the Church in Africa has an opportunity not only to be prophetic in word but in action. The clergy and leaders of the Church must be on the side of their people, not politicians or dictators. The Church cannot wait for the government to solve all the problems of her people, but she must step in to give her people a helping hand to solve their own problems" ("New Evangelization in Africa," 145). I note that, although Jesus nourished his people by word and deed, Jesus did not free his people, politically or economically speaking, from Roman domination and corruption.

70 Here I should clarify that I am not downplaying the resource of inspired Scripture, which mediates Christ. Stan Chu Ilo has rightly remarked, "The scriptural evidence was a testimony of lived experiences, and not a mere invention.... The evidence of the Word made flesh is an ongoing testimony attested to in the Church in all that she has and all that she is, including the Word that is written in Scripture" (Ilo, "Beginning Afresh with Christ in the Search for Abundant Life in Africa," in *The Church as Salt and Light*, 1–33, at 3). At the same time, Ilo might pay more attention than he does to the

role of Israel's Scriptures in shaping Christ's life and work, as well as in shaping the texts of the New Testament. Ilo goes on to critique Catholic theology for privileging European symbols and for seeking an unhelpful uniformity. He argues that it should be "left to African theologians to articulate a theology that is able to capture the imagination of the ordinary African Christians" (ibid., 32). I see this as true in one sense, but not in a way that isolates African Catholicism from the solemn dogmatic and moral teachings of the Catholic Church, and not in a way that leaves us with the situation of German theologians speaking to Germans, American theologians to Americans, and so on.

71 Utietiang, "New Evangelization in Africa," 145–46. At the same time, Ilo notes that "Radical Islamic advance is also perceived in Kenya, Eritrea, Ethiopia, Chad, Cameroun, Uganda, Sudan, and above all Nigeria" (Ilo, "Conclusion," 155).

72 I agree with Katongole that in a certain sense, "all politics is theological, in that it involves claims about life, reality, and the ultimate meaning of life" (ibid., 22). At the same time, however, theology or even ecclesiology is not politics in a this-worldly sense. Christ did not come to introduce the Roman empire to a better political and economic life, nor can the truth of Christianity be judged on the basis of whether the Constantinian order resulted in more just political and economic outcomes. Instead, as Katongole suggests through numerous concrete stories, it should be judged on the basis of whether it produces holy, cruciform witnesses to Christ, who bear this witness in the world and in the service of God and neighbor. The Church, as the family of such witnesses, may be able to heal and elevate the social order in particular contexts, though of course the leaders of the social order (and the populace as a whole) may and often will—whatever their professed Christianity—resist living in accord with Christ. Katongole finds such a perspective insufficient, insofar as in his view it fosters political quietism: see his commentary on such books as Kwame Bediako, *Christianity in Africa: The Renewal of a Non-Christian Religion* (Maryknoll, NY: Orbis Books, 1995); Bénézet Bujo, *African Theology in Its Social Context* (Nairobi: Pauline Publications Africa, 1999); and Paul Gifford, *African Christianity: Its Public Role* (Bloomington, IN: Indiana University Press, 1998)—as well as Pope John Paul II's *Ecclesia in Africa*. Katongole equally criticizes those who "identify the search for democracy as the essence of Christian mission" (*The Sacrifice of Africa*, 39), and I concur with him here. Katongole goes on to say, "What the different initiatives and programs confirm is that if conditions in Africa have

been stressful, it is not because African Christians and the Christian churches have been callous to the plight of the continent. Yet despite the growth of Christianity and the social activism of the churches, Africans in general are 40 percent worse off than they were in the 1980s. One then wonders: What accounts for the dismal social impact of Christianity in Africa? Why has Christianity, despite its overwhelming presence, failed to make a significant dent in the social history of the continent?" (ibid., 40). Augustine faced this same question when the Roman Empire, despite its conversion to Christianity, was crumbling in the early fifth century.

Chapter 9
Africae Munus, *Fr. Benedict Ssetuuma Jr., and the White Fathers on the Priestly Vocation Boom in Uganda and in Sub-Saharan Africa*

Joseph Lugalambi

In Jesus, some two thousand years ago, God himself brought salt and light to Africa. From that time on, the seed of his presence was buried deep within the hearts of the people of the dear continent, and it blossomed gradually and within the vicissitudes of its human history."[1]

Fr. Benedict Ssetuuma Jr. was a priest and a theologian from Masaka Diocese, Uganda. In his life and works, he reflected on, promoted, and defended the dignity of the priestly vocation. Fr. Ssetuuma was to participate in the conference on the 10th anniversary of Pope Benedict XVI's Apostolic exhortation *Africae Munus*[2] that took place at the University of Mary of the Lake in November 2021. However, Fr. Ssetuuma died on the morning of June 18th, 2021 while going to celebrate Holy Mass. In honor of his life as a priest and as a defender and lover of priestly vocations, this essay shall address the question of a priestly vocation boom in Uganda and in Sub-Saharan Africa against the fear of a false vocation boom. Although *Africae Munus* does not address the problem of the priestly vocation boom in Africa, we consider this topic pertinent to *Africae Munus* because priests serve the main concern of *Africae Munus*, namely, the administration of reconciliation, justice, and peace.

We proceed as follows. After a short introduction, we situate the current vocation boom in the tremendous work of the missionaries (that is, the White Fathers) that evangelized

Uganda and other parts of Sub-Saharan Africa. Next, we examine some paragraphs in *Africae Munus* on the training of priestly candidates and how to ensure that Africa and the entire Church gets enough priests to minister at the administration of reconciliation, justice and peace. We conclude this essay by looking at the life and writings of Fr. Ssetuuma on the vocation to the priesthood.

I. Introduction

In his work, *The Next Christendom: The Coming of Global Christianity*, Philip Jenkins envisions that Africa will have seven of the world's most populous nations by 2050.[3] Jenkins's work and many other studies indicate that sub-Saharan Africa is experiencing the fastest church growth in the world.[4] The increase in population and church growth in Africa has also brought a boom in vocations to priesthood and religious life. In fact, some African dioceses and religious congregations do not conduct vocation drives as is the case in the European and North American dioceses. The Vatican's statistics show that while the number of candidates to the priesthood across the globe decreased by 0.7 percent in 2017, Africa and Asia recorded an increase, with Africa contributing 27.1 percent to the total number of Major seminarians.[5] As Europe and North America continue to face a crisis of priests and priestly vocations, Africa on the other hand recorded a total number of 13,708 priests ordained in 2017 and 13,906 priests ordained in 2018.[6]

Although the increase in the number of priestly candidates in Uganda and sub-Saharan Africa should be an announcement of God's favor on Africa and a cause of joy and appreciation for the whole Church, Fr. Ssetuuma has observed that the vocation boom in Africa has, however, generated "unnecessary fear and panic" regarding the genuineness of such vocations.[7] The pessimists of the African vocation boom, Ssetuuma notes, fear that "many seminarians without proper conviction" join the seminary only to seek "comfort and good life there."[8] Fr. John Mary Waliggo, in his study on *The History of African Priests*,[9] made similar observations. Waliggo traced pessimism about African priestly vocations back to the beginning of missionary work in Africa. He notes that the first missionaries who worked in Africa between the 16th and 19th centuries saw the Tridentine priesthood as too high for the African man. This pessimism, however, was overcome by the White Fathers who arrived in Sub-Saharan Africa in the late nineteenth century. Their founder, Cardinal Lavigerie, was convinced that in order for the faith in Africa to flourish, the African people were to be evangelized by fellow Africans. He therefore tasked his missionaries to form native clergy. For this end, the White Fathers established seminaries in the provinces where they took root. Because of the White Fathers' conviction and commitment to produce an indigenous clergy, the number of priests and priestly candidates in Uganda and Sub-Saharan Africa has increased steadily since the ordination of the first two black priests on June 29th 1913.

II. The Coming of the Age of Priesthood in Uganda and in Sub-Saharan Africa

Until the Middle Ages, priestly formation was done through apprenticeship just as Christ formed his apostles, and later on through monastic and cathedral schools.[10] The apprenticeship system, however, lacked a uniform syllabus that priestly candidates followed. For this reason, many minor orders of subdeacons, acolytes, exorcists, porters, and lectors were established so as to observe the candidates and, if found worthy, to be promoted to subsequent higher orders and eventually to the priesthood.[11]

The move to formalize seminary formation was one the greatest achievements of the council of Trent (1545–1563). In the decree passed during the twenty-third session of the council, on 15 July 1563, the Tridentine fathers ordered the establishment of seminaries in all mission lands. The Tridentine Council fathers drew a curriculum for seminary formation in order to equip seminarists with knowledge and skills to ably defend the Catholic doctrine and to reform the moral lives of the priests that had been questioned by the Protestant Reformers.[12]

There were several attempts to establish seminaries in Africa. At the beginning of the nineteenth century, a female French missionary set up a seminary in West Africa to train local priests but, because of jealousy, she was forced to transfer the 23 seminarians with her to France in 1824. Only three became priests, but they exercised their priestly ministry in Europe.[13] Another attempt was by the Holy Ghost Fathers who established a seminary at Bagamoyo in 1869. This seminary, however, was closed by 1881.[14]

The first Catholic missionaries to Uganda, the White Fathers, arrived in 1879. They belonged to the Société des Missionaires d'Afrique (Missionaries of Africa) founded by Archbishop Lavigerie in 1868 with headquarters in Algiers.[15] They made their first headquarters in Buddu province, which later became the Catholic province in Uganda and in the whole of Sub-Saharan Africa. Lavigerie charged his missionaries to convert Africans mainly by the example of their lives. He wrote, "You will not convert nor sanctify others if you don't start by working courageously for your own sanctification."[16] For Lavigerie, a missionary's first task is to save his/her soul before saving others. By leading by example, a missionary's life (more than words) can be the greatest tool that invites others to embrace Christ. Lavigerie was convinced that for the faith to flourish in any mission land, missionaries were to form native clergy who would carry on the faith to subsequent generations.

There were two attempts to create indigenous priests in Uganda. The first was to train them from abroad and the second was to train them locally. The former failed and the latter succeeded.[17] After several attempts to form indigenous clergy from abroad failed, the White Fathers resolved to establish a local seminary in Buddu Province of Buganda. The first major seminary was started at Lubaga in June of 1891. Because of some challenges (religious wars between Catholics and Protestants, famine, sleeping sickness, etc.), the seminarians were moved to Villa Maria in 1892, back to Lubaga in 1893, to Kisubi in 1895, to Bukalasa at the end of 1905, and finally to the seminary which was settled at Katigondo on March 7th, 1911.

Waliggo highlights the following as the factors for flourishing of the African indigenous priests since the era of the White Fathers: First, the head of the White Fathers in Buddu province, Bishop Henry Streicher, insisted that Africa will be best evangelized by Africans and therefore promoted vocations to the priesthood. In his pastoral letter on the purpose of a seminary, he wrote that "to get one indigenous priest is for me more important than to convert ten thousand people."[18] Streicher's frequent visits to the seminary, appointing of his best priests to form seminarians, grading of students' end of year exams, etc., manifested the fact that he regarded the work of the seminary as the most important in ministry.[19] His efforts were supported by his superiors, his fellow missionaries and local Catholics.

The second reason for the flourishing of indigenous priesthood in Uganda is the fact that Baganda converts and local leaders cooperated very well with the White Fathers in strengthening their Church against the Protestant competitors. Third, the White Fathers' method of recruitment of priestly candidates and the seminary training incorporated some aspects of indigenous culture such as wearing ordinary tunics, working in gardens as part of their education, and playing traditional games and sports. Although candidates to the priesthood were to fully assimilate the Tridentine education, they were nevertheless not divorced from their people and culture.[20] Lavigerie charged the White Fathers to turn Africans into "Christians and apostles but not into French and Europeans."[21] After the ordination of the first two indigenous priests in 1913, priesthood was seen as possible and since then there has been a steady increase in the number of priestly candidates and ordinations.

The achievement of indigenous priests is also attributed to the efforts of the two great missionary popes, Benedict XV (1914–1922) and Pius XI (1922–1939). These popes encouraged establishment of local churches headed by indigenous priests in all mission lands. Pope Benedict XV, in his encyclical *Maximum Illud*, strongly encouraged missionaries to learn local languages and to train local clergy in mission lands. He strongly believed that local priests are more effective in attracting natives to the Faith since they know the language and can easily access places where missionary priests cannot.[22] Similar to Lavigerie, Pope Benedict XV believed that Africa would be best evangelized by fellow Africans. For him, effective evangelization requires contribution of the local priests who can easily interact with local people and help them engage in the Paschal Mystery in a more meaningful way. He therefore charged missionaries to prepare a well-trained indigenous clergy that will eventually take over leadership of local churches. The pope stressed that the indigenous clergy must not be trained merely to perform the humbler duties of the ministry such as acting as the assistants of the foreign priests. Rather, the indigenous clergy must be trained as European priests so that they are well equipped to take over "the spiritual leadership of their people."[23]

Pope Pius XI, in his missionary encyclical *Rerum Ecclesia*, reiterated the value of training local clergy and empowering them to take over leadership of their lands.[24] He charged the heads of missions to ensure equality between white missionaries and indigenous clergy. He cautioned heads of mission lands to reject any discrimination that considered indigenous priests to be inferior to the white missionaries.[25]

Although the effort of the White Fathers to train a local clergy was eventually a success, there were several challenges. For instance, there was pessimism about the success of getting African priests because both the missionaries and local natives saw the Tridentine priesthood as too high for an African man. Waliggo reports that one of the Buganda kingdom chief officials, Stanislas Mugwanya, told Bishop Streicher on behalf of the Catholics in Buganda that "you will never succeed in turning us or our children into priests as you plan."[26] Furthermore, many missionaries doubted whether African men would be able to observe celibacy after ordination since polygamy was widely accepted in Buganda and other parts of Sub-Saharan Africa. Despite these and many other challenges, Streicher's work bore fruit when the two Buganda men, Basil Lumu and Victor Mukasa were ordained priests on June 29th, 1913, at Villa Maria in Buddu province. These were the first two African priests of the new missionary era that opened the door to the African clergy. From 1921, African indigenous priests began to be appointed superiors of mission stations in Buddu. When the White Fathers evacuated Buddu province in 1934, the entire evangelizing work was left to the local clergy. In 1939, Buddu became the first African autonomous local Church with its own African Bishop, clergy, religious sisters and brothers, and catechists.[27]

III. *Africae Munus* and the Vocation to the Priesthood

Pope Benedict XVI published the post-synodal apostolic exhortation *Africae Munus* after the Second African Synod that took place in Rome in October of 2009. The theme of the Second Synod was "The Church in Africa in Service to Reconciliation, Justice and Peace."[28] *Africae Munus* builds upon the contents of the First African Synod convoked by Pope John Paul II in 1994.[29] In *Africae Munus*, Benedict XVI praises the apostolic zeal of missionaries who brought the light of Christ into Africa.[30]

Pope Benedict XVI recognizes Africa as the "spiritual lung" for a humanity that appears to be in a crisis of faith and hope."[31] He appreciates the central place of African Catholicism not only in world Catholicism, but also in the construction of a better place for African peoples especially in the urgent task of reconciliation, justice, and peace.[32] He argues that for *ecclesia* in Africa to be an effective agent for reconciliation, justice and peace, it should train pastoral agents at all levels especially at the grassroots. The formation of the clergy, Benedict continues, should be comprehensive and should involve all peoples in the leadership of the Church at all levels.[33]

Benedict XVI's predecessor, Pope John Paul II, taught that without priests the Church would not be able to live out the fundamental obedience to Christ's mandate to making disciples for all nations (cf. Matt. 28:19).[34] John Paul called upon the Church to help young men to discern the authenticity of their call to priesthood and respond to it generously so as to spread the gospel to all peoples. Similarly, Pope Benedict XVI tasks bishops, seminary staff, and all stakeholders of seminary formation to ensure quality rather than quantity of those being formed to the priesthood. He writes:

> The seminary staff and formators [should] work together, following the bishops' indications, to guarantee an integral formation of the seminarians entrusted to them. In selecting candidates, careful discernment and quality guidance must be ensured, so that those admitted to the priesthood will be true disciples of Christ and authentic servants of the Church. Care should be taken to initiate them in the unlimited richness of the Church's biblical, theological, spiritual, liturgical, moral and juridical patrimony.[35]

For Pope Benedict, "careful discernment and quality guidance" in selecting priestly candidates is not pessimism about the genuineness of priestly vocations. Rather, such caution ensures that the Church gets "true disciples of Christ and authentic servants of the Church." Although every priestly candidate receives his vocation from Christ through the Church as a gift, the bishops and all stakeholders of seminary formation should examine and ensure that candidates with the right motives are selected for the priestly ministry.[36]

In this fundamental task of forming a solid and zealous clergy, Benedict tasks African theologians to come up with "transforming theology" which can bring about "concrete pastoral ministry" to meet the challenges facing faith and life in Africa.[37] This theology, Benedict explains, should not be merely proof-texting, accumulation of data and regurgitation of Western theological terms, but a concrete and transformative African theological praxis. He writes:

> Dear brothers and sisters in Catholic universities and academic institutions, it falls to you, on the one hand, to shape the minds and hearts of the younger generation in the light of the Gospel and, on the other hand, to help African societies to understand the challenges confronting them today by providing Africa, through your research and analyses, with the light she needs.[38]

By calling upon Catholic institutions to form the young generation with a "transforming theology," the pope wants to ensure that the theology taught in Catholic institutions cultivates an authentic Christian culture. Fr. Matthew Lamb qualified such theology as the one that realizes "the intrinsic relation between the intellectual, moral, and spiritual formation."[39] Such a "transforming theology" should be characterized by an intrinsic relation between faith and reason, the past and the present, old and new.[40]

The pope calls upon seminarians to root themselves in gospel values in order to strengthen their commitment to Jesus Christ. He therefore tasks them to have a "profound union with Christ" through leading a life "of prayer" and "the human, spiritual and moral values assimilated during their time of formation."[41] Recalling John Paul II's *Ecclesia in Africa*, the Pope invites seminarians to develop "a correct understanding of their own culture while not being locked within their own ethnic and cultural limits."[42]

As far as the intellectual formation of the seminarians is concerned, Pope Benedict calls for a rebirth of intellectual life like "the prestigious School of Alexandria."[43] One of the challenges of the seminaries in Africa is lack of well-trained teachers and formators due to limited financial resources. Bishops are therefore forced to pick some simple, good, and prayerful priests and throw them into seminaries. For this reason, seminarians miss the opportunity of being immersed into the rich Catholic intellectual patrimony and are instead trained as practical pastoral agents. They end up not being able to fully defend the Church's doctrine and practice against some modern intellectual and moral problems.

Furthermore, the Holy Father stresses that for the African

clergy to be relevant and helpful in solving the African continent's problems, seminarians must be schooled in "social doctrine." Education in social doctrine, the pope continues, will "help the Church in Africa serenely to prepare a pastoral plan which speaks to the heart of Africans and enables them to be reconciled to themselves by following Christ."[44]

IV. Fr. Benedict Ssetuuma Jr.: Formator, Promoter, and Defender of Priestly Vocations

Fr. Ssetuuma was ordained a priest of the Masaka diocese on 3rd August 1996. After graduating with a doctorate in Missiology from the Faculty of Missiology at the Pontifical Urbaniana University in 2005, Fr. Ssetuuma spent the rest of his life as a professor of theology and formator of men for priesthood at Ggaba Seminary in Uganda. He was a Catholic gentleman with a sharp intellect. As his former professor and research supervisor, Prof. Francis Anekwe Oborji eulogized him, stating that Ssetuuma was "one of the rare geniuses, a hero ... mighty in brain and scholarship."[45] Fr. Ssetuuma's published works include, among others, the following: Benedict Ssetuuma Jr., "Mission As Integral Liberation In Africa" (Paulines Publications Africa, Nairobi 2004); *Mission As Liberation In Uganda* (PUU, Rome 2005); *Friendship An Effective Tool For Mission* (AMECEA Gaba Publications 2010); *Mission as Integral Liberation in Africa* (Hekima Publications, Nairobi 2003); *Inculturation: Towards an Integrated Approach for Ownership, Permanence and Relevance of Christianity for a People* (Angel Agencies, Kampala 2010); *Uganda at 50: Understanding and Presenting Our History* (Nuru Library, Uganda 2013); *Mission as Promotion of the Image of God* (Nuru Library, Uganda 2013); *Uganda: A Spiritual Lung of Africa* (Nuru Library, Uganda 2016). Benedict Ssetuuma, *Pope Benedict VI: A Simple Humble Servant Who Turned the Tide in Modern Church History* (Nuru Library, Uganda 2015); *Katigondo Major Seminary Through a Hundred Years* (1911–2011): *A Miracle and Pride of Modern Africa* (Katigondo National Seminary 2013), etc.

In his life as a priest and theologian, Ssetuuma promoted, defended and nurtured vocations to the priesthood. He was convinced that when God calls one to the priesthood, God does not revoke his call or regret it, even in cases of incompetence, fear or failure.[46] He was a man of no prejudice—he never judged seminarians from hearsay. One of the challenges of seminary formation in Uganda and in Africa is overcrowding and the incommensurate ratio of seminarians to formators.[47] The few formators in most African seminaries are also the teachers and spiritual directors of hundreds of seminarians. This makes accompaniment of seminarians as stipulated by the Vatican almost impossible.[48] Because of overcrowding in African seminaries, some formators are forced to adopt a policing approach based on fear and intimidation. Such formators use seminarians to spy on other seminarians. Fr. Ssetuuma was not such a priest and formator. In fact, he openly criticized the spying mentality in some seminaries and dioceses. He believed in his "boys," and gave them second chances when they messed up in their formation. Ssetuuma was convinced that God always makes the right choice of the individual he calls to the priesthood and reminded seminarians their responsibility to be obedient to God's voice and to respond to it with sincerity of heart.[49]

Although God has blessed Uganda and Africa with abundant vocations to the priesthood, Fr. Ssetuuma was convinced that the Church can never have enough priests given the nature of its mission of sanctifying the world. He never tired of encouraging and promoting many more vocations. He agreed with *Africae Munus* that Africa is still in need of many more priests to minister reconciliation, justice and peace. In Uganda for instance, the 2009 Uganda Catholic Directory indicated that there are 1,680 priests ministering to 13,760,000 in the 19 Catholic dioceses. This means that on average every priest served at least 8200 Catholics by then. This is too demanding for each priest.[50]

As a formator and teacher, Fr. Ssetuuma executed his duties with diligence and most times beyond expectation. Leading by example, he instructed seminarians to be true disciples of Jesus

Christ. He worked tirelessly to make St. Mary's Seminary Ggaba the best place to live in. Following the Church's documents on the formation of the clergy, Fr. Ssetuuma emphasized the importance of community life in priestly formation.[51] He reminded the seminarians that since a priest is called from the community to be its mediator with God (cf. Heb. 5:1–10), every seminarian and priest should be a man of communion.[52] He encouraged the African philosophy of "*ubuntu*," which Desmond Tutu described as "my humanity is inextricably bound up in yours."[53] To foster community life, Fr. Ssetuuma spent most of his free time working on the seminary farm so that his brothers—priests and seminarians—had enough milk and food. He put into practice the instructions of St. Paul to the Thessalonians regarding the importance of work (cf. 2 Thess. 3:6–15). For St. Paul, those who are unwilling to work should not eat (2 Thess. 3:10). In this way Fr. Ssetuuma taught seminarians to be servant leaders and to be self-reliant. He emphasized self-reliance as the best way to overcome the biting poverty in most parishes. He preached that an African priest should not only administer sacraments but should also be a man who subdues the earth (cf. Gen 1:28) by the work of his own hands. By encouraging community life and self-reliance, Fr. Ssetuuma taught seminarians to fight individualism and search for survival mentality[54]—which are some of the big challenges of the African diocesan priesthood.

As a teacher of theology and formator of seminarians, Fr. Ssetuuma emphasized that the realities of faith taught in the classroom should be lived out in the daily life. He knew that failure to live out the realities of faith in prayer and worship would render Catholic doctrines mere words and ideas. He warned his students to be aware that the intellectual and moral virtues disappear without the theological virtues of faith, hope, and charity. For him as for St. Augustine, theology is best done on the knees. Fr. Ssetuuma believed that a theology in which intellectual formation is separated from the spiritual formation is not worth the name theology.

In exercising his role as a formator, Fr. Ssetuuma decried clericalism which, according to Jordan Nyenyembe, is the "virus of

Christendom" that the African Catholic priesthood inherited from the West.[55] Priests with this "virus" see their role mainly as only "administrators of sacraments and the teachers of faith." Priests eaten by the "virus of Christendom" take themselves as "set apart from the rest of the faithful, superior in holiness" and "bionic superhumans." Fr. Ssetuuma decried clericalism not only because it destroys community life, but mostly because such men "tend to be judgmental, hypocritical and insensitive to the sufferings of lay people."[56]

Conclusion

"To get one indigenous priest," Bishop Streicher confessed in 1929, "is for me more important than to convert ten thousand people." With the support of the White Fathers and native Africans, Bishop Streicher made African Catholic priesthood possible in Buganda and in Sub-Saharan Africa. Since the ordination of the first two Baganda men on June 29th, 1913, the number of priestly candidates in Uganda and in Sub-Saharan Africa has increased steadily, and today Sub-Saharan Africa is experiencing a priestly vocation boom. This vocation boom is first and foremost a fruit of the work of the White Fathers who believed that Africa would be best evangelized by native Africans. Furthermore, the African emphasis on priority of family and community life fosters priestly vocations. The African philosophy of *ubuntu*, that is, *I am because we are, and since we are therefore I am,* has led to the flourishing of the Catholic priesthood in Uganda and Sub-Saharan Africa. For Africans, a priestly candidate is not only a child of his immediate family. Rather, he is a son of the entire community—Christians and non-Christians. Most African priests are very close to the people they serve: They make house-to-house visits, they celebrate marriages, funerals, and other thanksgiving Masses in peoples' homes. Such priestly simplicity, joy, and commitment attract many young boys to the Catholic priesthood.

Although Africa is often described in derogatory terms,[57] it is also referred to as the future of the Church because of its increasing number of priestly vocations and the solid faith of the African peoples. For this reason, Pope Benedict XVI describes Africa as "a spiritual lung for humanity."[58] For Africa to remain a "spiritual lung for humanity" and the future of the Church, it needs to nurture and promote priestly vocations to carry out the ministry of reconciliation, justice and peace, just as Fr. Ssetuuma did.

Chapter 9 Endnotes

1 Benedict XVI, *Address to Members of the Special Council for Africa of the Synod of Bishops* (Yaoundé, 19 March 2009): AAS101 (2009), 310.

2 See Pope Benedict VI, Post-Synodal Apostolic Exhortation on the Church in Africa in Service to Reconciliation, Justice and Peace, *Africae Munus* (November 19th, 2011). At the Holy See, https://www.vatican.va/content/benedict-xvi/en/apost_exhortations/documents/hf_ben-xvi_exh_20111119_africae-munus.html. Hereafter cited as *AM*.

3 Philip Jenkins, *The Next Christendom: The Coming of Global Christianity* (Oxford: Oxford University Press, 2002), 83–85, especially at 83.

4 J. J. Bonk, "Africa and the Christian Mission." Editorial Comment for the *International Bulletin of Missionary Research* 33 (2), p. 58. Also, J. Hanciles, "African Christianity, Globalization, and Mission: Marginalizing the Centre." In O. Kalu and A. Low (eds), *Interpreting Contemporary Christianity: Global Processes and Local Identities* (Grand Rapids: William B. Eerdmans Publishing Company, 2008), 77.

5 See the Presentation of the Pontifical Yearbook 2019 and the *Annuarium Statisticum Ecclesiae* 2017. At the Holy See, https://press.vatican.va/content/salastampa/en/bollettino/pubblico/2019/03/06/190306b.html. Accessed on June 1, 2022.

6 See Vatican, Catholic Church Statistics 2018. Available at http://www.fides.org/en/stats/64944–VATICAN_CATHOLIC_CHURCH_STATISTICS_2018.

7 Benedict Ssetuuma Jr., "In defence of the Vocations to the Priesthood in Uganda: Tackling the fear of a False Boom," in *Priesthood As A Mysterious and Amphibious Existence: Essays in Honour of Rev. Fr. Dr. Paul Masolo on His Silver Jubilee in the Priesthood and his 51st Birthday, Waliggo Journal* May 2010, Vol. 3.No. 1, p. 61–66, at 61.

8 See Ibid.

9 See John Mary Waliggo, *A history of African Priests* (Nairobi: Matianum Press Consultants, 1988).

10 John Mary Waliggo, "Historical Background on the Major Seminary Formation in Uganda since 1904 and since the Creation of the National Seminaries in the Mid 1960s," in the *Theological Reflections on Some Practical Aspects of Life in Uganda: Essays in Honor of Rev. Fr. Dr. Vicent Kanyoza on his Golden Jubilee in Priesthood and 80th Birthday,* eds., David W. Ssempungu, Benedict Ssetuuma, et al (Kampala: Angel Agencies, 2009), 13–28, at 13.

11 Waligo, *A history of African Priests* (Nairobi: Matianum Press Consultants, 1988), 2.

12 Waligo, "Historical Background on the Major Seminary Formation in Uganda," 14.

13 See M. J. Bane, *Catholic Pioneers in West Africa* (Dublin 1955), 114.

14 Waligo, *A history of African Priests,* 3.

15 For studies on work and mission of the White Fathers in East and Central Africa, see John Mary Waligo, *The Catholic Church in the Buddu Province of Buganda, 1879–1925* (Kampala: Angel Agencies, 2011); Roland Vizeau, *The White Fathers' Contribution to the Civilization of Central Africa through their Agricultural Activities and Improvement of Native Dietaries, 1879–1955* (STL Dissertation, Gregorian University, Rome, 1954); Brian Garvey, *The Development of the White Fathers' Mission Among the Bemba-Speaking Peoples 1891–1964'* (Doctoral Dissertation: London University, 1974.)

16 See the *Instructions of Cardinal Lavigerie to Missionaries in East Africa,* 1972. Hereafter cited as *ICL.*

17 Waligo reports that on October 9th 1890, the White Fathers presented fourteen boys from Uganda to Pope Leo XIII to be trained for the priesthood. Six of the boys were placed in the seminary of the White Father in Algiers whereas seven were sent to Malta after one, "Lwanga," was judged to be too old for novitiate. After one year, all were dismissed from the seminary "after having been found too slow to learn [and therefore] not ideal for priesthood." See Waligo, *A history of African Priests,* 6–8, especially at 7.

18 See *Lubaga Missionary Achieves,* Streicher's pastoral letter 'Omugaso Gw'a Seminario [The Utiity of the Seminary] of March 1929, circular 174.

19 Waligo reports that the missionaries that Bishop Streicher described as the best in his annual reports are the ones that he appointed in the seminary. See Waligo, *The Catholic Church in the Buddu Province of Buganda,* 104.

20 According to the instructions of Cardinal Lavigerie, priestly candidates were to be educated within their cultural environment.

21 *ICL*, April 1880, 284.

22 Pope Benedict XV, Apostolic Letter on the Propagation of the Faith throughout the World *Maximum Illud,* (30 November 1919), § 14: "There is one final, and very important, point for anyone who has charge of a mission. He must make it his special concern to secure and train local candidates for the sacred ministry. In this policy lies the greatest hope of the new churches. For the local priest, one with his people by birth, by nature, by his sympathies and his aspirations, is remarkably effective in appealing to their mentality and thus attracting them to the Faith. Far better than anyone else, he knows the kind of argument they will listen to, and as a result, he often has easy access to places where a foreign priest would not be tolerated." Also, § 17: "The Apostolic See has always urged the directors of missions to realize that this is a very serious obligation of their office and vigorously to put it into action. Here in Rome the colleges – both the old colleges and the newer ones – that train clergy for the foreign missions, have already shown their earnestness in the matter. This is particularly true of those training men for the Oriental rites...." Available at the Holy See, https://www.vatican.va/content/benedict-xv/en/apost_letters/documents/hf_ben-xv_apl_19191130_maximum-illud.html. Hereafter cited as *MI.*

23 *MI*, § 15.

24 See Pope Pius XI, Encyclical on Catholic Missions *Rerum Ecclesiae* (February 28th,1926), § 19: "Before everything else, we call your attention to the importance of building up a native clergy. If you do not work with all your might to attain this purpose, we assert that not only will your apostolate be crippled, but it will become an obstacle and an impediment to the establishment and organization of the Church in those countries. We gladly recognize and acknowledge the fact that in some places steps have already been taken to provide for these needs by the erection of seminaries in which native youths of promise are well educated and prepared to receive the dignity of the priesthood, and are trained to instruct in the Christian Faith members of their own race. But in spite of all this work, we are still a great distance from the goal which we have set for ourselves." Available at the Holy See, https://www.vatican.va/content/pius-xi/en/encyclicals/documents/hf_p-xi_enc_28021926_rerum-ecclesiae.html. Hereafter cited as *RE*.

25 *RE*, § 26.

26 See Waliggo, *The Catholic Church in the Buddu Province of Buganda,* 102.

27 Ibid., 101.
28 *AM*, §§ 1, 2.
29 Ibid., § 2.
30 See Ibid., § 113.
31 Ibid., § 13.
32 Ibid., § 3.
33 See *AM*, §§ 74–78. In addition to the training of "pastoral agents," Benedict XVI says that training of church leaders should be more centered on the social mission of the Church and that all members of the Church should be educated in the social teaching of the Church (§§ 109, 128, 134, 137).
34 John Pau II, Post-Synodal Apostolic Exhortation on the Formation of Priests in the Circumstances of the Present Day *Pastores dabo vobis* (25 March 1992), § 1. At the Holy See, https://www.vatican.va/content/john-paul-ii/en/apost_exhortations/documents/hf_jp-ii_exh_25031992_pastores-dabo-vobis.html. Hereafter cited as *PDV*.
35 *AM*, § 122. For other documents on seminary formation, see Decree on Priestly Training, Optatam Totius (October 28, 1965); decree on the ministry and life of priests presbyterorum ordinis (December 7, 1965); Pope Pius XI, Encyclical Letter on the Catholic Priesthood (*Ad Catholici Sacerdotii*) 1935; Pope Paul VI, Encyclical letter on the Celibacy of priests (*sacerdotalis coelibatus*), 1967; John Paul II, Post-Synodal Apostolic Exhortation on the Formation of Priests in the Circumstances of the Present Day (*Pastores dabo vobis*), 1992; John Paul II, Encyclical Letter *Veritatis Splendor* (1993); John Paul II, Apostolic Letter on Reserving Priestly Ordination to Men Alone (*Ordination Sacerdotalis*), 1994; John Paul II, Post-Synodal Apostolic Exhortation on Consecrated Life and its Mission in the Church and in the World *Vita consacrata* (1996); John Paul II, Encyclical Letter on the Relationship between Faith and Reason *Fides et ratio* 1988.
36 *PDV*, § 35.
37 *AM*, § 10.
38 Ibid., §135.
39 See Matthew L. Lamb, "From 1990: Will there be Catholic theology in the United States?" in the *American Magazine* May 26, 1990. Available at https://www.americamagazine.org/faith/2021/05/19/catholic-theology-lamb-doctoral-education-240685
40 For a good analysis of the intrinsic relation between faith and reason, ancient and present, see John Paul II' Encyclical Letter on the Relation between Faith and Reason *Fides et Ratio* (14 September 1988). At the Holy See, https://www.vatican.va/content/john-paul-ii/en/encyclicals/documents/hf_jp-ii_enc_14091998_fides-et-ratio.html. Also,

see Vatican II's emphasis on *Aggiornamento* and *Ressourcement*. For an explanation of these terms, see the Address of Pope Benedict XVI to the Bishops who participated in the second Vatican Ecumenical Council and Presidents of Episcopal Conferences (12 October 2012). Available at the Holy See, https://www.vatican.va/content/benedict-xvi/en/speeches/2012/october/documents/hf_ben-xvi_spe_20121012_vescovi-concilio.html. Also, Eduardo Echeverria, "Ressourcement," "Aggiornamento," and Vatican II in Ecumenical Perspective. Available at https://www.hprweb.com/2014/07/ressourcement-aggiornamento-and-vatican-ii-in-ecumenical-perspective/

41 *AM*, § 121

42 Ibid.

43 Ibid., § 137.

44 Ibid.

45 See the eulogy Prof. Francis Anekwe Oborji, Professor Ordinarius of Contextual theology, Pontifical Urbaniana University, Rome on June 19, 2021.

46 See Benedict Ssetuuma, "When God Calls," in Priesthood as Mysterious and Amphibious Existence, 11.

47 The following is the total number of seminarians per class in the four national major seminaries in Uganda as of June 2022: St. Thomas Aquinas Katigondo seminary has 235 students (an average of 78 students per class); Uganda Martyr's Seminary Alokorum has 215 students (an average of 72 students in each class); St. Mary's Ggaba seminary has a total of 212 students (an average of 53 students per class); and St. Paul's Seminary Kinyamasika has a total of 198 students (average of 50 students per class). I am grateful to seminarians George William Mukalazi, Jerome Ssebayigga, Deogratias Kabanda, and Wynand Namugera for providing me with these statistics.

48 For the guidelines on the formation of the clergy, see the Congregation for the Clergy's *The Gift of the Priestly Vocation: Ratio Fundamentalis Institutionis Sacerditalis* (London: CTS Publications, 2017), §§ 44–49. Hereafter cited as *RF*. For other documents on the formation of the clergy, see John Paul II, Post-Synodal Apostolic Exhortation *Pastores dabo vobis* (25 March, 1992); Second Vatican Council, Decree on the Training of Priests *Optatam totius;* Second Vatican Council, Decree on the Ministry and Life of Priests *Presbyterorum ordinis* (7 December 1965).

49 Benedict Ssetuuma, "When God Calls," in Priesthood as Mysterious and Amphibious Existence, 14.

50 See *Uganda Catholic Directory 2009* (Kisubi: Marianum Press, 2009), 43–358.

51 See *RF* 50, "Community life during the years of initial formation must make an impact on each individual, purifying his interior intentions and transforming the conduct of his life as he gradually conforms himself to Christ"; *OT*, § 5; *PDV*, §§ 60–66.

52 See also, *PDV*, §§60–64.

53 See Desmond Tutu, *No Future without Forgiveness* (New York: Doubleday, 2000), 31.

54 The "search for survival mentality "is where priests and seminarians, instead of concentrating on their pastoral ministry, look for other financial opportunities to sustain themselves. Most African dioceses lack a stable and sustainable financial arrangement for their clergy especially in sickness and old age. As a result, many look for "opportunities" outside their pastoral ministry in order to support themselves especially in the most vulnerable times.

55 See Jordan Nyenyembe, "Stewards of God's Mercy: Vocation and Priestly Ministry in Africa," *Journal of Global Catholicism* 1 (July 2017), 74–95. According to Nyenyembe, African Catholic priesthood inherited two viruses: the first is the "virus of Christendom" and the "virus of Chiefdom" or the "*Igwe syndrome*." Whereas the former was inherited from the West, the latter, "virus of chiefdom," is inherited from African traditions. The "virus of chiefdom" makes priests to take themselves as village chiefs, which eventually gives rise to personality cult.

56 Nyenyembe, Stewards of God's Mercy," 78.

57 One of the most famous descriptions of Africa is an image of the half-dead man on the roadside found in Luke 10:25–35. Such derogatory descriptions of Africa are due to the effects of colonialism, incessant conflicts, disease, and poverty. See Passion for Christ, Passion for Humanity, *Acts of the Congress on Consecrated Life* (Nairobi: Pauline Publications, 2005), 42. Also Benedict Ssetuuma Jr., *The Crying Old Man from the Sea*.

58 *AM*, § 13.

Chapter 10

Africae Munus *in the Light of Prophetic Praxis: A Liberation Theology for Africa? A Critical Engagement with Ratzinger*

Tegha Afuhwi Nji

Introduction: The Question at Stake

The current unsettling socio-political and economic situation of many African countries, compared against the religious landscape of the continent, seems to suggest strongly that theologians, especially of African extraction or those with intellectual or other ties to Africa, should pay closer attention to the question of liberation theology.[1] The exigency of this suggestion, one may argue, is notably heightened, were one to pause over the recommendations of Benedict XVI's post-synodal apostolic exhortation, *Africae Munus*, promulgated on November 19, 2011, after the second special synod of bishops for Africa, held in Rome in October 2009, on the theme, "The Church in Africa in the Service to Reconciliation, Justice, and Peace."[2]

This notwithstanding, any theologian, especially a Ratzingerian, willing to undertake the above-mentioned task is faced with the apparent stigma that the subject of liberation theology bears, some of which is at times, erroneously as I argue, attributed to Joseph Ratzinger himself.[3] This essay seeks to undertake the modest task of clarifying what exactly Ratzinger rejects in the so-called theologies of liberation and deciphering how this differs from a rejection of liberation theology as such This accomplished, I show how a reading of *Africae Munus*, ten years later, does in fact place upon the African theologian (and well-wishers) the onus of re-thinking the state of the question of liberation theology in and for the continent.

It is expedient to have here a summary mention of Ratzinger's criticism. In a March 1984 article titled "Liberation Theology," he describes liberation theology as "a fundamental danger for the faith of the Church."[4] However, and very importantly, he places significant caveats as to what sort of theology of liberation he critiques, restricting it only to those that are Marxist in character. He explains,

> The theology of liberation is an extraordinarily complex phenomenon. Any concept of liberation theology has to be able to span positions ranging from the radically Marxist to those that stress necessary Christian responsibility toward the poor and the oppressed in the context of sound ecclesiology, as did the documents of CELAM from Medellin to Puebla. Here, I am using the concept of 'liberation theology' in a more restricted sense, a sense which includes ***only*** those theologians who in some way have espoused a Marxist fundamental option.[5]

Without presuming to be able to reproduce an entirety of Ratzinger's take on liberation theology, for the purpose of this essay, pieced together here are five of Ratzinger's predominant criticisms of Marxist-inclined theologies of liberation: (i) their emptying of the Christian tradition into a scheme of socio-political practice;[6] (ii) their deployment of 'weaponized' Marxist ideologies and a hermeneutic founded upon history and experience rather than a hermeneutic of faith;[7] (iii) their transformation of orthopraxis into a new orthodoxy, such that action rather than faith becomes truth;[8] (iv) their blurring of the boundaries between churches and a false 'universalism' founded on praxis rather than faith[9] (v) their reduction of everything to the political context and making liberation into a concept and its guide political action.[10] With regard to this last point, Ratzinger has in hindsight Gustavo

Gutierrez's claim, which he quotes, that "Nothing remains outside political commitment. All exists with a political coloration."[11]

In the light of these criticisms, this essay in its reading of *Africae Munus* attempts to offer a new perspective on liberation theology for Africa which is both authentic and orthodox. As Ratzinger himself notes in the article, "Alongside the demonstration of error, and the danger of liberation theology, we have to also consider the question, what truth is hidden in the error, and how do we recover it completely."[12] As the Prefect of the Congregation of the Doctrine of Faith (CDF), we see Ratzinger setting underway this "recovery" process. This is abundantly clear in publications he overseed such as, "Instruction on Certain Aspects of the 'Theology of Liberation'"[13] "Notifications on the works of Father Jon Sobrino, SJ.: Jesucristo liberador. Lectura histórico-teológica de Jesús de Nazaret (Madrid, 1991) and La fe en Jesucristo: Ensayo desde las víctimas (San Salvador, 1999)."[14] It is this recovery process that this essay seeks to further in the light of *Africae Munus*, with the following question in mind: ***"Could our reading of Africae Munus map out a path of an authentic liberation theology for Africa and beyond?"***

Considering this question, the following preliminary notes are in order. In *Africae Munus*, I argue, we find an *integrative* Ratzinger-powered vision of liberation theology. Earlier on (1984), writing as Prefect of the CDF, Ratzinger had avowed that "Liberation is first and foremost liberation from the radical slavery of sin. Its end and its goal is the freedom of the children of God, which is the gift of grace. As a logical consequence, it calls for freedom from . . . slavery in the cultural, economic, social, and political spheres, all of which derive ultimately from sin."[15] Here, Ratzinger was pushing for a perspective of liberation which integrates the "spiritual or eschatological" and "practico-political" spheres, the result being a truly pastoral approach to the subject, whereby neither sphere gets subsumed in or by the other.

The consistent argument this essay makes, therefore, is that this integrative vision of Ratzinger finds concrete fruition, many years later, in *Africae Munus*, wherein, now as Pope Benedict XVI, he calls for a legitimate and urgent "transforming of theology into pastoral care, namely into a very concrete pastoral ministry in which the great perspectives found in sacred Scripture and Tradition find application in the activity of bishops and priests in specific times and places'"[16]—thereby building a Church in Africa (and beyond) in service to reconciliation, justice, and peace. In this call, Ratzinger is redefining *prophetic praxis* as truly the Church's mission without at the same time letting it dissolve into political action, simply. The Church is indeed *prophet*, that is, "one called" (from the Hebrew, *nābî'*), and her mission is to "speak on behalf of God" (from the Greek προφήτης) and to witness to the gospel message in the concrete conditions of life. In this mission, it is the Christian *ethos* or *praxis* that serves as a transforming principle for society. Accordingly, Ratzinger describes this gospel message as a message of freedom and a force for liberation.[17] This brief sketch of what is at stake in *Africae Munus*, vis-à-vis the program of liberation theology, already gives us warrant to anticipate an affirmative answer to the initial question posed—"Could our reading of *Africae Munus* map out a path of an authentic liberation theology for Africa and beyond?" In what follows we attempt an explication of this affirmation.

To achieve this end, therefore, this essay is structured into four parts. Part one is a deepening of the critical engagement of Ratzinger with liberation theology, especially the Latin American tradition and its prominent adherents such as Gustavo Gutierrez and Jon Sobrino, who happen to be two of Ratzinger's main interlocutors. This section is thematized as follows: "Potential dangers of a misconstrued liberation theology." Part two aims at constructing a vision of an *authentic* liberation theology (for Africa and beyond), built around five fundamental principles. Part three narrows in on "inaugurated eschatology" as the theological locus for developing the proposed *authentic* liberation theology. The final part is a resourcing of the category of "lament" as a model for a legitimate (African) perspective of liberation theology. In the conclusion, we revisit the question of the subject name, "liberation theology." Very importantly, each section is inspired and motivated by a "prophetic-practical" reading of *Africae Munus*.

I. Potential Dangers of a Misconstrued Liberation Theology

This section attends to the following question: "Why the stigma on the theology of liberation?" The argument here is that this stigma more than likely stems from the potential dangers associated with the subject matter, at least from a confessional (mostly Catholic) perspective. Three of these likely dangers include: political utopia, the problem of an earthly kingdom, and the narrowing of the biblical understanding of poverty. Hopefully, in the lines that follow we shall see how interrelated all three are.

I.i. Political Utopia

By political utopia we refer to that attempt by man to fashion for himself and by himself a perfect kingdom of justice and peace. It is a form of liberation which fails to be Christocentric but relies on what Ratzinger calls a "Marxist analysis," fueled by impatience and a desire for results.[18] Ratzinger's uneasiness with this model of liberation is understandable, specifically for its near-mythical deployment of the "'scientific analysis' of the structural causes of poverty" using Marxist tools and ideologies, with the assumption that society can be transformed by the mere application of this analysis.[19] In addition to Pope Paul VI's warning that a society thus transformed ends up becoming totalitarian,[20] Ratzinger's legitimate bone of contention against this model is that any theology of liberation construed on Marxist ideologies makes "class struggle" and "history" into the "determining principle."[21] Within such a system, "the only true consciousness, then, is partisan consciousness," while truth becomes partisan praxis.[22] Herein, "class struggle is presented as an objective, necessary law" effecting social change in all spheres—religious, ethical, cultural, and institutional—by the consequent adoption of necessary violence and opposition.[23]

It is probably beyond a guess that Ratzinger (as head of the CDF), in writing the *Instruction on Certain Aspects of the "Theology of Liberation"* (1984), had in mind the pioneering work of Leonardo Boff, *Church: Charism and Power* (1981), which, inarguably, employs such Marxist readings.[24] A trend that runs through the text culminates in chapter eight, wherein Boff sets up a class struggle between the "ecclesial base communities" (defined as grassroot churches or those not in power) and the "institutional or hierarchical Christianity" (those in power). Boff claims that this struggle mirrors the class struggle in a typical capitalist society wherein some are rich (dominating class), and others are poor (the dominated). He re-interprets the traditional four "notes" of the Church—unity, holiness, catholicity, apostolicity—as serving the interest of the dominant class in masking the real class tensions in the religious-ecclesiastical realm. According to him, this class struggle results in a sharpened sense of liberation amongst the lower class (base communities) who, he argues, are faithful to the gospel of Christ, hinged on love, hope, fraternity, mutual service, and trusting surrender to the Father.[25]

For all the merits due to him, Boff's is a faulty ecclesiology. He does not have an integrative vision of the Church wherein all are equally sons and daughters of God around the Eucharist, nor does he show how the institutional dimension of the Church fits into the "new order" he advocates.[26] Rather, he ends up promoting "class struggle" as the effective principle of change and not the love of God or dialogue. Boff fails in the same way Marx does, for should this "revolution" succeed, he does not stipulate how the Church should live thence, in much the same way as Marx succeeded in showing how to overthrow the existing order but did not say how matters should proceed thereafter.[27] In Boff's analysis of the "new Church" he desired, on pages 120 through 122 of the referenced text, the Eucharist is conspicuously missing. Rather, what takes central place and makes for unity is the mission of liberation. Of course, justice becomes a social agenda, and the base communities (which he later calls the Church of the poor, Church of the people, etc.,) become a "social class"[28] that has realized its need of revolutionary struggle for liberation from the oppressive hierarchy or institutional Church.[29]

On a broader scale, the result of the adoption of such a Marxist system, vis-à-vis the faith and theological explanation of the faith, is the unfortunate "politicization of faith's affirmation and theological judgments."[30] When this happens, the question is no longer about the consequences and political implications of the truths of faith, which are respected beforehand for their transcendent value. Rather, every affirmation of faith or of theology is subordinated to a political criterion, which in turn depends on class struggle, the "new" driving force of history.[31] This constitutes what Ratzinger calls a "secular faith in progress" or hope in the historical process devoid of faith. This, in his words still, is a "political utopia."[32] The ultimate result is a historicist immanentism, upon which is founded an earthly kingdom of man.

Besides a pure secularization of the faith or the kingdom of God, there is another danger of blurring the *dis-continuum* between the historical or present reality of the kingdom of God and the eschatological consummation of that kingdom, such that the latter simply becomes a progressive intensification or growth of the former. When this happens, the decisive aspect of the *adventus novum ultimum* (borrowing Moltmann's words) is lost.[33] Though it is hard to find a Catholic liberation theologian who explicitly and completely endorses this view, there are, however, unnuanced statements here and there which approximate it when critically examined. For instance, in advocating for the overcoming of the "kingdom–God" duality, Jon Sobrino tends to overstretch the *continuum* between "God's reign" and the "earthly kingdom" such that the distinctively *new* or the *eschatological more* of the coming kingdom of God is blurred.[34] There is a need to hold in continuous tension the *continuity* and *discontinuity* of the "present" and the "not-yet" dimensions of the kingdom of God without at the same time creating an opposing dualism.

It would seem, as Cyril O'Regan aptly points out, that even Jürgen Moltmann's "theology of hope" comes under the scrutiny of Ratzinger for what O'Regan calls Moltmann's *soft Marxism*. In his interpretation of Ratzinger's *Eschatology: Death and Eternal Life,* O'Regan points to two key passages: First is Ratzinger's insistence that "The kingdom of God is not a political norm of political activity, but it is an ethical norm of this activity" (59); and the second is the line Ratzinger draws between the path followed by Jesus and that of the Zealots (60). The thrust of our argument here basically accords with O'Regan's contentions that, "influenced by Solovyov's and Dostoyevsky's reflection on the anti-Christ—an influence that is still in full-force in his encyclical *Spe Salvi* (2007) and in *Jesus of Nazareth*—Ratzinger judges that an interpretive stance overdetermined by political rectification yields to the temptation of confusing the kingdom of God with the kingdom of the world. As he does so, he is conscious that he is supporting Augustine's political theology that is anathema to Bloch and on his authority the object of critique in Moltmann."[35] Let us pursue a bit further this temptation toward historicist immanentism which Ratzinger sees as crystalizing in this "new" emerging danger of an altogether earthly kingdom.

I.ii. An Earthly Kingdom

The fundamental principle guiding our reflection here is Christ's own words denouncing an earthly kingdom as the goal of his mission. At his trial before Pilate, Jesus affirmed, "My kingdom is not of this world." (John 18:36). A historicist immanentism fails to account for this proclamation and denunciation of Christ. While some theologians (such as Jon Sobrino) have rightly read Jesus' actions as prophetic against the structures of sin and effectual for the establishment of a just social order, this same reading, if unnuanced, poses a danger to orthodoxy when the kingdom of God is identified with social order or when human liberation in history is made into the subject of its own development, that is, a process of self-redemption by means of class struggle.[36] The direct consequence of such a view is "temporal messianism," which is one of the most radical expressions of the "secularization of the Kingdom of God and of its absorption into the immanence of human history."[37] This is similar to the Zealot's politicization of

Israel's eschatology by interpreting Israel's hope as a fundamentally political program.[38] In the words of the Pastoral Constitution of Vatican II on the Church in the Modern World, *Gaudium et Spes,* "Among the forms of modern atheism is that which anticipates the liberation of man especially through his economic and social emancipation"—a liberation by solely human effort.[39]

An even subtler expression of the danger we here consider is experienced when the kingdom of God is simply appended to an already constructed robust social structure. Arguably, this tendency creeps in here and there in Boff's *Church: Charism and Power*. In his description of the liberation of the "Church of the people," his struggling social class, he notes,

> This people becomes the People of God in the measure to which, forming communities of faith, hope, and love inspired by Jesus' message of complete fraternity, they try to make concrete the reality of a people comprised of free, fraternal, and participating individuals. This historical reality is not only a product of a balanced social movement, but theologically it signifies the anticipation of and preparation for the kingdom of God and the eschatological People of God.[40]

Boff's error here is that he prefaces a "balanced social movement" as a preparation for the kingdom of God rather than see the kingdom of God as that undergirding and orienting social transformation.

I.iii. Narrowing the Biblical Understanding of Poverty and Introduction of Partiality in God

There is a true danger of reading God's preferential option for the poor or oppressed in a way that introduces "partiality" in God. Reading off the exodus event, for instance, Sobrino characterizes God as being partial to an oppressed people, revealing himself to them, not to all, liberating them, not everyone. He then qualifies this partiality as God's self-revelation.[41] This way of reasoning shuts out everyone else—particularly, the rich and perceived oppressor—from the love of God; and this is contrary to the nature of God. But the point we are making is that while God's liberation of an oppressed people may well be his manifestation of his justice to the oppressor, it may at the same time likewise be an invitation to repentance, for God's saving grace is open to all. What further confounds the problem in such a reading is that poverty is often limited to material poverty or physical/economic dispossession. Poverty of spirit—detachment and the rightful use of one's wealth—doesn't seem to count much. For as Sobrino argues, the mere co-existence of the rich and poor is insulting and intolerable. There is no room for honestly gotten wealth.[42] More disturbing is the fact that the materially rich, regardless of how they got their wealth, almost have no means of redemption: they are shut out of God's saving grace.

I think Gutierrez makes a more nuanced argument than Sobrino. According to Gutierrez, as Christians who believe in the God of Jesus Christ, we must prefer the poor, but at the same time we cannot say the non-poor are not relevant to us. This would not be a Christian attitude.[43]

The above nuances notwithstanding, Ratzinger offers a general criticism of liberation theologies' neglect or repudiation of evangelical poverty and its transformation of the fight for the rights of the poor into a class struggle.[44] One wonders what this critique by Ratzinger might mean for a stance such as Gerald West's. In discussing the perception of God in his 1985 article, "African Theologies of Liberation," West notes that the central problem in Third World countries is not atheism but "an idolatrous submission to systems of oppression" and the central question posed to any faith tradition is whether and to what extent that tradition deifies the ideologies used to sacralize structures of oppression.[45] There is most certainly a need here for a healthy mean between the danger perceived by West and that which Ratzinger warns of; in other words, between the "the sacralization of oppression" and "the secularization of religion." One way out could be to ensure that the faith tradition itself does not become a site of struggle between the oppressor and the oppressed,[46] but the very criterion by which to adjudicate right social order, lest we run the risk of falling into the ideological conundrums of a Marxist social analysis.

Lastly, in the light of Christ's poverty—self-emptying on the cross—Ratzinger further criticizes some liberation theologies' exclusively political interpretation of Christ's death which robs it of its value for salvation and the whole economy of redemption.[47]

What then is left of Liberation Theology? Any way forward?

The above-discussed potential dangers of liberation theology are in no way to stigmatize the latter nor to perpetrate a stigmatized "single story" of liberation theology. Rather, these only help us to now articulate what would be the authentic principles of liberation that serve as corrective to the above misconstrual. The basic question driving these liberation theologies, one could say, is precisely that of making sense of the gospel message in their different contexts of poverty or suffering. If Jesus fails to speak to these different situations, then he certainly would not be the Jesus of Scripture. For example, speaking from an African-American liberationist perspective, the Protestant theologian James Cone makes a legitimate case in this regard. He avows that liberation theology is all about an exegetical, prophetic, and keen reading of Scripture and tradition in response to the concrete socio-political condition of the oppressed Black Americans.[48]

If these contextual questions are legitimate and make a claim on our honest attention, then, while noting the above-mentioned dangers, we must likewise take cognizance of the value of liberation theology or at least the direction to which it turns our gaze—"recovering the truths therein," as Ratzinger puts it. To this effect I discuss below *five pillars or leitmotifs of authentic liberation theology*. We can already note here that the vision of justice, peace, and reconciliation of *Africae Munus* challenges the above-mentioned dangers and offers us the raw material, so to speak, for building an authentic liberation theology hinged on these five pillars. For instance, *Africae Munus* affirms the following: that the mission of the Church is not political in nature (no. 23); that the kingdom of God is the basis for working for reconciliation, justice, and peace (no. 26); that the Church is invited to prophetic action in the face of injustice, wars, conflicts, racism, and xenophobia (nn. 12, 15); that the transforming principle of society is Christ and the Holy Spirit and not some "scientific analysis" (nn. 12, 17–18, 23); and more generally, primacy is given to the spiritual as opposed to the social, and it is the kingdom of God which orients the social order and not the other way round.

Notice how these points could form a safeguard against the above-mentioned dangers to which a Marxist-inspired liberation theology is susceptible; and how they accord with the Ratzingerian prism with which we seek to understand liberation. Pragmatically, we could define this "liberation" as follows: A holistic and total freedom, including, in the first place, spiritual deliverance from sin, but also deliverance from the social consequences or effects of sin in the social, economic, political, and cosmological dimensions.

Let us attempt an analysis of this concept of liberation under the said five pillars:

II. Recasting the Concept of "Liberation": Five Pillars or Motifs of Liberation Theology in the Light of *Africae Munus*

II.i. Overcoming the "Political–Spiritual" Dualism: An Integrative Dynamism

A fundamental presupposition in articulating an authentic theology of liberation is the *creative overcoming* of dualisms, particularly, the "political–spiritual" dualism. The root of this dualism was already present in the fifteenth and sixteenth century grace–nature debates, resulting in no small measure from Cajetan's (1469–1534) "mis-interpretation" of Thomas Aquinas on the said question. Spurred by an otherwise well-meaning desire to preserve the gratuity of grace, Cajetan introduced the category of *pure nature*, as opposed to "graced nature."[49] Arguably, the genealogy of many sheds of dualism—be it the natural and supernatural, or spiritual and the profane, Church and world, temporal and eschatological, or the political and spiritual dualisms—date back to the era proceeding from the birth of Cajetan's pure nature. In fact, the legitimacy of Henri de Lubac's *Mystery of the Supernatural* is could be aptly articulated in terms of its momentous effort to address that fundamental dualism which had completely separated the supernatural from the natural. And as Gutierrez observes, there had grown therefrom a "distrust of the world and an ecclesio-centrism."[50]

Attempting at recasting an authentic vision of liberation theology, we certainly are engaged in the process of overcoming these tempting dualisms in preference for both the "non-linear continuity" and "non-severing discontinuity" between these pairs of categories. In other words, liberation theology properly construed neither adopts the view that collapses the distinction between the political and the spiritual nor that which completely separates them and keeps them apart. It seeks the middle ground. It is within such a middle course—an integrative dynamism—that one can make sense of the claim that the kingdom of God or the divine reign of God impacts and shapes the social and political realm without at the same time being collapsed into the latter. It is such an integral view that it is found in the affirmations of *Africae Munus* as regards the mission of the Church, namely, that the Church's mission is neither political nor apolitical. The text reads,

> Through her Justice and Peace Commissions, the Church is engaged in the civic formation of citizens and in assisting with the electoral process in a number of countries. . . . It is worth repeating that while a distinction must be made between the role of pastors and that of the lay faithful, the Church's mission is not political in nature. The Church wishes to be the sign and safeguard of the human person's transcendence.[51]

Creatively integrated here are the following dimensions or categories: the political and the spiritual, the temporal and transcendent, the Church and the world. By overcoming a Boff-style competitive ecclesiology and any such "Church–world" dualism, this text offers us an impetus for a theological liberationist reading of *Africae Munus*. While not becoming political by nature, the Church in Africa was being invited to engage the *polis* and its politics as it reflects on the theme of reconciliation, justice, and peace. This reflection ought to bring her "face to face with her "theological and social responsibility" and her "public role and place" in Africa today."[52] This shuns the danger of passivity.

The Church is called to a praxis motivated by the word of God. "Authentic hearing," the synod fathers note, "is obeying and acting."[53] This praxis is variably defined throughout the document, for example, as bringing the message of the Gospel to the heart of the African societies (no. 15); as responding to the challenges of war, conflicts, racism, and xenophobia (no. 12). Furthermore, the document exhorts that, "Acting in concert with all other components of civil society, the Church must speak out against the unjust order that prevents the peoples of Africa from consolidating their economies and 'developing according to their cultural characteristics.'"[54] It is thus that she fulfills her mission as "salt of the earth" and "light of the world."[55] It is worth noting that these coincide with the genuine aspirations, goals, and motif of any authentic liberation theology. Hence, we find here an impetus for a liberationist reading of *Africae Munus*.

II.ii. Extension of the Kingdom of God in History

Without reducing Christianity in the Middle Ages to this limitation, Ratzinger locates within this period the danger of reducing Christianity to an individualistic other-worldliness, born from an overly anxious view of the *Dies irae*. This anxiety made the urgent question become that of personal salvation and the "last things." *Sed contra*, Ratzinger delineates the task of modern Eschatology as, "to marry perspectives, so that person and community, present and future, are seen in their unity."[56] It is on this sort of reading of eschatology and salvation that we build an authentic liberation theology. Herein shines forth the necessary extension of the kingdom of God into the temporal, that is, the marrying of the present and the future, such that the eschatological hope of the consummation of the reign of God has implications for the present moment. Granting this, the ultimate liberation from sin, constitutive of the eschatological hope, affects both the personal and social, present and future dimensions of human existence. Consequently, Gutierrez is most certainly in good company in affirming that liberation is ultimately about the communion of man with God and with his fellow man, which happens in history but is oriented by the eschatological hope of the Kingdom of God.[57]

Commenting on this permeation of the social or historical dimension of human existence with the gospel message, *Africae Munus* proposes genuine conversion or *metanoia*, as a necessary means. It is to such conversion that Christ constantly calls the Christian, who, attentive to the "school of the heart" in the sacrament of Reconciliation, gradually forges an adult Christian life that is attentive to the moral and spiritual dimensions of his actions, and thus becomes capable of "confronting the difficulties of social, political, economic and cultural life."[58] A practical example the document offers is the "liberation of women following the example of Christ's own esteem for them" in a culture that is slow in appreciating the equal dignity of man and woman.[59] Therefore, where sincere conversion brings about the virtues of love, justice, and peace, there already is the inauguration of the kingdom of God as present-but-not-yet-realized, in accord with the programmatic proclamation of Jesus in Mark 1:15, "The kingdom of God has come near. Repent and believe the good news!" We shall return to this theme in greater detail.

II.iii. Christocentrism and Christ's Radical Identification with the Poor and Oppressed

The following words of Pope Saint John Paul II during the homily at his inaugural Mass are significant here: "Do not be afraid. Open, I say open wide the doors for Christ. To his saving power open the boundaries of states, economic and political systems, the vast fields of culture, civilization, and development. Do not be afraid. Christ knows 'that which is in man.' He alone knows it."[60] For our context, the implicit message in these words is the truth that true liberation is the work of Christ to which he calls the Church to participate. It is Christ who liberates from sin and its effect. It is he who is the Kingdom of God personified; it is in him that all our sufferings, frustrations, cares, and anxieties are resolved. He alone offers us rest. This is the truth the Pontiff presupposes when he invites all to submit all facets of human life to the reign of Christ the King. It is this same Christocentric motif we find in *Africae Munus* which locates "Christ at the heart of African life [as] the source of reconciliation, justice, and peace."[61] The very arrangement of the document, especially part one, chapter one, reveals the following inner logic: It is Christ who makes us just in order that we might live in justice and build a just society, and living justly constitutes the promotion of his kingdom among men.[62] The point here, therefore, is that genuine liberation ought to be Christocentric.

Affirming the above-stated principle, Gutierrez speaks of a Christo-finalized history. Liberation, he maintains, is the work of Christ. "The work of Christ is a new creation . . . [it is] simultaneously a liberation from sin and from all its consequences: despoliation, injustice, hatred. . . . Creation and salvation therefore have, in the first place, a Christological sense: all things have been created in Christ, all things have been saved in him (cf. Col. 1:15–20)."[63] Nuancing such Christo-centrism, Ratzinger writes, "Jesus is opposed to any form of righteousness, whether political or ethical, that tries to achieve the Kingdom of God by its own volition. He contrasts such self-made righteousness with a redemption which is pure gift. . . . However, we must also maintain that the Kingdom of God does find expression in ethical categories.[64] Similarly, in *Spe Salvi*, he avows, "Certainly we cannot 'build' the Kingdom of God by our own efforts—what we build will always be the kingdom of man with all the limitations proper to our human nature. The Kingdom of God is a gift, and precisely because of this, it is great and beautiful, and constitutes the response to our hope."[65] This affirmation of *Spe Salvi* is reformulated years later in *Africae Munus*, as follows: "purification and inner development towards true humanity cannot exist without God."[66] While furthering the above critique of the dangers of a political utopia and the establishment of an earthly kingdom, the call here is for an integration of God's gratuity and human effort without conflation or separating of the two in a false synergism. Should this point be taken seriously, the result is an understanding of the Kingdom of God which finds concrete expression in history without becoming reducible to it or connatural with it.

Another aspect of the necessary Christocentric turn in any genuine theology of liberation is the definition of "concern for the poor" in terms of Christ's radical identification with the poor and oppressed. Having purged Sobrino's description of the poor of any reductionism, it offers us a beautiful interpretation of the last judgment scene in Matthew 25:31–46. Herein, Jesus identifies himself most intimately with the poor and needy, saying, "Whatever you did for one of the least of these brothers and sisters of mine, you did for me." In Sobrino's reading, by that very identification, the poor become Christ's very body. In other words, Jesus is saying that the place we meet God is in the poor.[67] Our argument, therefore, is that it is such a vision of the poor and not a humanist or Marxist analysis that ought to be the basis of genuine liberation theology.

II.iv. Historicity and the Eschatologization of Biblical Promises of Liberation

Following in the cue of the Latin American liberation theologians, James Cone identifies biblical models and warrants for liberation theology such as the exodus, the Incarnation, Jesus's agenda in Luke 4:18, and the prophetic promises of liberation. Through a liberationist reading of the prophets (especially Amos, Hosea, Micah, Isaiah, and Jeremiah) and other texts such as the Psalms and Proverbs, Cone discusses the urgency of justice on behalf of the poor and weak, and Yahweh's commitment to the latter.[68]

With respect to the exodus model, Cone argues for black people's hope and belief that as God delivered Moses and the Israelites from Egyptian bondage, so too will he deliver them from slavery in North America.[69] The incarnational model hinges on God deigning to be with us in our wretchedness, taking on our condition of oppression and slavery as his own.[70] Also, for Cone, Jesus' agenda in Luke 4:18—"to set at liberty those who are oppressed"—includes black Americans, and hence has consequences for black theology.[71]

All these biblical models testify to God's benevolent intervention in history, in the historical process of a given people. In a sense, creation and history are the foreground of liberation. Thus, one can legitimately talk of the historicity of the biblical promises of liberation. Paul's affirmation that "God was in Christ reconciling the world to himself" (2 Corinthians 5:19) grounds God's activity of reconciliation in the concrete reality of the cosmos. However, God's intervention in a people's historical, social, economic, and political life—such as in the exodus—is always in view of a transcendental purpose, that they may become God's own people through whom salvation will reach the ends of the earth, and all peoples would be called to eschatological hope. Here, we see yet another integrative dynamism that holds in creative tension the "historicity of biblical promises" and the "eschatologization" of the same.[72] Accordingly, the CDF instructs that an authentic interpretation of the exodus event must not lose sight of these two dynamics to the event. It criticizes a reduction of the exodus to a political liberation while at the same time affirming its true historicity and political dimension.[73]

II.v. Jesus' Prophetic Action and the Existential Claim of the Gospel

Jesus is the prophet par excellence who proclaims the truth of God, the Good News of the nearness of the Kingdom of God, and calls all peoples to conversion. This prophetic mission of Jesus is of necessity existential in character, precisely in that it affects the here and now, it challenges our way of life and orients us toward its fulfillment. Benedict XVI captures this most eloquently in his very first papal encyclical, saying, "Being Christian is not the result of an ethical choice or a lofty idea, but the encounter with an event, a person, which gives life a new horizon and a decisive direction."[74] As he explains further, referencing John's gospel, this "decisive direction" gets identified with the call to eternal life—"God so loved the world that he gave his only Son, that whoever believes in him should have eternal life." (John3:16).[75]

The existential claim of the gospel message cast in the light of prophetic praxis is by far the most adopted theological category among liberation theologians (especially of Latin American extraction or orientation). For instance, in chapter six of *Jesus the Liberator,* Sobrino uses the term *"praxis"* to delineate Jesus' debates and encounters with the political, religious, and social power structures of his day—Scribes, Pharisees, the rich, the priests, and rulers—denouncing and unmasking their idolatry coded in vanity, hypocrisy, and oppression of the poor. The poor for Sobrino are the privileged addressees of the Kingdom of God.[76] Sobrino distinguishes—formally rather than substantively—between Jesus' "Messianic signs" announcing God's kingdom and these "prophetic praxes" which denounce the "anti-Kingdom."[77] By anti-kingdom he means the social and religious rules and practices by the "power structure" which dictate a vision of God contrary to the true vision of God proclaimed by Jesus. Accordingly, then, for Sobrino, unlike the legalistic, hypocritical, and oppressive Jewish interpretation of the law and manipulation of religion for selfish gains, Jesus' God is a God of life who liberates, who prefers mercy to sacrifice, for whom true service and worship not merely *can be* but must *necessarily* be service of humankind.[78]

While agreeing with Sobrino's interpretation of Jesus' mission as both proclamation of the kingdom of God and refutation of the anti-kingdom, I find his distinction between Jesus' "Messianic signs" and "prophetic praxes" rather artificial and unnecessary. In my opinion, it creates an unnecessary dualism in Jesus' saving activity. The whole person of Jesus is one prophetic and Messianic sign, whether in his announcing of the Kingdom of God or in his denouncing of the anti-kingdom. Viewing it this way precludes the danger of slipping into a separation between the "Jesus of faith" (the Messiah, Christ) and the "Jesus of history" (the prophet who challenges the social order). Jesus' criticism of the social order and the religious and political powers of his day was precisely because he was the Christ announcing the kingdom of God. Liberation theology, properly construed, therefore, cannot and should not separate both actions; for if that happens, then, it runs the risk of caricaturing Jesus Christ into a social or political revolutionist. Rather, as already intimated, Jesus' engagement with the polis was only as far as it was the arena within which the kingdom of God was inaugurated in history. Today, it is this kingdom that ought to define and orient the social order, and not the other way round.

In the spirit of *Africae Munus* paragraph 17, this understanding of the Kingdom–world relationship does not admit of passivity in the face of social injustice but has existential implications. Even Jesus' very example is instructive here: Jesus was truly prophet and Messiah, but never a political Messiah, yet he was a Messiah whose prophetic teachings and message challenged religious and political systems built on injustice. Jesus was no political revolutionary as many wanted him to be, yet he set ablaze upon the earth the revolution of love, a love capable of "creating a just order in the spirit of the beatitudes."[79] Standing before Pilate, Jesus declared that his kingdom was not of this world, yet this world (all of creation) is the stage within which the kingdom of God unfolds in time, maturing toward its perfection in the eschaton. Similarly, the synod fathers professed that while God's justice revealed to us in the beatitudes will be perfected in the kingdom of God at the eschaton, "God's justice is already manifest here and now, wherever the poor are consoled and admitted to the banquet of life."[80]

From these discussions on the five pillars of an authentic liberation theology, what stands out as a uniting category is the "inaugurated kingdom of God," extending into history but transcending it at the same time. The transcendent dimension defines, transforms, and orients history toward its eschatological *telos.* This is the only meaningful liberationist reading of scripture and the kingdom of God vis-à-vis history and the social order in which the kingdom does not become an earthly, immanentist, or a political one. In what follows we expatiate on this category of the "inaugurated kingdom (eschatology)" and how it provides a fitting theological locus for the articulation of an authentic theology of liberation.

III. Proposing "Inaugurated Eschatology" as the Theological Locus for an Authentic Liberation Theology

For the synod fathers, the beatitudes provide the blueprint for creating a just social order which accords with the mind of Christ and divine justice. They form the link between the human/earthly and divine planes in a certain sense. The beatitudes are how earth gets modeled on heaven and leans toward its perfection in the eschatological fulfillment in beatific life. For this reason, the synod fathers talk of "Creating a just order in the spirit of the Beatitudes."[81] They note,

> The disciple of Christ, in union with his Master, must help to create a just society where all will be able to participate actively, using their particular talents, in social and economic life . . . Christ does not propose a revolution of a social or political kind, but a revolution of love, brought about by his complete self-giving through his death on the Cross and his resurrection. The Beatitudes are built upon this revolution of love (cf. Matthew5:3–10). They provide a new horizon of justice, **inaugurated** in the paschal mystery, through which we can become just and can build a better world. God's justice, revealed to us in the Beatitudes, raises the lowly and humbles those who exalt themselves. It will be perfected, it is true, in the kingdom of God which is to be fully realized at the end of time. But God's justice is

> already manifest here and now, wherever the poor are consoled and admitted to the banquet of life.[82]

Beautifully held in tension here is the present-and-not-yet-realized reality of the Kingdom of God. More recently, the Theologian John Thiel has rightly observed that both New Testament exegesis and theological speculations in the last century are agreed that the most appropriate Christian understanding of salvation takes the form of "inaugurated eschatology."[83] Cyril O'Regan is one of those who support this theological reading of eschatology after the fashion of Ratzinger. Thiel meticulously situates "inaugurated eschatology" as a response against Charles H. Dodd's "realized" or "this-worldly" eschatology.[84] Dodd is not a liberation theologian, yet he espouses a view that has often been cited as the characteristic limitation of some Liberation Theologies. Within the framework of a "this-worldly" eschatology, the kingdom of God is presented as an earthly reality with no eschatological "more."

In an email correspondence with Matthew Levering, he characterized this lack of an eschatological "more" in some liberation theologies as an "immanentism" that focuses on earthly politics, which can in turn weaken a congregation's interest in the actual teaching and work of Jesus. What is evident thus far is that in a liberation theology devoid of the eschatological "more," the kingdom of God would coincide with a "good earthly political-economic structure," which would be realizable even in a thoroughly secularized state, and at times by purely human efforts (political utopia). This is far from what *Africae Munus* is proposing. As already mentioned, the eschatological vision of *Africae Munus* is that of an "inaugurated eschatology." A further look into the document strengthens this claim. The document admonishes the African bishops against a politicization of their ministry and an absolutization of African culture spurred by the illusion that human efforts alone can bring the kingdom of eternal happiness to earth.[85] While recognizing the mutual co-existing or inter-penetrating nature of the two realms, they must nonetheless not be thought of as co-extensive. À la Moltmann, there is a decidedly *novum ultimum*, a quintessential "more" to the yet-to-be-realized eschatological realm.[86] This *novum* does not issue from the history of the old; but at the same time, what is eschatologically new itself creates its own continuity with the old, since the latter is not annihilated.[87]

Put differently, inaugurated eschatology espouses the view that eternal life, and consequently the kingdom of God, "has been 'inaugurated' through God's raising of Jesus, an event that begins the graceful gift of salvation already in history. That gift, however, continues to be unwrapped and appreciated anew in all the moments of history as the power of the resurrected life wins its victory in time over the powers of sin and death."[88] Of particular relevance here is the progressive expansion of the Kingdom of God, like the yeast that silently mixes throughout the dough, causing it to rise.[89] This "rising" of the kingdom of God in history is exemplified in the "victory in time over the powers of sin and death."[90] This is the transforming effect the disciple of Christ is called to have on the historical process, permeating it with the gift of Christ's word and grace. In so doing, he truly becomes "salt to the earth" and "light of the world" (Matt. 5:13,14), which is the urgent vocation addressed to the African Church by *Africae Munus*.[91] Fulfilling this vocation means becoming a part of the transforming effect of the Kingdom of God which, as Sobrino asserts, is the "ultimate reality" which not only relativizes but also critiques the social order.[92] In the end, this means taking a path of conversion and repentance, enabled by the gift of grace.[93]

Concretely, *Africae Munus* recognizes the co-extensiveness of her mission as evangelizer and promoter of God's Kingdom through the call to conversion and repentance, on the one hand, and her mission of working for a more just, humane, and equitable community of brothers and sisters, on the other hand.[94] Paragraphs 81–83 detail how the Church's mission relates to the "the good governance of states" within the social, cultural, and political realms. At an even broader level, the 1971 World Synod of Catholic Bishops affirmed the co-extensiveness of the Church's mission and preaching of the gospel with action on behalf of justice and participation in the transformation of the world,[95] even as *Gaudium et Spes* speaks of the earthly and heavenly cities existing together and interpenetrating each other.[96] It is needless to add how the aspirations of authentic theologies of liberation closely resemble this. But the argument we are making here is that it is precisely this vision of an "inaugurated eschatology" that warrants the Christian's engagement with the temporal order. For the *telos* of the Church's mission is the very accomplishment of the Kingdom of God and the salvation of humanity in and through Jesus Christ, who is in his person "the goal of human history, the focal point of the longings of history and of civilization."[97] The consummation of history in Christ constitutes the eschatological hope that orients and propels history itself, and of course all human aspirations for a better social order. This is the Christian hope, an active hope which keeps the world open to God.[98]

Therefore, the human aspiration for a just society constitutes a horizontal hope which finds grounding only in a vertical hope, which, if not taken seriously, the historical struggle for liberation becomes unsustainable. It makes sense then to support Cone's insightful argument that Black Theology, while taking history with utmost seriousness, ought not to and does not limit liberation to history.[99] Liberation, as we have argued all along, must be moved away from a historical immanentist view and away from a political utopia. Liberation is not simply what oppressed people can accomplish alone; it is basically what God has done and will accomplish both in and beyond history.[100] Such a view of liberation at last takes seriously the cross and resurrection of Christ as those mysterious events with ultimate liberative power *in* and *beyond* history, the very events which create the new space of hopeful existence within which a horizontal hope of liberation is made possible.

At this point, it is fitting to end our analysis with a particularly African appropriation of such an authentic liberation theology being proposed here.

IV. Lament: A Model of Liberation Theology for Africa

A place to go for a detailed bibliography on African liberation theologies is Gerald West's "Africa's Liberation Theologies: An Historical-Hermeneutical Analysis."[101] The said author identifies four main strands of African liberation theologies. The earliest form emerged alongside missionary and colonial incursions into Africa. The main thrust here was a push back against European denigration of African religion and culture, the seizure of African lands and resources, and the Europeanization of Christianity. It was modeled as inculturation liberation theology, or simply African theology.[102] The second form, common to southern Africa, including Tanzania and South Africa in particular, is Black theology, or simply liberation theology (following the Latin American designation) where the emphasis is on the political and economic (and racial, in the case of South Africa) dimensions of the struggle against varying forms of colonialism. The third strand is African feminist theology, growing out of both African theology and Black theology. The fourth form focuses on matters of identity and empire.[103] In both the third and fourth strands of African liberation theologies, we still find the deployment of social analysis and social sciences in ways that we have critiqued above.

In what follows, I am proposing the category of *Lament* as a fitting expression of an authentic liberation theology within the African context, integrating the five pillars of liberation discussed above. The prevalence of suffering and oppression on the one hand, and on the other hand, a real human helplessness in the face of that suffering, legitimizes the African's near-natural disposition to lament before God. Lament as a model of liberation is grounded in a *theocentric* spirituality prior to any conceptualization.[104] For the incurably religious African, to use the words of John Mbiti, God is a given. Paraphrasing the words of The Ecumenical Association of Third World Theologians (EATWOT), we could therefore say that "The question about God in the world of the oppressed African is not knowing whether God exists or not, but knowing on which side God is."[105] In the face of her oppression, the African laments to the God he believes in, loves, and trusts as a helper close at hand. This belief is expressed in song, prayer, and a general attitude of worship. Take for example the following lyrics of the worship song, "You say you will carry my load" by the Liberian Gospel artist, Kanvee Adams:

> You say, you will carry my load . . . Now I am in your presence. I will never let you go unless you bless me . . . That is why I am in your presence . . . My help comes from the Lord who made heaven and earth . . . As long as it is God who shares, every man must have his own portion . . . They that wait on the Lord shall renew their strength . . . I will wait daddy until you give me my own portion . . . My God will arise, and you will see me lifted so high.[106]

This song is an expression of confidence in God to act on behalf of the oppressed, something common in the African imagination. It is indeed a prevalent spiritual disposition. It is this disposition that grounds the subsequent conceptualization of a theology of lament which we propose as an authentic African expression of liberation theology.

Bearing in mind *Ecclesia in Africa's* likening of Africa to the victim of robbers, left to die by the roadside (cf. Lk 10:25–37),[107] let us use the gruesome example of the ongoing war in Cameroon with origins in the country's French and British colonial past. As of 2019, over 260 villages had been burnt, over a million people had either fled the country as refugees or were internally displaced; and it isn't over yet.[108] The carnage is unspeakable. Some have helplessly watched their elderly and ailing grandparents and relations burnt to death in their homes as they were unable to escape the raids. On February 14, 2020, government forces and armed ethnic Fulani killed about 21 unarmed civilians in the village of Ngarbuh, including 13 children and 1 pregnant woman.[109] On October 24, 2020, a similar atrocious act was repeated in the city of Kumba, killing six school children in class and wounding six others. More recently, on October 14, 2021, a gendarme killed a five-year old girl, Enondiale T. Carolaise, in the city of Buea. What can helpless Christians do before such evil, injustice, and wickedness. What can the Church do? Should she "take up arms?" No! She can't! She believes in the sacredness of life! Her weapon is her lament! This applies to whatever form of oppression in the African continent at large.

Inspired by Emmanuel Katongole's *Born from Lament,* I must say that Africa's hope is in her lament. She must never stop lamenting, for not to lament is a sign of death. But as long as she laments, then, there is hope that someone, above all, her God, will hear her someday. Lament is like wrestling with God—"Why, Lord, do you stand far off? Why do you hide yourself in times of trouble?" (Psalm 10:1). Such lament births a renewal of the hope that deliverance and help come from God. Thus, lament becomes a theological practice of engaging God from within the midst of political, social, or economic ruins.[110] It is precisely in this sense that we must understand *Africae Munus'* description of the Church as sentinel. Her task as sentinel is twofold. Firstly, she must make the voice of Christ heard. Secondly, like the *narrator* in the Book of Lamentations,[111] "for the sake of Christ and in fidelity to the lesson of life which he taught us," she must "be present wherever human suffering exists and to make heard the silent cry of the innocent who suffer persecution, or of peoples whose governments mortgage the present and the future for personal interests."[112] Thus, the Church helps, "slowly but surely to forge a new Africa."[113]

Injustice and suffering are the result of the brokenness of creation, and God took upon himself in Christ this brokenness so that he might redeem all of creation. Therefore, to lament is to enter into the mystery of Christ within which we are transformed. And since it is God alone who can deliver creation from its brokenness, it makes sense, then, that in the African worldview of lament and liberation, God should be the principal addressee and not some political power. The latter is addressed only secondarily. This theocentrism is evident in what Katongole calls the "the contours of lament," that is, the inner structure or logic of lament deducible from an analysis of the plaintive Psalms. There are five characteristic features here: Address to Yahweh; complaint (description of the problem); request (asking for God's intervention); motivation (appealing to God's righteousness, mercy or promises); and confidence or praise (confession of trust in God's help).[114] This theocentric attitude evades Ratzinger's criticism of a political messianism, which thrives "on the false hopes that political powers or systems could satisfy the deepest longings of the human person, whereas in fact, God alone can."[115]

Lament as a category of liberation, therefore, brings together the two interpenetrating realities of the kingdom of God: the present and future. The "future hope" of liberation by God, in history and beyond history, is that which sustains lament. Lament is rooted in faith in God's transcendence and in his power and willingness to intervene on behalf of the oppressed. It does not end up being passive, rather, it is prophetic and practical. Lament is prophetic in its ceaseless condemnation of evil and all forms of oppression against which it is directed. It is practical in its engagement with the concrete reality of a people's lives in an attempt to forge a better social order. Lament identifies with the poor and marginalized, even as God would, and challenges the systems and powers responsible for their oppression. It does all these with the confidence that liberation is possible not on account of the "hardened hearts" of the political systems but on account of God, who, even though desiring the conversion of the oppressor, nevertheless always delivers the poor and oppressed from the hard-hearted Pharaoh. Such a vision of liberation radically redefines social action or advocacy. The latter ceases to be an optional human endeavor, becoming an obligation of divine origin, a call to participate in making the world a place where God's reign extends. This never includes the path of violence. In fact, in the very logic of Christ's lament, violence has no place—it was Christ who stopped the unfolding of violence. He absorbed all and refused to give it back. In return he gave out love—"Father, forgive them for they do not know what they are doing" (Lk

23:34). This seems utter weakness and foolishness, but it is the power of God to save the world (1 Corinthians 1:18).

In much the same way as Cone distances Black theology of liberation and its discourse on the poor and oppressed (enslaved blacks in North America) from a Marxist analysis, so too does an alternative African theology of liberation modeled on lament distance itself from such analysis.

Conclusion

In summary, this essay has attempted to demonstrate that liberation theology, properly understood, is about a moral order that is shaped and defined by a concrete and realistic hope of the "more than historical," but a hope which nonetheless breaks into history, transforms it, and orients it toward the eschatological. It is as von Balthasar notes, that Christian hope, theological hope, goes beyond this world, but it does not pass it by. Rather, it takes the world with it on its way to God, who has graciously prepared a dwelling in himself for us and for the world. This implies that the Christian in the world is meant to awaken hope, particularly among the most helpless; and this in turn means that he must create such humane conditions that will actually allow the poor and oppressed to have hope.[116]

If we are correct thus far, Christianity is not the lonely path of avoiding sin, or of a calculative observance of the law in view of a future reward. No! It is the joyful fellowship of brothers and sisters sharing everything in common, breaking bread and enjoying the fellowship of Christ in the Holy Spirit (Acts 2:42). This certainly is not an entirely "other-worldly" reality but precisely a "this-worldly" community that is constituted in view of its consummation in the eschatological reality of God's kingdom. In this reading, the words of St. James are even more meaningful, "Faith without works is dead" (James 2:7). But we must immediately add, that while faith without works is dead, works without faith are nothing but a mere self-serving humanistic optimism.

Lastly, in the face of the attendant dangers sometimes associated with "liberation theology," one wonders if this necessitates a new terminology to depict what we have attempted in this paper to describe as an authentic or alternative liberation theology. And if that be the case, what name would that be? Ratzinger's usage of two slightly different appellations for the subject matter leaves a careful reader curious. It would seem that when he critiques the subject, he titles it, "Liberation Theology" as in his public article prior to the CDF *Instructions*, while calling it "Theologies of Liberation" when he delineates the contours of liberation properly understood, such as in the CDF *Instructions*. While his intention might not be clear solely from these texts, this at least leaves open the question of name for the subject matter.

Until we can find an alternative terminology—if necessary—I propose a more generous reading and engagement with liberation theology or theology of liberation as a means of achieving the above-stated Ratzingerian project of "recovery," which we have attempted thus far.

Chapter 10 Endnotes

1 Ten years after, while there has been registered progress in the implementation of *Africae Munus*, the situation of reconciliation, justice, and peace in Africa still leaves much to be desired. Africa still suffers enormously from hunger, disease, war, neo-colonialism, and other forms of injustice. There are at least 15 countries with active armed conflicts in sub-Saharan Africa (as of 2019): Burkina Faso, Burundi, Cameroon, the Central African Republic (CAR), Chad, the Democratic Republic of the Congo (DRC), Ethiopia, Kenya, Mali, Mozambique, Niger, Nigeria, Somalia, South Sudan, and Sudan. The conflict dynamics, and ethnic and religious tensions, are often rooted in a combination of state weakness, corruption, ineffective delivery of basic services, competition over natural resources, inequality and a sense of marginalization. cf. Stockholm International Peace Research Institute (SIPRI), "Armed Conflict and Peace Processes in Sub-Saharan Africa | SIPRI," accessed December 2, 2021, https://www.sipri.org/yearbook/2020/07.

2 Benedict XVI, *Africae Munus: Post-Synodal Apostolic Exhortation on the Church in Africa in Service to Reconciliation, Justice and Peace* (Benin:

Libreria Editrice Vaticana, 2011), https://www.vatican.va/content/benedict-xvi/en/apost_exhortations/documents/hf_ben-xvi_exh_20111119_africae-munus.html.

3 For a feel of how uncritical some of these assertions regarding Ratzinger's rapport with liberation theology are, see Nikolas Kozloff's popular-styled article, "The Pope's Holy War Against Liberation Theology," in *Nacla* (April 30, 2008). https://nacla.org/news/popes-holy-war-against-liberation-theology. Retrieved on June 11, 2022.

4 Joseph Ratzinger, "Liberation Theology," in *Catholicism in Crisis* (September 1984): 367 – 374. Citing 367. A different translation is available in *The Ratzinger Report: An Exclusive Interview on the State of the Church* (San Francisco: Ignatius Press, 1985), pp. 174–186.

5 Cf. Ibid., 367. Emphases are mine.

6 Cf. Ibid., 368.

7 Cf. Ibid., 367, 369, 374.

8 Cf. Ibid., 374.

9 Cf. Ibid., 368. Here, he directly critiques the efforts and claims of liberation theologian, Hugo Assman, a former Catholic priest who (at the time of his writing) was teaching as a Protestant in a Protestant department of theology while continuing to claim that he is beyond confessional boundaries.

10 Cf. Ibid., 368.

11 Cf. Ibid. Unfortunately, Ratzinger does not reference the Gutierrez text he is quoting from.

12 Ratzinger, "Liberation Theology," 368.

13 Published on August 6, 1984.

14 Published on Nov. 26, 2016.

15 CDF, "Instruction on Certain Aspects of the 'Theology of Liberation,'" August 6, 1984, https://www.vatican.va/roman_curia/congregations/cfaith/documents/rc_con_cfaith_doc_19840806_theolo gy-liberation_en.html. Quoting here from the Introduction. Cf. Section X, no. 7; Section IV, no. 12.

16 *Africae Munus*, no. 10. The Pontiff quotes here from his 2009 address to the Roman Curia. Cf. Benedict XVI, Address to the Roman Curia (21 December 2009): AAS 102 (2010), 35.

17 CDF, *Instruction on Certain Aspects of the "Theology of Liberation,"* introduction.

18 Cf. CDF, *Instruction on Certain Aspects of the "Theology of Liberation,"* Section VII.

19 Cf. Ibid., Sec. VII, nn. 1–3.

20 Cf. Ibid., Sec. VII, nn. 4–5, 7.

21 Cf. Ibid., Sec. VII, nn. 1–3.

22 Cf. Ibid., Sec. VIII, no. 4.
23 Cf. Ibid., Sec.VIII, nn. 7, 8.
24 Cf. Leonardo Boff, *Church, Charism and Power: Liberation Theology and the Institutional Church*, trans. John W. Diercksmeier (Eugene, Oregon: Wipf & Stock, 2011). Originally published in 1981.
25 Cf. Leonardo Boff, *Church: Charism and Power,* chapter 8. See pages 62–63, 116–117,
26 In his analysis of the "new Church" on pages 120–122 the Eucharist is conspicuously missing. Rather, what takes central place and makes for *unity* is the "mission of liberation."
27 Benedict XVI, *Spe Salvi,* no. 21.
28 Cf. Leonardo Boff, *Church: Charism and Power,* 123.
39 Cf. CDF, Instruction on Certain Aspects of the "Theology of Liberation," Sec. IX, no. 10.
30 Cf. Ibid., Sec. IX, no. 6.
31 Cf. Ibid.
32 Cf. Joseph Ratzinger, *Eschatology: Death and Eternal Life,* trans. Michael Waldstein, ed. Aidan Nichols (Washington, D.C.: The Catholic University of America Press, 1988), 13.
33 The Reformed Theologian, Jürgen Moltmann may be wrong in many respects, but he aptly articulates the *novum,* the novelty which the advent of the kingdom of God brings about. It is not simply a transformation of the present (old) but the advent of a radically new (future), which only God can bring about. Cf. Jürgen Moltmann, *The Coming of God: Christian Eschatology,* trans. Margaret Kohl (Minneapolis: Fortress Press, 1996); 28, 29, 30.
34 Jon Sobrino, *Jesus the Liberator: A Historical-Theological View,* trans. Paul Burns and Francis McDonagh (Maryknoll, New York: Orbis Books, 1993), 123.
35 Cyril O'Regan, "Benedict XVI: Eschatology as Mirror and Lamp," Church Life Journal, April 19, 2021, https://churchlifejournal.nd.edu/articles/benedict-xvi-eschatology-as-mirror-and-lamp/.
36 Cf. CDF, Instruction on Certain Aspects of the "Theology of Liberation," Sec. IX, no. 3.
37 Ibid., Sec. X, 6.
38 Cf. Ratzinger, *Eschatology*, 28.
39 Cf. Vatican II Council, Pastoral Constitution on the Church in the Modern World *Gaudium et Spes* (December 7, 1965), no. 20. See Gustavo Gutiérrez, *A Theology of Liberation: History, Politics, and Salvation,* Revised Edition with a new Introduction (Maryknoll, N.Y: Orbis Books, 1988). 22, 23.
40 Leonardo Boff, *Church: Charism and Power,* 117.

41 Cf. Jon Sobrino, *Jesus the Liberator: A Historical-Theological View,* 82, 83.
42 Cf. Ibid., 172, 173. See 170–174.
43 Cf. Gustavo Gutierrez, "Poverty as a Theological Challenge," in *Mediations in Theology: Georges De Schrijver's Wager and Liberation Theologies,* ed. J. Haers and F. P. de Guzman (Leuven ; Dudley, MA: Peeters Publishers, 2003). 178–179.
44 Cf. CDF, Instruction on Certain Aspects of the "Theology of Liberation," Sec. IX, 9–10.
45 Cf. Gerald West, "*African Theologies of Liberation,*" in Virginia Fabella and Sergio Torres (Eds.), *Doing Theology in a Divided World: Papers from the Sixth International Conference of the Ecumenical Association of Third World Theologians, January 5,* First Edition (Maryknoll, N.Y: Orbis Books, 1985), p. 103.
46 Cf. Ibid., 103. Cf. Gary S D Leonard, ed., *The Kairos Documents: A Theological Commentary on the Political Crisis in South Africa* (Johannesburg: The Kairos Theologians, Sept. 25th, 1985). Frist edition (pp. 16, 18–21). Second edition (pp. 56, 58–61). Online at: . (Accessed on November 21, 20)
47 Cf. CDF, Instruction on Certain Aspects of the "Theology of Liberation," Sec. X, no. 12.
48 Cf. James Cone, *God of the Oppressed* (Maryknoll, New York: Orbis Book, 1997), 8–9, 15–16, 105.
49 De Lubac is particularly known for this historical attribution of "pure nature" to Cajetan. Cf. Henri de Lubac, *The Mystery of the Supernatural* (New York: Crossroad, 1998), 3–4, 7. [Originally published as *Le Mystère du Surnaturel,* 1965].
50 Cf. Gustavo Gutiérrez, *A Theology of Liberation,* 43.
51 *Africae Munus,* no. 23. Referencing *Deus Caritas Est,* 28–29; and *Gaudium et Spes,* 40.
52 *Africae Munus,* no. 17.
53 *Africae Munus,* no. 16.
54 *Africae Munus,* no. 79.
55 Cf. *Africae Munus,* no. 3. This is the sub-theme of the Exhortation.
56 Ratzinger, *Eschatology,* 12. See pp. 10–11.
57 Cf. Gustavo Gutiérrez, *A Theology of Liberation,* 103.
58 *Africae Munus,* no. 32.
59 *Africae Munus,* no. 57. Referencing Matthew15:21–28; Lk 7:36–50; 8:1–3; 10:38–42; John4:7–42. Also see Benedict XVI, *Meeting with Catholic Movements for the Promotion of Women* (Luanda, 22 March 2009): Insegnamenti V/I, 484. Online at: https://www.vatican.va/content/benedict-xvi/en/speeches/2009/march/documents/hf_ben-xvi_spe_20090322_promozione-donna.html.

60 John Paul II, Homily of His Holiness John Paul II for the Inauguration of His Pontificate (at St. Peter's Square on Sunday, 22 October 1978), no. 5.
61 *Africae Munus*, title of Section II of Chapter I.
62 Part one = "Behold, I make all things new" (Rev 21:5) [no. 14]. Chapter I = In service to reconciliation, justice and peace." This is sub-divided into: I. Authentic servants of God's word [15–16] and II. Christ at the heart of African life: The source of reconciliation, justice and peace [17–18]. This is further divided into: A. "Be reconciled with God" (2 Cor 5:20b) [19–21]; B. Becoming just and building a just social order [22–23], {further divided into: 1. Living in accordance with Christ's justice [24–25] and 2. Creating a just order in the spirit of the Beatitudes [26–27]}; and C. Love in truth: the source of peace [28], further divided into 1. Concrete fraternal service [29] and 2. The Church as a sentinel [30].
63 Gustavo Gutiérrez, *A Theology of Liberation*, 90.
64 Cf. Ratzinger, *Eschatology*, 31.
65 Benedict XVI, Encyclical Letter *Spe Salvi* (November 30, 2007), no. 35.
66 Cf. *Africae Munus*, no. 19.
67 Cf. Jon Sobrino, *Jesus the Liberator*,
68 Cf. James Cone, *God of the Oppressed*, 65. See chapter 4, "Biblical Revelation and Social Existence."
69 Cf. Ibid., 209–210. See pp. 27, 150–151.
70 Cf. Ibid., 33, 71.
71 Cf. Ibid., 43, 150.
72 By eschatologization we refer to the spiritual interpretation and future-looking or transcendent interpretation of the biblical promises and actions of divine liberation, especially of the Old Testament.
73 CDF, "Instruction on Certain Aspects of the 'Theology of Liberation,'" Sec. IV, 3. The text reads: The "theologies of liberation" make wide use of readings from the book of Exodus. The exodus, in fact, is the fundamental event in the formation of the chosen people. It represents freedom from foreign domination and from slavery. One will note that the specific significance of the event comes from its purpose, for this liberation is ordered to the foundation of the people of God and the Covenant cult celebrated on Mt. Sinai. That is why the liberation of the Exodus cannot be reduced to a liberation which is principally or exclusively political in nature.
74 Benedict XVI, Encyclical Letter *Deus Caritas Est* (December 25, 2005), no. 1.
75 Cf. Ibid.
76 Cf. Sobrino, *Jesus the Liberator*, 173, 175.

77 Cf. Ibid., 160–2.
78 Cf. Ibid., 163, 165, 168–9.
79 Cf. *Africae Munus*, nn. 26–27.
80 *Africae Munus*, no. 26.
81 *Africae Munus*, no. 26.
82 *Africae Munus*, no. 26. Emphasis mine.
83 John E. Thiel, *Icons of Hope: The "Last Things" in Catholic Imagination*, 1st edition (Notre Dame, Indiana: University of Notre Dame Press, 2013). 21.
84 Cf. C. H. Dodd, *The Parables of the Kingdom*, (NY: Scribner, 1961), 33 as cited in Footnote 33 in Thiel's *Icons of Hope*, Chapter one.
85 Cf. *Africae Munus*, 102.
86 Cf. Jürgen Moltmann, *The Coming of God: Christian Eschatology*, trans. Margaret Kohl (Minneapolis: Fortress Press, 1996), 29, 30.
87 Cf. Ibid.
88 John Thiel, *Icons of Hope*, 21–22.
89 Cf. Matthew 13:33.
90 John Thiel, *Icons of Hope*, 21–22.
91 This is the scriptural passage that serves as a sub-title for the Post-Synodal Apostolic Exhortation *Africae Munus*.
92 Cf. Jon Sobrino, *Jesus the Liberator*, 107
93 Cf. Ratzinger, *Eschatology*, 30.
94 This is articulated in the very first paragraph of the document and is integrally developed throughout.
95 World Synod of Catholic Bishops, *Justice in the World* (1971), no. 6. Par 36 reads, "The Church has received from Christ the mission of preaching the Gospel message, which contains a call to people to turn away from sin to the love of the Father, universal kinship and a consequent demand for justice in the world. This is the reason why the Church has the right, indeed the duty, to proclaim justice on the social, national and international level, and to denounce instances of injustice, when the fundamental rights of people and their very salvation demand it."
96 *Gaudium et Spes*, no. 40.
97 *Gaudium et Spes*, 45.
98 Benedict XVI, *Spe Salvi*, no. 34.
99 Cf. James Cone, *God of the Oppressed*, 147.
100 Cf. Ibid., 147.
101 Gerald West, "Africa's Liberation Theologies: An Historical-Hermeneutical Analysis, in *ResearchGate*, online at: https://www.researchgate.net/publication/285228493. Published: November 2015.
102 These sentiments are expressed in works such as: Takatso Mofokeng, "Black Christians, the Bible and Liberation," in *Journal of Black*

Theology in South Africa, vol. 2, no. 1 (May 1988): 34–42. Online at: https://www.sahistory.org.za/sites/default/files/DC/BtMay88.1015.2296.002.001.May1988.7/BtMay88.1015.2296.002.001.May1988.7.pdf.

103 Cf. Gerald West, "Africa's Liberation Theologies: An Historical-Hermeneutical Analysis," abstract.

104 Quoting from the Dominican theologian, Marie-Dominique Chenu's *Une école la théologie: Le Saulchoir*, Gutierrez speaks of the primacy of spirituality over theology – "to understand a theology, you must go to the spirituality behind the theology." Cf. Gustavo Gutierrez, "Poverty as a Theological Challenge," 181.

105 Fabella, V., & Torres, S. (Eds.). (1985). Doing theology in a divided world. Maryknoll: Orbis Books, 190. Cf. Gerald West, 103.

106 Kanvee Adams, "You say you will carry me." Online at: https://www.youtube.com/watch?v=wLvF6mbYwt8. Accessed on October 30, 2021.

107 John Paul II, Post-Synodal Apostolic Exhortation *Ecclesia in Africa* (September 14, 1995), no. 41. See *Africae Munus*, no. 9.

108 Cf. CHRDA, Full Report: Cameroon's Unfolding Atrocities (published on June 3, 2019). https://static1.squarespace.com/static/5ab13c5c620b859944157bc7/t/5cf685bc19d167000186c6fb/1559659972339/Cameroon%27s+Unfolding+Catastrophe+%28June+2019%29_report.pdf. (Accessed on Nov. 21, 2020).

109 https://www.hrw.org/news/2020/02/25/cameroon-civilians-massacred-separatist-area (Accessed on Nov. 19, 2020).

110 Drawing here from Emmanuel Katongole, *Born from Lament: The Theology and Politics of Hope in Africa* (Michigan: Wm. B. Eerdmans Publishing Co., 2017), 45.

111 There are in all five voices in this text, so beautifully illustrated by Katongole: there is the narrator who relates the destitution of the city (1:1–11,15,17; 2:1–19); daughter Zion, the city personified as the weeping mother recounting her own destructing with cries of intense grief (1:9,11–22; 2:20–22); another is a "strong man" (sometimes identified as the prophet Jeremiah) who describes his own experience of the devastation (chapter 3); there is the "poet" who expresses poetically the collapse of both domestic and civil life in the destroyed city; and lastly, there is the "collective voice" of Jerusalem, the entire community of the people. Cf. Katongole, *Born from Lament*, 45.

112 *Africa Munus*, no. 30.

113 Cf. Ibid.

114 Katongole, *Born from Lament*, 105–106.

115 cf. Tegha Nji, "Ratzinger and the Future of African Theology: Motivation and Aspirations," in *Cameroon Concord:* http://www.cameroonconcordnews.com/ratzinger-and-the-future-of-african-theology-motivation-and-aspirations/ (Accessed November 11, 2020).

116 Hans Urs von Balthasar, *Theo-Drama, Vol. 4: The Action* (San Francisco: Ignatius Press, 1994), 176.

Chapter 11
Justice, Africae Munus*'s Clarion Call: A Canon Law Perspective*
Denis Tameh

Introduction

> The Church-Family, the dwelling place of Christ, the Word of the Father, feels called to serve the justice of the kingdom. First of all, she must live this justice within herself, i.e., in her members, so that Africa's brothers and sisters will choose the arduous road to redemption and follow it.[1]

> From their rebirth in Christ, there exists among all the Christian faithful a true equality regarding dignity and action by which they all cooperate in the building up of the Body of Christ according to each one's own condition and function. (c. 208)[2]

The two quotes above capture the soul of this essay, which sets out to examine how the church's role as salt of the earth and light of the world in relation to justice can only be attained when she takes seriously within the church the *vera aequalitas* of all the *christifideles*. If the *munus* of the Church in Africa is to be authentic arbiters of reconciliation, justice, and peace, how can she accomplish this, or how can she be the salt of justice and the light of justice if there is within the Church no justice at all? Therefore, the very first *munus* of the Church in my estimation is that she becomes that beacon of justice so that the light of justice from within her can illumine the continent of Africa. And the Church in Africa can become that light when she realizes the full implications of the juridic act of baptism, which makes the baptized subjects of rights and obligations within the Church. It is through baptism that one is constituted a person juridically in the church.[3] In no. 6 of *Africae Munus,* the Pope reminds us that the unifying theme of the synod are the words of Christ: "You are the salt of the earth . . . you are the light of the world."[4] But the Latin adage, "*Nemo dat quod non habet*" forces the Church to ask the question whether she can be an instrument of justice if she is not just.

1.0. What Is Justice?

Plato gave a definition of justice which was later adopted by Roman law, and which forms the basis of our understanding of what justice is today: giving to each his due. A definition which Cicero immortalized in these words: "*iustitia suum cuique distribuit.*"[5] That is, justice renders to everyone his due. This was codified in the Justinian *Corpus Iuris Civilis* by using the definition of another jurist, Ulpian, who wrote that "Justice is a habit whereby a man renders to each one his due with constant and perpetual will." (constans et perpetua voluntas ius suum cuique tribuendi).[6] In the beginning of the *Institutiones,* he states the purpose of law: "*iuris praecepta sunt haec: honeste vivere, alterum non laedere, suum cuique tribuere.*"[7] (To live honestly, not to injure another, to give each his due.) It is the same definition the pope uses of justice in *Africae* Munus when he writes that justice obliges us to render each his duc.[8]

Another fundamental key to understanding how the Roman view of justice laid the groundwork for subsequent canonical and civil understanding of justice lay in the use of the word *ius.* This word has no exact equivalence in the English language. But very often it is translated to mean one of the following: Justice, right, jurisprudence, jurist, jurisdiction, law. The Roman jurists, in defining *ius,* always linked it to the idea of justice. Celsius defined it as "ars boni et aequi," that is, the art of goodness and fairness.[9]

The jurist Paulus defines it as "id quod semper aequum ac bonum est," that is, what always is fair and good.[10] Just as medicine is the art of healing, so law is the art of doing justice. And law, like medicine, is to be sought for its own benefit. With the introduction of the particle *directum* in the legal vocabulary, the juridical and moral dimensions of justice were united. For *directum* means directed or guided. Thus, *ius directum* became the law that determines the right direction, the good way for social cohesion and intercourse.[11] From *directum* comes the English word, right, the German word, *recht*, the Spanish word *derecho*, the French *droit*, the Italian *diritto*. Thus, we see in this the modern understanding of the inescapable union between justice and right, or law and morality. For *ius* expresses the general principles and foundation of law, the origin of law which, in the Catholic tradition, is referred to as natural law; and *directum* expresses the relation between the *ius* and morality. Aquinas' definition of *ius* takes into account this relationship between *ius* and *directum*. He defines *ius* as that which directs man in his relations to others according to some kind of equality or rightness.[12] This means that *ius*, though intimately linked with justice, precedes justice logically. For it stems from our human nature which makes us equal and therefore entitled to rights.

It is this understanding of justice that sets the framework for the Church's interaction *ad intra et ad extra*. That is with society and within the Church. If the task of the *Ecclesia in Africa* is to ensure that justice, peace and reconciliation reign she must continuously ask the question "what is justice, what is right?" not only in society but also within the Church. For if justice is the virtue of giving each his own (his rights), in order to be put in motion, it is precisely necessary that someone's own (what is his by right) exists. If not, how can we give someone what is his own, what is his by right?[13] What makes one a subject of rights in the Church as pointed out earlier is baptism. Before delving into the canon law contribution to the notion of justice, it is important to briefly examine the vision of justice as spelt out in *Africae Munus*.

2.0. The Vision of Justice in *Africae Munus*

The theme of this document, "You are the salt of the earth . . . You are the light of the world," provides the blueprint or the signposts directing the Church on the highway to the citadel of justice. And it is from this theme that the canonical orientation of this presentation as a Church of justice which looks within first, is born. To be a light of justice for the world, the oil of justice must be put within the lamp of the Church for it to shine. The Church must be a place where rights are protected, and justice served. Only in that way can she make all things new (Rev 21:5).

2.1. A Church in Service of Reconciliation, Justice and Peace

What is the relationship between reconciliation, justice, and peace? Pope John Paul II in his message for the celebration of the World Day of Peace in 2002 provided an answer, an answer which revealed the centrality of justice in establishing peace and having reconciliation and forgiveness. He wrote: "True peace is the work of justice. . . . Peace is the fruit of that right ordering of things with which the divine founder has invested human society and which must be actualized by man thirsting for an ever more perfect reign of justice."[14] Thus, as Augustine says the peace built in this world is the peace of right order, the tranquillitas *ordinis.*[15] Only where there is right order can we be sure that rights and responsibilities are guaranteed, that there is a just distribution of benefits and burdens. The Spanish canonist, Javier Hervada, expressed it thus: "When is there peace except when the rights of each person, each community, each people and each nation are recognized and respected?[16] But for justice and peace to be complete, there also must be forgiveness or reconciliation which heals and rebuilds troubled human relations from their foundations. For a society that is only just according to Hervada is an intolerable society. For if a person is only given what is just, there would be no friendship, no solidarity, nothing that allows for the normal and adequate development of social life.[17] In forgiveness we have a kind of *sanatio* of justice, a healing from the roots.

2.2. The Application of the Principle of Subsidiarity in Building a Just Social Order

Africae Munus emphasizes that one of the requirements for a just social order is the grave duty of forming upright consciences that are receptive to the demands of justice, and so help build a just social order by their responsible conduct.[18] This requires that each member of the people of God have the necessary autonomy to contribute to the just social order. That in essence is what the principle of subsidiarity is. As a result, the Church is not seen simply as the Church of the *Episcopus* or the *Presbyteros* but a Church in which all of the people of God in their diversity of vocations participate in their own unique way in the building up of the social order. This principle of subsidiarity is also a core foundation in canon law, which considers it as one of its *lex fundamentalis*.[19] In this vision for justice in Africa then, there is a role for the priest as an indispensable coworker with the bishop to bring about justice; there is a role for the missionaries and societies of religious life, and there is the role for the lay faithful whom justice requires that they be given adequate formation in the faith so that they can truly become agents of justice. *Africae Munus* sees the implementation of a just social order not simply as the task of the clerics or the religious but that of the whole Church. In this way, it fulfills the vision of the Code Revision process, which saw in the principle of subsidiarity a way in which justice can be mirrored in the Church, which is the people of God as they participate according to their unique charisms. For the Church to be a sentinel making the voice of Christ,[20] the voice of justice heard requires that all of her members be involved.

2.3. Justice Rooted in the Person of Christ

This is the unique Christian contribution to the idea of justice within the African continent. The Holy Father reminds Africa that Christ does not propose a revolution of a social or political kind, but a revolution of love brought about by a complete self-giving. This vision of justice is what Christian jurists have always considered important. Hervada argued that it is not justice that justifies a commitment, but love for humans. Justice is the minimum to which we are all obliged in relationships among humans; and the minimum cannot be the ideal.[21] This notion of justice is what Benedict XVI articulated in these words: "Charity goes beyond justice, because to love is to give, to offer what is mine to the other; but it never lacks justice, which prompts us to give the other what is his."[22] Thus the ideal of justice is Christ who is love—take him away and our notion of justice is truncated because it would lack mercy, charity and forgiveness. This conclusion is pointed out clearly by Benedict XVI when he writes: "Not only is justice not extraneous to charity, not only is it not an alternative or a parallel path to charity: justice is inseparable from charity and intrinsic to it."[23] It is this vision of justice that *Africae Munus* points at. A vision that speaks the truth with love, that offers fraternal service with love, that calls for a metanoia of authentic conversion.

However, this vision of justice can only be implemented when the Church herself is a *sedes justitia,* a seat of justice. This explains why canon law views the concept of justice within the church as a pastoral tool for the salvation of souls.

3.0. Canonical Vision of Justice and Its Application to *Africae Munus*

Pope John Paul II, in promulgating the 1983 code, explained why the code was so necessary for the Church. He said: "As a matter of fact, the Code of Canon Law is extremely necessary for the Church. Since the Church is organized as a social and visible structure, it must have norms in order that the mutual relations of the faithful may be regulated according to justice based upon charity, with rights of individuals guaranteed and well defined."[24] It is with this in mind that the Code Revsion *Coetus* came out with certain fundamental principles to serve as the basis of the new Code. Among these principles were the following that are of significant value to the understanding of justice in the Church: The principle of subsidiarity as seen already; the Pneumatic-Charismatic principle which, building upon *Gaudum et spes* and *Dignitatis Humanae* emphasized the dignity of the human person and sought to have this codified in legal language under the protection of rights in the Church; and the principle of fundamental Christian equality and coresponsibility which had its basis in *Lumen Gentium* 9 (the fundamental equality of all the baptized). According to this principle, the law should not reflect a stratified ecclesiology, dividing the people of God, but rather its complementarity.[25] Thus, rights and duties within the Church, which constitute an essential part of justice, occur within a specifically theological or spiritual context: the Church as the community of faith established by Christ as the sacrament of salvation until the fulfilment of the kingdom of God through the return of Christ.[26]

Principle 6 and 7 of the Code Revision Process clearly outline the importance of justice in the Church, which manifests itself in the respect of rights. Principle 6 states: "The use of power in the Church must not be arbitrary, because that is prohibited by natural law, by divine law, and by ecclesiastical law. The rights of each one of Christ's faithful must be acknowledged and protected, both those which are contained in natural and divine positive law and those derived from those laws because of the social condition which the faithful acquire and possess in the Church."[27] Principle 7 stipulated that the principle must be proclaimed in canon law that juridical protection applies equally to superiors and to subjects so that any suspicion of arbitrariness in ecclesiastical administration will entirely disappear. This end can only be achieved by avenues of recourse wisely provided by the law which allow a person who thinks his or her rights have been violated at a lower level to have them effectively restored at a higher level.[28] In the mind of the Church, justice must be felt at all levels and structures. Rights must be vindicated, and the Church has to be seen as the protector and guarantor of rights for her members.

3.1. Justice within the Church as a Means to Manifest the Reality of Salvation to the World.

Canon 208 states a general principle derived from *Lumen Gentium* 32 that a true equality in dignity and action exists among all the faithful. This fundamental equality does not remove differences among the faithful but shows the interrelation among the faithful which is essential for justice in the Church. In this way the Church can be that sentinel of justice that *Africae Munus* wants it to be.

Just as natural law requires that each person be given his or her rights by virtue of being human, ecclesiastical law requires that each person be given his or her fundamental rights by virtue of not only being human, but most especially of being baptized and incorporated in the Body of Christ. It is for this reason that the 1983 Code of Canon Law was very particular about the rights of all within the Church. The previous code only mentioned the rights of the clerics (cc. 118–144), religious (cc. 592–631), and barely that of the laity. But the 1983 Code not only mentioned these rights of the laity but described them. Among them are the right to privacy (c. 220), right to a good name and reputation, the right to freedom from coercion in choosing a state of life (c. 219), the right to proclaim the divine message of salvation and foster the spread of the gospel (cc. 210–211), the right to vindicate one's rights in a competent forum (c. 221), the right to educate the children (c. 266§2), the right to acquire knowledge of Christian doctrine (c. 228), and the right to marry (c. 1058).

It is important to note that within the Church, the issue of rights and obligations takes on a solemn gravity, because the rights of one group often are the obligations of another group. More specifically, some of the rights of the faithful are obligations of the clerisy such that, when the cleric fails in his obligations, he injures the rights of the faithful and creates a scenario of injustice. Canon 213 for example makes it a right of the Christian faithful to receive spiritual assistance, especially of the Word and sacraments, from the pastors. This becomes an obligation which can result in an injustice when the pastor is negligent in providing this assistance. Justice then demands that the norms of canon 1389§2 be applied to restore justice where culpable negligence is proven. The right to freely found and direct associations for the purpose of charity requires the obligation of the authority to give the authorization according to the norms of law (c. 215). The right to a Christian education by which the faithful are taught to mature in the faith requires an equal obligation on the part of the clergy to provide this education (c. 217) while being faithful to the deposit of faith, so that to teach what is contrary to divine and catholic faith would be an injustice. The right to choose one's state in life within the Church without any coercion requires the obligation of the Church to provide to all the faithful, all the states of life available in the Church. In the area of social justice and charity, the faithful who work for the Church have a right to a decent remuneration appropriate to their condition so that they can provide decently for their families (c. 231§ 2). This becomes an obligation for the Church, who, in failing to do that, cannot be truly a sentinel of justice.

3.2. How Are Rights to Be Protected in the Church So That Justice May Reign?

Canon 1341 outlines the purpose of sanctions in the Church. Among other things, it aims at restoring justice. Other reasons are the repair of scandal and reform of the offender. The restoration of justice is so central in the canonical world view of sanctions and procedures because, when the peace of the community is disturbed and the common spiritual or temporal good of the Church is deprived to some person, there is a disequilibrium created that may end up hampering the salvation of souls. It is for this reason that we have, in the code, processes such as the procedure for the transfer and removal of pastors (cc. 1740–1752) to ensure that the rights of the pastors are respected by their bishops; procedures for recourse so that those who feel that their rights have been violated by their superiors can appeal to have them vindicated (c. 1732). For one of the objects of trial in canon law is the vindication of rights of physical or juridic persons (c. 1400). This is also true of the nullity process in marriage, whereby it is a demand of justice that the Church should ensure that those who are free to marry can do so, or those who are in invalid marriages should have the freedom to marry again. Canon law, therefore, provides a necessary medium by which the Church can shine the bright light of justice within, so that she can become the sentinel for African society in matters of justice.

Conclusion

Having seen the important task laid before the African Church with respect to justice and reconciliation, it is high time the Church looked inward to better fulfill this *munus* with diligence and effectiveness. The Church which *Africae Munus* says should be the salt of the earth and the light of the world cannot be these if within her justice is not seen to be done. Justice as envisioned by *Africae Munus* is only possible when the Church breathes with the two lungs of justice ad intra et ad extra. The Church can only talk of justice and the respect of rights effectively in the continent when she too ensures that the rights of all within the Church are respected. Canon law provides the medium whereby the respect of rights and the implementation of justice within the Church takes place. In that way she would not be a blurred light or sentinel, but one that truly shines from the mountain tops, so that through her service to justice, both within and without, the supreme law of the Church is made manifest: the salvation of souls.

Chapter 11 Endnotes

1 *Instrumentum Laboris*, Synod of Bishops Special Assembly for Africa: The Church In Africa in Service to Reconciliation, Justice and Peace, (Vatican City: Libreria Editrice Vaticana, 2009).

2 *Codex Iuris Canonici auctoritate Ioanis Pauli PP. II promulgatus* (Vatican City: Libreria Editrice Vaticana, 1983) c. 208. English translation from the *Code of Canon Law, Latin-English Edition: New English Translation* (Washington, DC: CLSA,1998). All subsequent English translations of canons from this code will be taken from this source unless otherwise indicated.

3 C. 96: Baptismo homo Ecclesiae Christi incorporatgur et in eadem constituitur persona, cum offciis et iuribus quae christianis, attentat quidem eorum condicione, sunt propria, quartenus in ecclesiastica sunt communion et nisi obstet lata legitime sanction. The notion of juridic personality is distinct from the naturalistic definition of person as *substantia* as we find in Boethius. Here it refers more to the supernatural understanding of person who is in full communion with the church, having a concrete state of life with rights and duties proper to that state. Cf. John McIntyre. "Physical and Juridic persons" *New Commentary on the Code of Canon Law*, ed. John P. Beal et al. (Bangalore: Theological Publiations, 2010) 140.

4 Benedict XVI, Apostolic Exhortation *Africae Munus* 6 (Vatican City: Libreria Editrice Vaticana, 2010).

5 Cicero, *De Natura Deorum*, III, 38.

6 Justinian, *Digest*. 1.1.10 in Watson, Alan, ed., *The Digest of Justinian* (Philadelphia: University of Pennsylvania Press, 1985).

7 Ibidem

8 *Africae Munus*, 24.

9 Digest. 1.1.1

10 Digest. 1.1.11

11 Rafael Domingo, Roman Law, Basic Concepts and Values in *SSRN Electronic Journal* (2017) 9.

12 Summa Theologiae, p.2, q. 2, art.57,1.; De Veritate 23,6.

13 Javier Hervada, *What is Law? The Modern Response of Juridical Realism. An Introduction to Law*, (Montreal: Wilson &Lafleur 2009) 25.

14 John Paull II, No Peace without Justice, No Justice without Forgiveness (2002). Also Cf. Vatican II, Pastoral Constitution *Gaudium et spes*, December 7, 1965: *AAS* 58 (1966) 1097–1098 English translation in *Vatican Council II: The Conciliar and Post Conciliar Documents*, ed. Austin Flannery, 2nd ed. (Northport, NY: Costello Publishing, 1996).

15 De Civitate Dei, 19, 13.
16 Javier Hervada, 23.
17 Ibidem, 40.
18 *Africae Munus*, 22.
19 Thomas Green, The Revision of Canon Law: Theological Implications, *Theological Studies*, 656.
20 *Africae Munus*, 30.
21 Javier Hervada, 41.
22 Benedict XVI, *Caritas in Veritate* 6 (Vatican City: Libreria Editrice Vaticana, 2009)
23 Ibidem
24 John Paul II, Apostolic constitution *Sacrae Disciplinae Leges* (Vatican City: Editrice Libreria Vaticana 1983).
25 Thomas Green, 630.
26 Robert Kaslyn, "the People of God," *New Commentary*, 254.
27 James Coriden, "A Challenge: Making the Rights Real, *Jurist* 45 (1985) 7: *Communicationes* I (1969) 83.
28 Ibid.